It's another winner from the CGP lab...

There are only three ways to make sure you're fully prepared for the
Grade 9-1 GCSE Combined Science exams — practise, practise and practise.

That's why we've packed this brilliant CGP book with realistic exam-style
questions for every topic, and we've got all the practicals covered too.

And since you'll be tested on a wide range of topics in the real exams, we've also
included sections of mixed questions for Biology, Chemistry and Physics!

CGP — still the best! ☺

Our sole aim here at CGP is to produce the highest quality books —
carefully written, immaculately presented and dangerously close to being funny.

Then we work our socks off to get them out to you
— at the cheapest possible prices.

Contents

✓ Use the tick boxes to check off the topics you've completed.

How to Use This Book..1

Topic B1 — Cell Level Systems

Cells and Microscopy..2
Light Microscopy..4
More on Light Microscopy..5
DNA..6
Enzymes..7
Investigating Enzyme Activity....................................9
Respiration...10
Biological Molecules..12
Photosynthesis..13
The Rate of Photosynthesis.....................................14

Topic B2 — Scaling Up

The Cell Cycle and Mitosis......................................17
Cell Differentiation and Stem Cells.......................18
Diffusion, Active Transport and Osmosis............19
Exchanging Substances..21
Exchange Surfaces...22
The Circulatory System..24
The Blood Vessels..25
The Blood...26
Plant Transport Systems and Transpiration.......27
More on Transpiration..28
Investigating Transpiration......................................29

Topic B3 — Organism Level Systems

The Nervous System..31
Hormones and Negative Feedback Systems......34
Hormones in Reproduction.....................................35
Hormones for Fertility and Contraception.........36
More on Contraception..37
Controlling Blood Sugar Level................................38

Topic B4 — Community Level Systems

The Carbon Cycle..40
The Nitrogen Cycle and the Water Cycle...........41
Ecosystems and Interactions Between Organisms...42

Topic B5 — Genes, Inheritance and Selection

Genes and Variation..44
More on Variation and Genetic Variants.............45
Sexual Reproduction and Meiosis.........................46
Sex Determination and Asexual Reproduction.........47
Genetic Diagrams...48
Classification...50
Evolution and Natural Selection............................51
Evidence for Evolution..52

Topic B6 — Global Challenges

Investigating Distribution and Abundance.........53
Using Keys and Factors Affecting Distribution.........55
Using Transects...56
Human Impacts on Ecosystems.............................57
Maintaining Biodiversity...58
Selective Breeding...59
Genetic Engineering..60
Health and Disease...62
How Disease Spreads..63
Reducing and Preventing the Spread of Disease.....65
The Human Immune System..................................66
Vaccines and Medicines...67
Investigating Antimicrobials...................................68
Comparing Antimicrobials......................................69
Developing New Medicines....................................70
Non-Communicable Diseases................................71
Treating Cardiovascular Disease...........................73
Stem Cells in Medicine..74
Using Genome Research in Medicine.................75

Topic C1 — Particles

States of Matter..76
The History of the Atom..77
The Atom..78
Atoms, Isotopes and Ions..79

Topic C2 — Elements, Compounds and Mixtures

The Periodic Table..80
Electron Shells..81
Ionic Compounds..82
Simple Molecules..84
Giant Covalent Structures and Fullerenes..........86
Polymers...87
Properties of Materials...88
Metals...89
States, Structure and Bonding............................90
Purity..92
Purification Techniques..93
Chromatography..96
Relative Masses...98
Molecular and Empirical Formulas......................99

Topic C3 — Chemical Reactions

Conservation of Mass..101
Chemical Formulas..102
Chemical Equations...103
Moles..106
Calculating Masses..108
More Mole Calculations.....................................110
Concentration...112
Endothermic and Exothermic Reactions...........114
Bond Energies..115
Acids and Bases..117
Strong and Weak Acids.....................................119
Reactions of Acids...120
Making Salts..122
Oxidation and Reduction...................................124
Electrolysis...125
Electrolysis of Copper Sulfate...........................127
Tests for Gases..129

Topic C4 — Predicting and Identifying Reactions and Products

Group 1 — Alkali Metals....................................130
Group 7 — Halogens..131
Group 0 — Noble Gases....................................133
Reactivity of Metals..134

Topic C5 — Monitoring and Controlling Chemical Reactions

Reaction Rates...136
Collision Theory...139
Catalysts..140
Dynamic Equilibrium..141

Topic C6 — Global Challenges

Extracting Metals from their Ores.....................143
More on Extracting Metals.................................144
Life-Cycle Assessments....................................145
Recycling Materials..147
Crude Oil..148
Cracking...150
The Atmosphere...151
The Greenhouse Effect and Global Warming...152
Pollutants...154
Water Treatment..155

Topic P1 — Matter

The History of the Atom and Atomic Structure....156
Density..157
Particle Theory and States of Matter.................158
Specific Heat Capacity.......................................159
Specific Latent Heat...160
Pressure of Gases...161

Topic P2 — Forces

Speed and Velocity..162
Acceleration...163
Investigating Motion...164
Distance-Time Graphs.......................................165
Velocity-Time Graphs...166
Forces and Free Body Force Diagrams............168
Scale Diagrams and Forces..............................169
Newton's First and Second Laws of Motion.....171
Friction and Terminal Velocity............................173
Inertia and Newton's Third Law of Motion........174
Momentum and Conservation of Momentum....175
Mass, Weight and Gravity.................................177
Mechanical Energy Stores.................................178
Work Done and Power.......................................179
Forces, Elasticity and Hooke's Law...................181

Topic P3 — Electricity and Magnetism

Static Electricity 183
Current and Potential Difference 184
Circuits and Resistance 185
Circuit Devices 187
Series and Parallel Circuits 188
Energy and Power in Circuits 190
Magnets and Magnetic Fields 191
Electromagnetism 192
Magnetic Forces 193
Motors 195

Topic P4 — Waves and Radioactivity

Wave Basics 196
Wave Experiments 198
Reflection and Refraction 199
More on Reflection 201
More on Refraction 202
EM Waves and Their Uses 203
Isotopes and Radioactive Decay 206
Radiation Properties and Decay Equations 207
Electron Energy Levels 208
Half-Life 209
Dangers of Radioactivity 210

Topic P5 — Energy

Conservation of Energy 211
Efficiency 212
Energy Transfer by Heating 213
Reducing Unwanted Energy Transfers 214
Mechanical and Electrical Energy Transfers ... 215

Topic P6 — Global Challenges

Everyday Speeds and Accelerations 218
Stopping Distances and Reaction Times 219
Energy Sources 220
Electricity and the National Grid 223
Wiring in the Home 224

Mixed Questions

Biology Mixed Questions 225
Chemistry Mixed Questions 233
Physics Mixed Questions 239

Published by CGP

Editors:
Jane Ellingham, Mary Falkner, Robin Flello, Emily Forsberg, Emily Garrett, Paul Jordin, Christopher Lindle, Rachael Marshall, Chris McGarry, Ciara McGlade, Rachael Rogers, Sophie Scott, Camilla Simson, Sean Walsh, Jonathan Wray

Contributors:
Bethan Parry, Alison Popperwell

With thanks to Katherine Faudemer and Emily Howe for the proofreading.
With thanks to Jan Greenway for the copyright research.

ISBN: 978 1 78294 518 5

Page 153 contains public sector information licensed under the Open Government Licence v3.0.
http://www.nationalarchives.gov.uk/doc/open-government-licence/version/3/
Data to construct graph on page 153 provided by the JPL PODAAC, in support of the NASA's MEaSUREs program.

Clipart from Corel®
Illustrations by: Sandy Gardner Artist, email sandy@sandygardner.co.uk
Printed by Elanders Ltd, Newcastle upon Tyne

Based on the classic CGP style created by Richard Parsons.

Text, design, layout and original illustrations © Coordination Group Publications Ltd. (CGP) 2016
All rights reserved.

Photocopying this book is not permitted, even if you have a CLA licence.
Extra copies are available from CGP with next day delivery • 0800 1712 712 • www.cgpbooks.co.uk

How to Use This Book

- Hold the book <u>upright</u>, approximately <u>50 cm</u> from your face, ensuring that the text looks like <u>this</u>, not this. Alternatively, place the book on a <u>horizontal</u> surface (e.g. a table or desk) and sit adjacent to the book, at a distance which doesn't make the text too small to read.
- In case of emergency, press the two halves of the book together <u>firmly</u> in order to close.
- Before attempting to use this book, familiarise yourself with the following <u>safety information</u>:

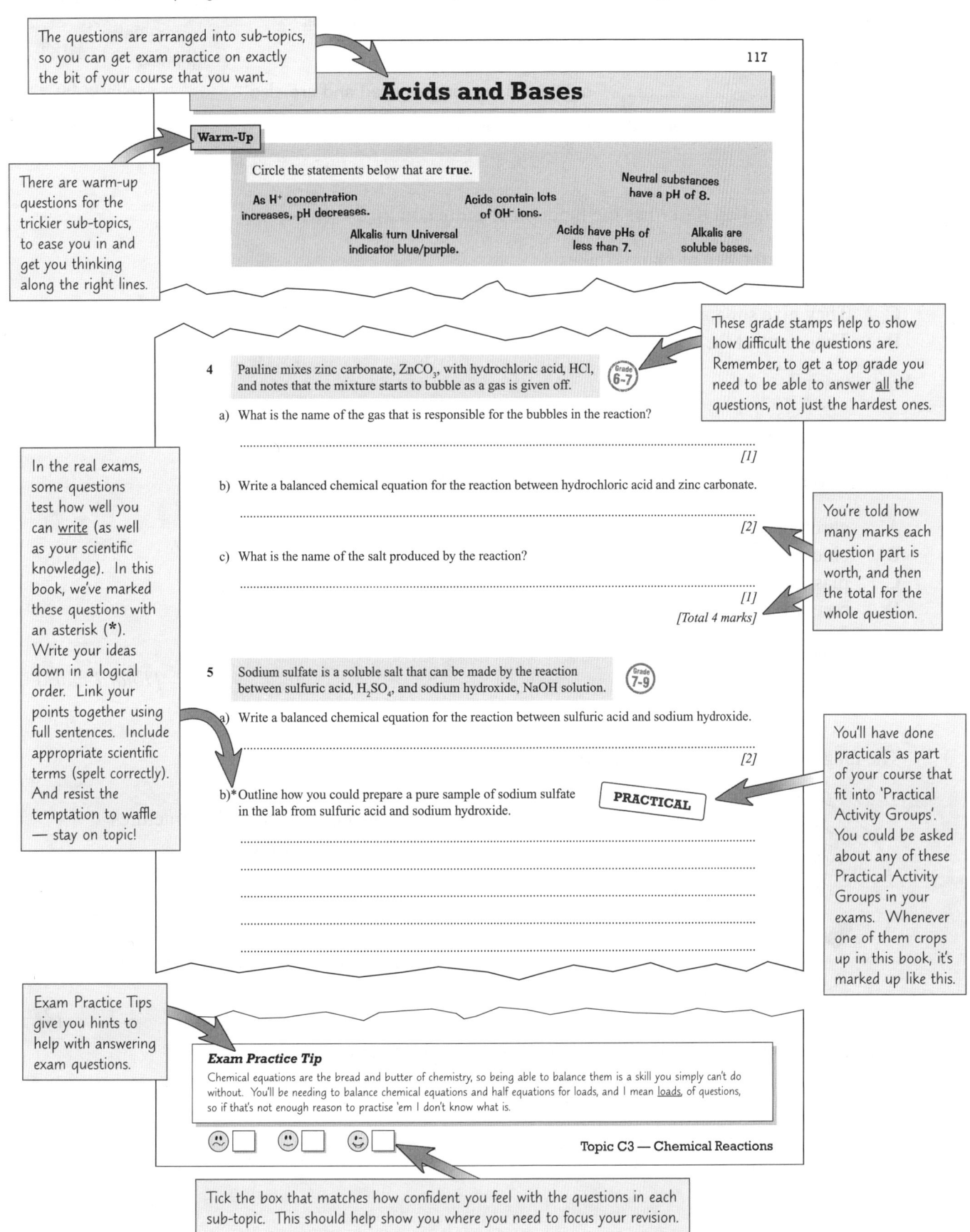

The questions are arranged into sub-topics, so you can get exam practice on exactly the bit of your course that you want.

117

Acids and Bases

Warm-Up

There are warm-up questions for the trickier sub-topics, to ease you in and get you thinking along the right lines.

Circle the statements below that are **true**.

As H⁺ concentration increases, pH decreases.

Acids contain lots of OH⁻ ions.

Neutral substances have a pH of 8.

Alkalis turn Universal indicator blue/purple.

Acids have pHs of less than 7.

Alkalis are soluble bases.

These grade stamps help to show how difficult the questions are. Remember, to get a top grade you need to be able to answer all the questions, not just the hardest ones.

4   Pauline mixes zinc carbonate, $ZnCO_3$, with hydrochloric acid, HCl, and notes that the mixture starts to bubble as a gas is given off.   (Grade 6-7)

   a) What is the name of the gas that is responsible for the bubbles in the reaction?

   ....

   [1]

In the real exams, some questions test how well you can write (as well as your scientific knowledge). In this book, we've marked these questions with an asterisk (*). Write your ideas down in a logical order. Link your points together using full sentences. Include appropriate scientific terms (spelt correctly). And resist the temptation to waffle — stay on topic!

   b) Write a balanced chemical equation for the reaction between hydrochloric acid and zinc carbonate.

   ....

   [2]

   c) What is the name of the salt produced by the reaction?

   ....

   [1]

   [Total 4 marks]

You're told how many marks each question part is worth, and then the total for the whole question.

5   Sodium sulfate is a soluble salt that can be made by the reaction between sulfuric acid, H_2SO_4, and sodium hydroxide, NaOH solution.   (Grade 7-9)

   a) Write a balanced chemical equation for the reaction between sulfuric acid and sodium hydroxide.

   ....

   [2]

   b)* Outline how you could prepare a pure sample of sodium sulfate in the lab from sulfuric acid and sodium hydroxide.   **PRACTICAL**

   ....
   ....
   ....
   ....
   ....

You'll have done practicals as part of your course that fit into 'Practical Activity Groups'. You could be asked about any of these Practical Activity Groups in your exams. Whenever one of them crops up in this book, it's marked up like this.

Exam Practice Tips give you hints to help with answering exam questions.

Exam Practice Tip

Chemical equations are the bread and butter of chemistry, so being able to balance them is a skill you simply can't do without. You'll be needing to balance chemical equations and half equations for loads, and I mean <u>loads</u>, of questions, so if that's not enough reason to practise 'em I don't know what is.

☹ ☐   ☺ ☐   ☻ ☐   Topic C3 — Chemical Reactions

Tick the box that matches how confident you feel with the questions in each sub-topic. This should help show you where you need to focus your revision.

How to Use This Book

Topic B1 — Cell Level Systems

Cells and Microscopy

PRACTICAL

Warm-Up

Use the words on the right to correctly fill in the gaps in the passage.
You don't have to use every word, but each word can only be used once.

Most .... organisms are made up of many cells,
for example, ... and ....
However, ... organisms are single-celled and are also
.... and simpler. They include ....

plants   bacteria
smaller   larger
animals
prokaryotic
eukaryotic   simpler

1 Which statement best describes the function of mitochondria? *Grade 4-6*

A   They are the site of photosynthesis.
B   They are the site of respiration.
C   They give support to the cell.
D   They control the cell's activities.

Your answer ☐

[Total 1 mark]

2 Which of the following would you find embedded in a cell membrane? *Grade 4-6*

A   chromosomes
B   chlorophyll
C   plasmids
D   receptor molecules

Your answer ☐

[Total 1 mark]

3 The diagram below shows a eukaryotic cell. *Grade 4-6*

a) What name is given to the structures labelled **X** on the diagram?

....
[1]

b) Label the nucleus and cell membrane on the diagram.
[2]

c) Describe how the contents of the nucleus allow it to carry out its function.

....

....
[2]

[Total 5 marks]

Topic B1 — Cell Level Systems

4 The diagram below shows a prokaryotic cell. *(Grade 4-6)*

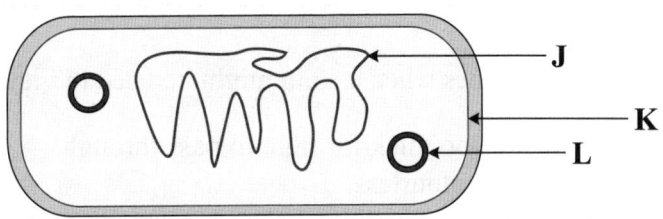

a) Name structures **J**, **K** and **L** shown on the diagram.

J ....

K ....

L ....
[3]

b) Name **one** structure within a prokaryotic cell that contains genetic material.

....
[1]

c) Describe **one** difference between bacterial cells (prokaryotic) and animal cells (eukaryotic) other than their size.

....

....
[1]
[Total 5 marks]

5 Cells are observed using microscopes. *(Grade 6-7)*

a) A scientist uses a light microscope to view plant cells. The chloroplasts appear green. Describe the function of chloroplasts and state why they appear green.

....

....
[2]

b) Electron microscopes can also be used to view plant cells.

   i) How do magnification and resolution compare between electron and light microscopes?

   ....

   ....
   [2]

   ii) How has electron microscopy increased our understanding of how plant cells work?

   ....

   ....

   ....
   [2]
   [Total 6 marks]

Topic B1 — Cell Level Systems

Light Microscopy

PRACTICAL

1 Which statement best describes when a stain might be used to view a sample of tissue?

    A   When the specimen is too thick for light to pass through.
    B   When the specimen is colourless.
    C   When there aren't many sub-cellular structures present in the cells.
    D   When a cover slip is not being used.

Your answer ☐

[Total 1 mark]

2 A student wants to use a light microscope to view a sample of cells that she has prepared. The diagram below shows a light microscope.

a) Give the name and function of the parts labelled **X**, **Y** and **Z** on the diagram.

    X ....

    Y ....

    Z ....
[3]

b) The individual steps taken when viewing a slide under a microscope are given below.
Place the steps in order by writing the numbers **1-5** in the boxes.

	Use the coarse adjustment knob to bring the stage up to just below the objective lens.
	Select the lowest-powered objective lens.
	Use the fine adjustment knob to get a clear image of the specimen.
	Use the coarse adjustment knob to move the stage downwards to focus the image.
	Clip the slide onto the stage.

[2]

c) The student follows the steps above but finds that the image is too small to see the internal structures of the cells. Outline the steps she should take to get a bigger image of the cells using the light microscope.

....

....
[2]

[Total 7 marks]

Topic B1 — Cell Level Systems

More on Light Microscopy

1 A student observed a sample of cells under a microscope. *Grade 4-6*

a) The student used an eyepiece lens with a magnification of ×10 and an objective lens with a magnification of ×40. What is the total magnification of the image?

answer = ...
[1]

b) By using the same eyepiece lens but a different objective lens the student changed the magnification of the image to ×100. Which objective lens did he use?

- **A** ×10
- **B** ×40
- **C** ×100
- **D** ×400

Your answer ☐

[1]
[Total 2 marks]

2 A student observed blood cells under a microscope. He takes a measurement of the width of one of the cells. The real width of the cell is 12 μm. *Grade 6-7*

a) What is the real width of the cell in mm?
1 mm = 1000 μm. Give your answer in standard form.

answer = ... mm
[2]

b) Another blood cell viewed under the microscope measured 0.0074 mm across.
What is the width of the cell in nm?
1 mm = 1000 μm
1 μm = 1000 nm

answer = ... nm
[2]
[Total 4 marks]

Exam Practice Tip

Don't panic if you have to give an answer in standard form. Just remember that the first number needs to be between 1 and 10. Then all you have to do to work out the power of 10 is count how many places the decimal point has moved. Don't forget to pop in a negative sign if the decimal point has moved to the right.

Topic B1 — Cell Level Systems

DNA

Warm-Up

Draw lines to match each word or phrase on the left with the description on the right.

polymer	joins the two strands of DNA together
DNA	the genetic material of an organism
base pairing	the spiral shape of a DNA molecule
double helix	a long chain of repeating molecules

1 Which of the following shows a complementary base pair? *Grade 4-6*

  A A-G
  B G-C
  C T-T
  D C-T

Your answer ☐

[Total 1 mark]

2 Complete the following sentence about the structure of DNA. *Grade 4-6*

DNA is a polymer made up of monomers called:

  A sugars
  B amino acids
  C nucleotides
  D bases

Your answer ☐

[Total 1 mark]

3 The diagram below shows the structure of a DNA nucleotide. *Grade 6-7*

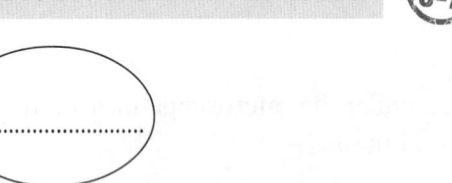

a) Complete the missing label on the diagram.

[1]

b) Describe how DNA nucleotides can differ from one another.

....

....

[2]

[Total 3 marks]

Topic B1 — Cell Level Systems

Enzymes

1 Enzymes help to control chemical reactions in our cells. Look at the table below. Which row best describes enzymes?

	are affected by pH	speed up reactions	get used up during reactions	all have the same shape
A	✓	✓		
B			✓	
C	✓	✓		✓
D		✓	✓	✓

Your answer ☐

[Total 1 mark]

2 The diagram shows an enzyme before and after it has been exposed to a high temperature.

a) Name the part of the enzyme labelled **X**.

....
[1]

b) Explain how the high temperature has affected the enzyme and how this will affect its activity.

....
....
....
....
[4]
[Total 5 marks]

3 Two different species of bacteria have slightly different versions of the same enzyme. Enzyme **A** is from a species of bacteria found in a hot thermal vent and enzyme **B** is from a species of bacteria found in soil. A scientist investigated the effect of temperature on the rate of reaction for both enzymes. The results are shown on the graph below.

— line 1
···· line 2

Suggest which line represents enzyme **A**. Give reasons for your answer.

....
....
....
....
[Total 3 marks]

Topic B1 — Cell Level Systems

4 A lipase is an enzyme that breaks down lipids into fatty acids and glycerol. The optimum pH of pancreatic lipase is approximately pH 8. The action of lipase results in the release of fatty acids, in the investigation this causes the pH of the test solution to decrease.

Grade 7-9

A student mixed pancreatic lipase solution with milk and recorded the change in the pH of the solution. She took readings every two minutes for ten minutes. The results are shown in the table below.

Time (minutes)	0	2	4	6	8	10
pH	9.2	8.8	8.5	8.0	7.6	7.3

a) Using the change in pH, calculate the mean rate of reaction during the ten minutes.

Mean rate of reaction = ... units of pH/minute

[2]

b) The student then investigated the effect of enzyme concentration on the action of lipase. At the end of her experiment she sketched the graph below, showing how the rate of reaction changed.

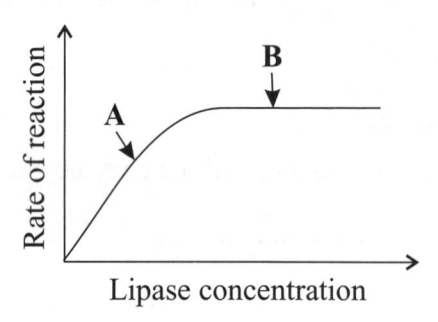

Explain what is happening at the points labelled **A** and **B** on the graph.

A ....

....

....

B ....

....

....

[4]

c) Explain **one** problem with using change in pH as a way of measuring the rate of the reaction.

....

....

....

[2]

[Total 8 marks]

Exam Practice Tip

Lots of the questions in the exams will be based on experiments. Some of them will be testing your practical skills, but some of them will just be getting you to apply your knowledge of a topic (e.g. how enzymes work) in a practical setting.

Topic B1 — Cell Level Systems

Investigating Enzyme Activity — PRACTICAL

1 The enzyme amylase is involved in the breakdown of starch into simple sugars.

A student investigated the effect of temperature on the activity of amylase in starch solution. Amylase and starch solution were added to test tubes **X**, **Y** and **Z**. The test tubes were placed in water baths of different temperatures, as shown in the table on the right. Spotting tiles were prepared with a drop of iodine solution in each well. Iodine solution is a browny-orange colour but it turns blue-black in the presence of starch.

Test tube	Temp (°C)
X	32
Y	36
Z	48

Every 30 seconds, a drop of the solution from each of the test tubes was added to a separate well on a spotting tile. The resulting colour of the solution in the well was recorded in the table below.

Time (s)	30	60	90	120	150
Tube **X**	Blue-black	Blue-black	Blue-black	Browny-orange	Browny-orange
Tube **Y**	Blue-black	Browny-orange	Browny-orange	Browny-orange	Browny-orange
Tube **Z**	Blue-black	Blue-black	Blue-black	Blue-black	Blue-black

a) State the temperature at which the rate of reaction was greatest. Explain your answer.

....

....

....
[2]

b) Suggest an explanation for the results in tube **Z**.

....

....
[1]

c) i) In any experiment, it is important to control the variables that are not being tested. State how the student could control the pH in the test tubes.

....
[1]

ii) Give **two** other variables that should be controlled in this experiment.

....

....
[2]

d) The student repeated her experiment at 37 °C and got the same results as she got for her experiment at 36 °C. Suggest **one** way in which she could determine whether the rate of reaction is greatest at 36 °C or 37 °C.

....

....
[1]

[Total 7 marks]

Topic B1 — Cell Level Systems

Respiration

1 Which statement best describes aerobic respiration?

    A   It is a universal chemical reaction that transfers energy from the breakdown of glucose.
    B   It is an endothermic reaction that transfers energy from the breakdown of glucose.
    C   It is an exothermic process that transfers energy from the breakdown of ATP.
    D   It is an endothermic process that allows plants to use energy from the Sun to make glucose.

Your answer ☐

[Total 1 mark]

2 Respiration is a process that goes on in all living organisms.

  a) Which of the following is a reactant in aerobic respiration?

    A   water
    B   carbon dioxide
    C   lactic acid
    D   oxygen

Your answer ☐

[1]

  b) Give **one** product of aerobic respiration.

....

[1]

[Total 2 marks]

3 The air that a person inhales has a different composition from the air that they exhale. The table shows the percentages of different gases in the inhaled air and in the exhaled air.

  a) Explain the difference in the values for the percentage of oxygen in inhaled and exhaled air.

	Inhaled air (%)	Exhaled air (%)
Nitrogen	78	78
Oxygen	21	16
Carbon dioxide		
Other gases	0.9	0.9

....

....

....

....

[1]

  b) Explain how the percentage of carbon dioxide would differ between inhaled and exhaled air.

....

....

[2]

[Total 3 marks]

Topic B1 — Cell Level Systems

4 One method of making alcoholic beer involves breaking down barley grains to produce sugar. Yeast (a type of fungus) and water are later added to the sugar, and the mixture is left to allow the yeast to ferment. During the fermentation process, it is important that the mixture is held in a sealed container.

a) Write the word equation for the respiration reaction that takes place when making beer.

.... → .... + ...
[2]

b) Suggest why a tight seal on the container is important in the beer-making process.

....

....
[2]

[Total 4 marks]

5 A scientist was measuring the effects of exercise on respiration. He asked a male volunteer to jog for 10 minutes on a treadmill. The speed of the treadmill was increased over the course of the 10 minutes, so that he was gradually working harder, until at the end he felt unable to do any more exercise. The graph below shows the oxygen consumption (the amount of oxygen used by the body per minute) of the man during the exercise.

a) Describe how oxygen consumption changed during the exercise.

....

....
[2]

b) In the final two minutes of the exercise, the man was respiring anaerobically.

i) Comment on the relative yields of ATP produced in aerobic and anaerobic respiration.

....
[1]

ii) Explain how the graph shows the period of time when the man was respiring anaerobically.

....

....

....
[2]

[Total 5 marks]

Topic B1 — Cell Level Systems

Biological Molecules

1 Which of the following molecules is a monomer?

  A protein
  B starch
  C amino acid
  D lipid

  Your answer ☐

[Total 1 mark]

2 Cell membranes contain structures called glycoproteins. As shown in the diagram below, glycoproteins are composed of both protein and carbohydrate.

The cell uses enzymes to regularly break down and rebuild glycoproteins.

a) State the type of monomer produced when the cell breaks down the carbohydrate portion of glycoproteins.

....
[1]

b) State the type of monomer the cell needs in order to rebuild the protein portion of glycoproteins.

....
[1]

[Total 2 marks]

3 Some bacterial species produce lipase (an enzyme that breaks down lipids). Two different species of bacteria were placed separately on an agar plate. The agar contained a lipid which made it cloudy. The plate was then left overnight. The results are shown in the diagram.

a) Bacteria that break down lipids are able to use the products of the reaction to transfer energy to the cell. Name the process the cells use to do this.

....
[1]

b) Use the diagram to suggest which species of bacteria contains lipase. Explain your answer.

....
....
....
[2]

c) Suggest why the pH on the surface of the clear zone might be lower than on the rest of the agar.

....
....
[2]

[Total 5 marks]

Topic B1 — Cell Level Systems

Photosynthesis

Warm-Up

Complete the following passage using words on the right. You do not need to use all the words.

Photosynthesis is carried out by organisms such as algae and ………………………… . It uses energy transferred by ………………………… to produce ………………………… . This energy is absorbed by subcellular structures called ………………………… .

mitochondria
glucose
green plants
fungi
chloroplasts
minerals
fructose
light

1   Photosynthesis is a chemical reaction, which allows photosynthetic organisms to generate their own food source.

   a) Write the word equation for photosynthesis.

   ……………… + ……………… → ……………… + ………………

   [2]

   b) Photosynthesis is an endothermic reaction. This means that:

   A energy is transferred from the environment during the reaction.
   B energy is transferred to the surroundings during the reaction.
   C energy is made during the reaction.
   D energy is broken down during the reaction.

   Your answer ☐

   [1]
   [Total 3 marks]

2   The sugar produced in photosynthesis can be broken down to transfer energy as part of respiration in a plant.

   a) Give **one** other way in which a plant uses the sugar produced by photosynthesis.

   ………………………………………………………………………………………………………
   [1]

   b) Explain why photosynthesis is important for the majority of life on Earth.

   ………………………………………………………………………………………………………
   ………………………………………………………………………………………………………
   ………………………………………………………………………………………………………
   ………………………………………………………………………………………………………
   [3]
   [Total 4 marks]

Topic B1 — Cell Level Systems

The Rate of Photosynthesis

1 The distance of a plant from a light source affects the plant's rate of photosynthesis.

a) Name the mathematical law that governs the relationship between light intensity and distance from a light source.

....
[1]

b) A plant is 40 cm away from a light source. The plant is moved so that it is 20 cm away from the same light source. Describe how the intensity of light reaching the plant will change.

....
[1]

[Total 2 marks]

2 The graph below shows how temperature affects the rate of photosynthesis in a green plant.

a) Describe and explain the shape of the curve between points **A** and **B**.

....
....
....
....
[2]

b) Describe and explain the shape of the curve between points **B** and **C**.

....
....
....
....
....
[3]

[Total 5 marks]

Topic B1 — Cell Level Systems

3 *Myriophyllum* is an aquatic plant. A student decided to investigate the effect of light intensity on the rate of photosynthesis in *Myriophyllum*.

The student set up a test tube containing a solution of sodium hydrogencarbonate next to a lamp. She then took a cutting of *Myriophyllum* and placed it in the test tube. Finally, she sealed and attached a gas syringe to the test tube and measured the amount of gas collected from the test tube in two hours. She repeated this for four more test tubes at different distances from the lamp. Her results are shown in the table below.

Test tube	Distance away from light (cm)	Gas collected (cm^3)	Rate of gas production (cm^3/h)
1	0	1.50	0.75
2	10	1.40	0.70
3	20	1.20	0.60
4	30	0.70	0.35
5	40	0.20	X

a) Name the gas collected in the gas syringe.

....
[1]

b) Calculate the rate of gas production in **Test tube 5**.

X = ... cm^3/h
[1]

c) i) Using the results in the table, describe and explain the effect of the distance from the lamp on the rate of gas production in *Myriophyllum*.

....
....
....
....
[3]

ii) Suggest **one** way in which you could increase your confidence in the answer you gave to part c) i).

....
[1]

d) Explain why it is important that the test tubes are all next to the same lamp.

....
....
....
[2]

[Total 8 marks]

Topic B1 — Cell Level Systems

4 A student carried out an experiment to investigate the effect of changing the concentration of carbon dioxide on the rate of photosynthesis in a green plant. The results were plotted on the graph shown below.

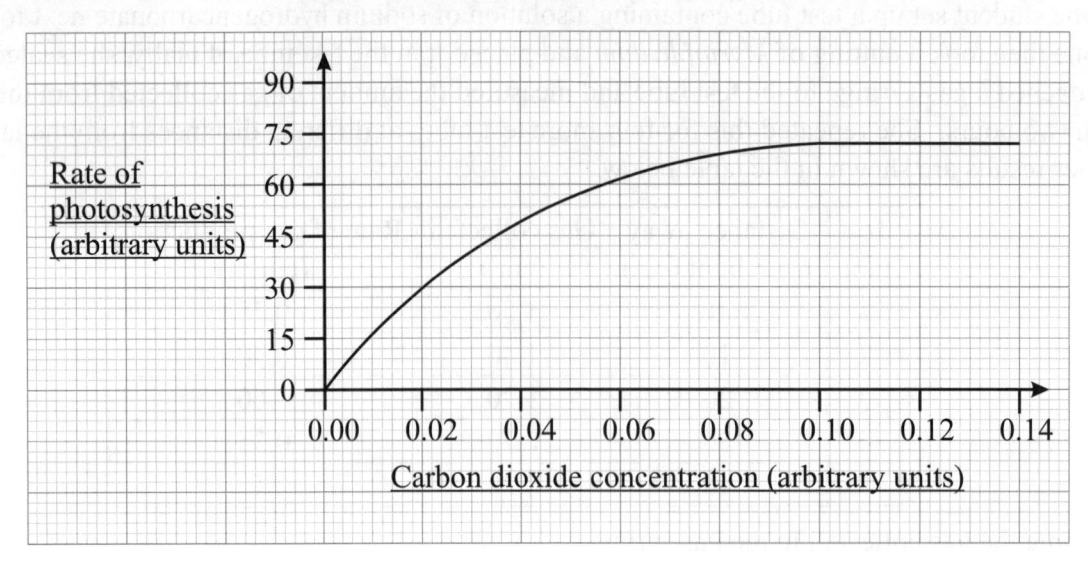

Grade 6-7

a) Describe the trend shown in the graph.

....

....

....

....
[2]

b) At a certain point, the CO_2 concentration is no longer limiting the rate of photosynthesis. Suggest **two** factors that could be limiting the rate at this point.

....
[2]

c) In the space below, sketch a graph to show how light intensity affects the rate of photosynthesis.

[2]

[Total 6 marks]

Exam Practice Tip

There's a lot to learn about limiting factors and the rate of photosynthesis. It's a good idea to practise drawing the graphs to show the effect of light intensity, carbon dioxide concentration and temperature on the rate of photosynthesis. Also, make sure you know how to investigate the effect of these factors on photosynthesis in the lab.

Topic B1 — Cell Level Systems

Topic B2 — Scaling Up

The Cell Cycle and Mitosis

1 How many new cells are produced when a cell divides by mitosis?

    A   2
    B   4
    C   8
    D   10

Your answer ☐

[Total 1 mark]

2 Which of these statements about the cell cycle is **true**?

    A   Mitosis occurs twice during one turn of the cell cycle.
    B   The cell cycle involves several growth stages in addition to mitosis.
    C   Cells divide once by meiosis as well as once by mitosis during the cell cycle.
    D   The cell cycle only occurs in animals. Plants use a different process.

Your answer ☐

[Total 1 mark]

3 Mitosis can be split into several stages.
The diagram below shows one of these stages.

a) Describe what is happening during the stage of mitosis shown in the diagram above.

....

....
[2]

b) Describe what happens to the cell after the stage of mitosis shown in the diagram above.

....

....
[2]

c) What must have happened to the cell's DNA before mitosis could take place?
Explain why this is necessary.

....

....
[2]

[Total 6 marks]

Cell Differentiation and Stem Cells

1 Stem cells are unspecialised cells that can become different types of specialised cells. *(Grade 4-6)*

a) Which of these is the name of the process by which a cell becomes specialised?

    A   mutation
    B   adaptation
    C   functionalisation
    D   differentiation

Your answer ☐

[1]

b) What is the benefit to plants and animals of having specialised cells?

....

[1]

[Total 2 marks]

2 Scientists can use stem cells to grow new cells, on which they can then test new drugs. *(Grade 6-7)*

a) Suggest **one** reason why scientists may prefer to use embryonic stem cells for research rather than adult stem cells.

....

....

[2]

b) In terms of their function, how do adult stem cells and embryonic stem cells differ?

....

....

[2]

[Total 4 marks]

3 The shoot tip of a plant can be used to grow a whole plant, through a process called micropropagation which is often used in scientific research. *(Grade 7-9)*

Using your knowledge of plant stem cells, explain how this process can generate whole plants.

....

....

....

....

[Total 3 marks]

Topic B2 — Scaling Up

Diffusion, Active Transport and Osmosis

Warm-Up

The diagram on the right shows three cells. The carbon dioxide concentration inside each cell is shown. Draw arrows between the cells to show in which directions the carbon dioxide will diffuse.

carbon dioxide concentration = 0.2% carbon dioxide concentration = 1.5%
carbon dioxide concentration = 3.0% ← cell

1 Osmosis is a form of diffusion. Complete the following definition of osmosis. *(Grade 4-6)*

Osmosis is the net movement of .... molecules across a partially permeable membrane from a region of .... water potential to a region of .... water potential.

[Total 3 marks]

2 In which **one** of these scenarios is osmosis occurring? *(Grade 4-6)*

A A plant is absorbing water from the soil.
B Sugar is being taken up into the blood from the gut.
C Water is evaporating from a leaf.
D Oxygen is entering the blood from the lungs.

Your answer ☐

[Total 1 mark]

3 Diffusion, osmosis and active transport all involve the movement of molecules. *(Grade 6-7)*

Draw arrows in the boxes underneath the diagram on the right to illustrate the net movement of the following:

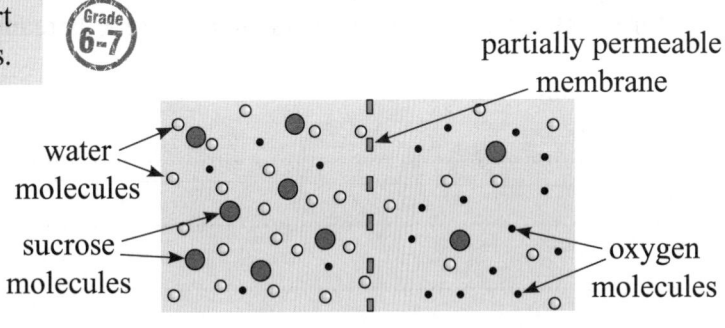

a) sucrose molecules moving by active transport:

[1]

b) water molecules moving by osmosis:

[1]

c) oxygen molecules moving by diffusion:

[1]

[Total 3 marks]

Topic B2 — Scaling Up

4 The cell membrane is important in controlling what substances can enter or leave a cell. The diagram below shows some molecules diffusing across a cell membrane.

a) Describe the process of diffusion.

....

....
[2]

b) Which molecule shown in the diagram represents a protein?

A   molecule **W**
B   molecule **X**
C   molecule **Y**
D   molecule **Z**

Your answer ☐

[1]
[Total 3 marks]

5 Amino acids are absorbed in the gut by active transport. The diagram below shows amino acids being absorbed into the bloodstream across the epithelial cells of the gut.

a) Using the diagram above, explain why active transport is necessary for the absorption of amino acids into the bloodstream.

....

....

....

....
[3]

b) Explain why there are lots of mitochondria present in the epithelial cells of the gut.

....

....
[1]
[Total 4 marks]

Exam Practice Tip

Make sure that you've got diffusion, osmosis and active transport sorted — learn their definitions and make sure that you're crystal clear on the differences between them. If you don't bother I reckon you'll kick yourself after the exams...

Exchanging Substances

1. A student was investigating the effect of size on the uptake of substances by diffusion. He cut different sized cubes of agar containing phenolphthalein (a pH indicator) and placed them in beakers of alkaline solution. The student timed how long it took for the alkali to diffuse through to the centre of each cube (and so completely change the colour of the agar).

   The table shows the relationship between the surface area and volume of the agar cubes.

   a) Calculate the values of **X**, **Y** and **Z** in the table.

Cube size (cm)	Surface area (cm^2)	Volume (cm^3)	Simple ratio
2 × 2 × 2	24	8	3 : 1
3 × 3 × 3	**X**	**Y**	2 : 1
5 × 5 × 5	150	125	**Z** : 1

   X = ... cm^2

   Y = ... cm^3

   Z = ...
   [3]

   b) Predict which cube size took the longest to change colour. Give **one** reason for your answer.

   Cube size ....

   Reason ....
   [1]
   [Total 4 marks]

2* All organisms need to exchange substances with the environment in order to survive. Outline how multicellular organisms and single-celled organisms exchange substances, and explain why they exchange substances differently.

   ....

   [Total 6 marks]

Topic B2 — Scaling Up

Exchange Surfaces

1 Leaves are adapted for gas exchange. The diagram below shows a cross-section of a leaf.

a) Name the openings in the leaf labelled **X**.

.... [1]

b) Describe the movement of gases into and out of the leaf that are a result of photosynthesis taking place.

....

.... [3]

c) What are **two** functions of air spaces in the leaf?

....

.... [2]

[Total 6 marks]

2 Ventilation helps to supply gases to gas exchange surfaces in animals.

a) Other than ventilation, state and explain **two** features of an effective gas exchange surface in animals.

....

....

.... [4]

b) The alveoli in the lungs are an example of a gas exchange surface. The diagram on the right shows an alveolus and a capillary.

i) Which row of the table shows the correct concentrations of gases in the blood at point **Z**?

	Oxygen concentration	Carbon dioxide concentration
A	high	high
B	low	high
C	high	low
D	low	low

Your answer ☐ [1]

ii) At point **Y** is the net diffusion of carbon dioxide into or out of the blood?

.... [1]

[Total 6 marks]

Topic B2 — Scaling Up

3 The roots of plants are covered in millions of root hair cells which are specialised for the exchange of water and mineral ions.

a) Explain how root hair cells take up water from the soil.

....
....
....
....
[2]

b) The concentration of mineral ions is often higher in the plant than the soil. Name the process by which the roots take up mineral ions.

....
[1]
[Total 3 marks]

4 The small intestine is where the products of digestion are absorbed into the blood. State and explain **two** ways in which the structure of the small intestine enables it to carry out its function effectively.

....
....
....
....
....
....
[Total 4 marks]

5 Emphysema is a disease that weakens and breaks down the walls of the alveoli. Suggest why a person with emphysema may have a lower concentration of oxygen in their blood than a person who doesn't have the disease.

....
....
....
....
[Total 3 marks]

Exam Practice Tip
It may seem obvious, but if you're asked to explain how the structure of something relates to its function, don't just dive straight in and rattle off what it looks like. You need to focus on the function and then pick out the individual structures that could help it to carry out that function. For each structure, make sure you give a clear explanation of how it helps.

Topic B2 — Scaling Up

The Circulatory System

Warm-Up

Use the words on the right to correctly fill in the gaps in the passage.
You don't have to use every word, but each word can only be used once.

coronary
carbon dioxide
oxygen
mitochondria
pulmonary
cardiac
plasmids

The heart is made up of .... muscle. These muscle cells contain lots of .... to provide the cells with ATP. They also need their own blood supply to deliver nutrients and .... Blood is supplied to the heart by the .... arteries.

1 Humans have a double circulatory system, in which the heart pumps blood around the body through a network of veins and arteries. The diagram below shows the human heart.

   a) Name the parts of the heart labelled **X** and **Y**.

      X: ....

      Y: ....
                                                                                        [2]

   b) Put the following stages in order to describe how blood flows through the right side of the heart by writing the numbers **1** to **5** in the boxes. The first one has been done for you.

	Blood is forced through a valve into the right ventricle.
	Blood enters the pulmonary artery, and heads towards the lungs.
	The atrium contracts.
	The ventricle contracts, forcing blood through a valve.
1	Deoxygenated blood flows into the right atrium from the vena cava.

                                                                                                                                            [2]

   c) Explain why the human circulatory system is described as a double circulatory system.

      ....

      ....

      ....
                                                                                                                                            [3]

   d) Explain the **benefits** to humans of having a double circulatory system.

      ....

      ....

      ....

      ....

      ....
                                                                                                                                            [3]

[Total 10 marks]

Topic B2 — Scaling Up

The Blood Vessels

1 Blood is carried around the body in blood vessels.
Different types of blood vessel perform different functions.

Grade 6-7

The diagrams below show three different types of blood vessel.

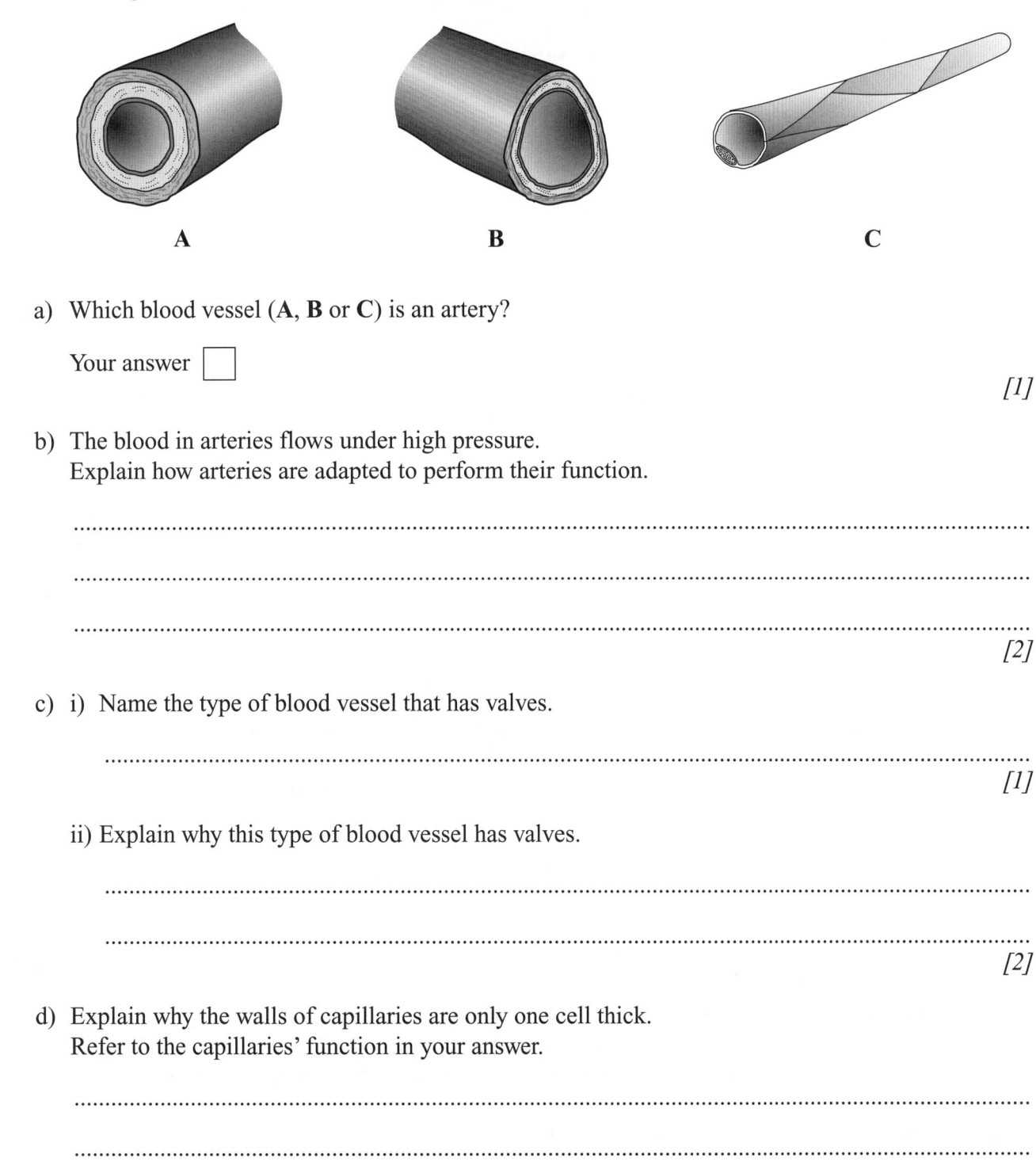

A   B   C

a) Which blood vessel (**A**, **B** or **C**) is an artery?

Your answer ☐

[1]

b) The blood in arteries flows under high pressure.
Explain how arteries are adapted to perform their function.

....

....

....

[2]

c) i) Name the type of blood vessel that has valves.

....

[1]

ii) Explain why this type of blood vessel has valves.

....

....

[2]

d) Explain why the walls of capillaries are only one cell thick.
Refer to the capillaries' function in your answer.

....

....

....

....

[2]

[Total 8 marks]

Topic B2 — Scaling Up

The Blood

1 Blood is made up of several different components. *(Grade 6-7)*

The components of blood can be separated by spinning them at high speed.
The diagram below shows a tube of blood that has been separated in this way.

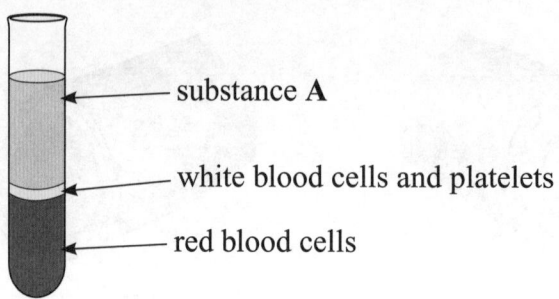

- substance **A**
- white blood cells and platelets
- red blood cells

a) Identify the substance labelled **A**.

....

[1]

b) Substance **A** transports the blood cells, as well as nutrients and other substances, around the body. Give **three** examples of substances, other than cells, which are transported in substance **A**.

....

....

[3]

[Total 4 marks]

2 Red blood cells carry oxygen in the blood to other tissues in the body. *(Grade 7-9)*

a) Explain how the structure of red blood cells make them well adapted to their function.

....

....

....

....

[3]

b) Thalassaemia is a genetic condition which can cause people to have less haemoglobin than normal in their red blood cells. One of the symptoms of this condition is tiredness. Suggest why a decreased amount of haemoglobin in a person's red blood cells may result in tiredness.

....

....

....

....

[4]

[Total 7 marks]

Topic B2 — Scaling Up

Plant Transport Systems and Transpiration

Warm-Up

Use the words below to correctly fill in the gaps in the passage.
You don't have to use every word, but each word can only be used once.

perspiration   leaves   translocation stream   mineral ions   transpiration stream
roots   translocation   transpiration   sugars   evaporation   stem

The process by which water is moved up a plant is called ………………………… . It is caused by the ………………………… and diffusion of water from a plant's surface, most often from the ………………………… . This causes a constant ………………………… to flow through the plant as more water is drawn up from the ………………………… to replace the lost water. Another process, called …………………………, is the transport of ………………………… and other food substances around the plant.

1   Plants have two separate types of transport vessel. They are shown in the diagrams below.

Vessel A   **Xylem vessel**

a) i) What type of vessel is vessel **A**?

   ……………………………………………………………………………………………………
   [1]

   ii) What is the function of vessel **A**?

   ……………………………………………………………………………………………………
   ……………………………………………………………………………………………………
   [1]

b) i) Describe the structure of xylem walls and what benefit they give to plants.

   ……………………………………………………………………………………………………
   ……………………………………………………………………………………………………
   [2]

   ii) Describe the involvement of xylem in transpiration.

   ……………………………………………………………………………………………………
   ……………………………………………………………………………………………………
   [1]

   [Total 5 marks]

More on Transpiration

1 The diagram below shows part of the surface of a leaf at high magnification. *Grade 4-6*

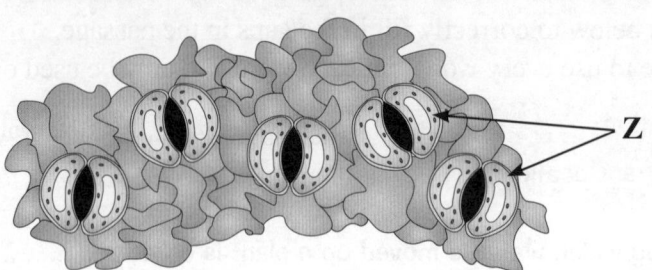

a) Name the cells labelled **Z** in the diagram.

....
[1]

b) The cells labelled **Z** are responsible for the opening and closure of the stomata. Describe how these cells change in order for the stomata to close.

....
[1]

c) What is the purpose of stomata opening and closing?

....
[1]
[Total 3 marks]

2 The table below shows the diameter of eight open stomata. Four stomata were measured on two separate leaves (**A** and **B**). *Grade 7-9*

	Diameter of stomata (µm)
Leaf A	25.2, 20.1, 18.7, 17.9
Leaf B	14.7, 12.8, 14.1, 13.2

a) Calculate the mean stomatal diameter for each leaf.

Leaf **A** = ... µm   Leaf **B** = ... µm
[2]

b) Leaves **A** and **B** are from the same species. Suggest which leaf had its stomatal measurements taken at a **lower** light intensity. Explain your answer.

....

....

....

....
[3]
[Total 5 marks]

Topic B2 — Scaling Up

Investigating Transpiration — PRACTICAL

1   A group of students were investigating the effect of air flow on the rate of transpiration. They set up a simple potometer as shown in the diagram below and kept the light intensity in the room constant. *(Grade 6-7)*

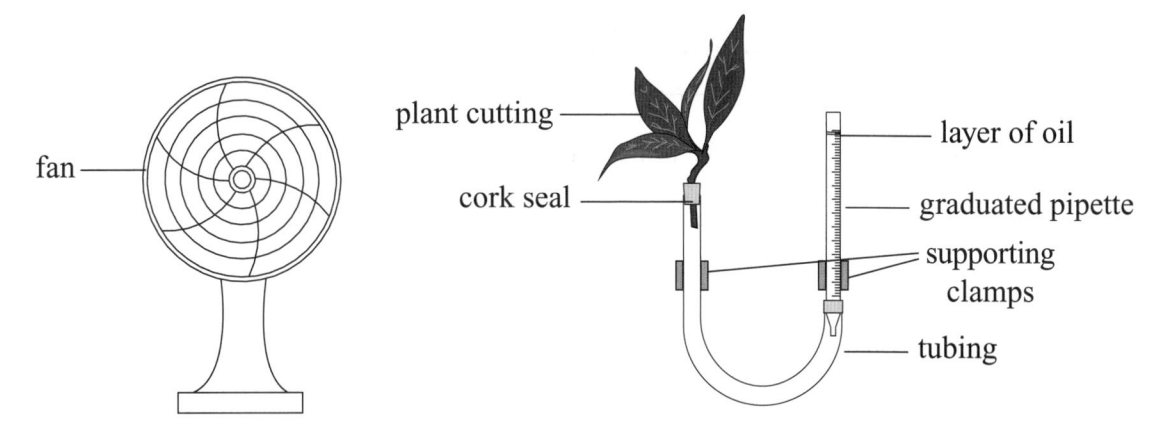

The students recorded the change in the volume of water in the pipette over 30 minutes, in normal conditions. They repeated this five times. They then carried out these steps with the fan turned on to simulate windy conditions. Their results are shown in the table below.

	Environmental condition	Repeat 1	2	3	4	5	Mean
Water uptake in 30 minutes (cm^3)	Still Air	1.2	1.2	1.0	0.8	1.1	1.1
	Moving Air	2.0	1.8	2.3	1.9	1.7	1.9

a) Draw a bar chart to show the mean water uptake for still air and moving air.

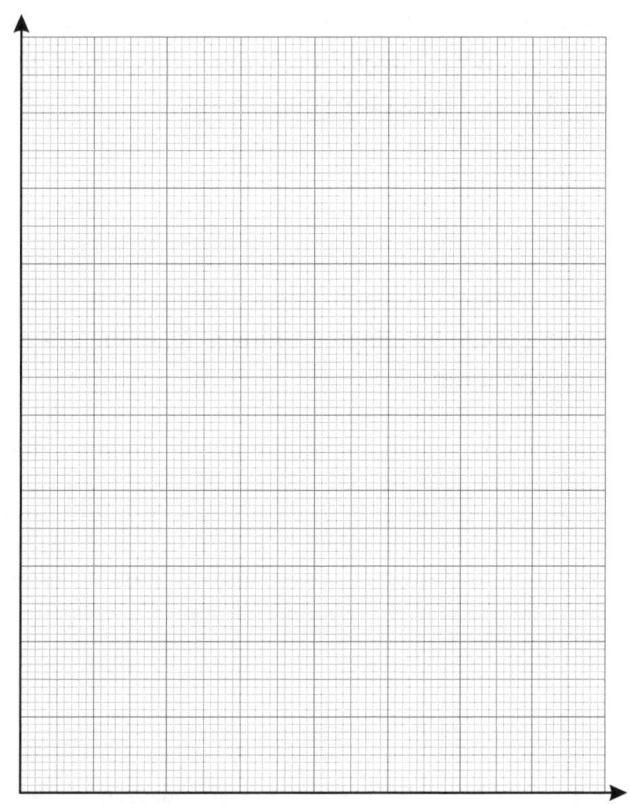

[3]

Topic B2 — Scaling Up

b) Calculate the range of the results for still air.

range = ... cm³
[1]

c) Describe the relationship between air flow around the plant and transpiration rate.

....
[1]

d) Explain the effect of air flow on the transpiration rate.

....

....

....
[2]

e) The rate of transpiration can be calculated using the formula:

$$\text{rate of transpiration} = \frac{\text{mean volume of water uptake}}{\text{time taken}}$$

Calculate the rate of transpiration for the plant in moving air. Give your answer in cm³/hr.

transpiration rate = ... cm³/hr
[2]

f) Another group of students carrying out the same experiment forgot about keeping the light intensity in the room constant. After the first repeat, one of the students turned on a light positioned near the apparatus. What effect do you think this would have on the water uptake in the remaining repeats? Give a reason for your answer.

....

....
[2]

g) Suggest how this experiment could be adapted to investigate the effect of changing the light intensity on the rate of transpiration.

....

....

....
[2]

[Total 13 marks]

Exam Practice Tip

Don't panic if you don't recognise the exact apparatus used in an exam question. As with many other bits of scientific kit, there are several different types of potometer. They all perform the same task, but some do it in a different way to others. If an exam question does use apparatus that you've not learnt about, you'll always be given all the info you need.

Topic B2 — Scaling Up

Topic B3 — Organism Level Systems

The Nervous System

Warm-Up

Circle the examples that are reflex reactions.

Pedalling a bike.   The pupils widening in dim light.

Dropping a hot plate.   Running to catch a bus.   Writing a letter.

1   Which of the following sentences about reflex reactions is correct?

    A   Reflex reactions are slow and under conscious control.
    B   Reflex reactions are slow and automatic.
    C   Reflex reactions are rapid and automatic.
    D   Reflex reactions are rapid and under conscious control.

Your answer ☐

[Total 1 mark]

2   The diagram below shows part of the human nervous system.

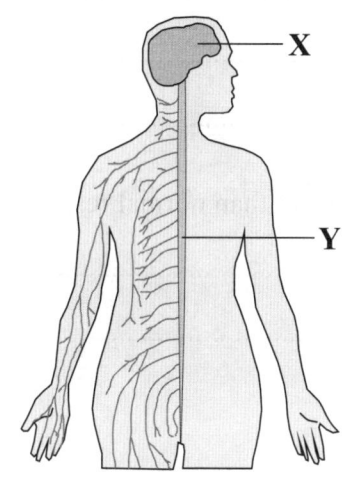

a) Name the structures labelled **X** and **Y** on the diagram.

X ....

Y ....
[2]

b) i) Which part of the nervous system do structures **X** and **Y** form?

....
[1]

ii) Describe the role of the part of the nervous system formed by structures **X** and **Y**.

....

....
[2]

[Total 5 marks]

Topic B3 — Organism Level Systems

3 Mohini put her finger near a candle flame. She quickly moved her hand away from it. The diagram below shows the reflex arc involved in this movement.

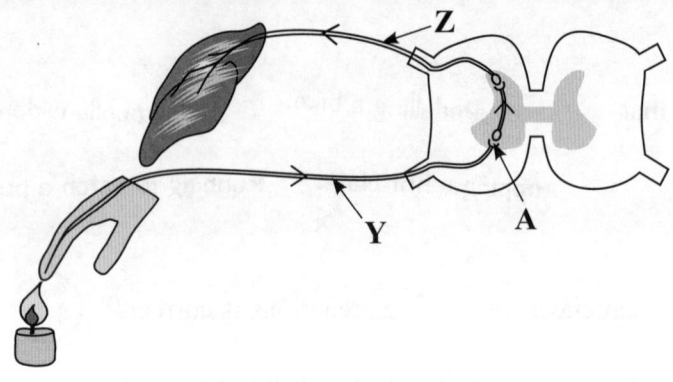

Grade 6-7

a) i) Name structures **Y** and **Z**.

Y ....

Z ....
[2]

ii) Structure **A** is the junction between two neurones. Name structure **A**.

....
[1]

b) In the reflex arc shown in the diagram above, state:

the stimulus ....

the effector ....
[2]

c) What makes reflex actions quicker than normal responses?

....

....
[1]
[Total 6 marks]

4 Information is passed along neurones as electrical impulses.

Grade 6-7

a) Name the long part of a neurone that impulses travel along.

....
[1]

b) Explain a structural feature of a neurone which can help speed up the transmission of impulses.

....

....
[2]
[Total 3 marks]

Exam Practice Tip

The pathway that nervous impulses take in a reflex arc is always the same — from receptor to effector. Learn the full details of the pathway involved and you'll be able to tackle any question on reflexes, even if it's a reflex you've not learnt.

Topic B3 — Organism Level Systems

5 Stimulants, such as caffeine, increase the rate at which nerve impulses travel. An investigation was carried out to assess the impact of different caffeinated drinks on reaction time.

Grade 7-9

The investigation involved measuring reaction time using a ruler drop test. In this test, a ruler is held above a student's outstretched hand by another person. The ruler is then dropped without warning and the student catches the ruler as quickly as possible. The distance down the ruler where the student caught it is used to calculate their reaction time in seconds (s).
Three different students (Students **1** to **3**) consumed a different caffeinated drink — each one contained a different amount of caffeine. Each student then undertook three ruler drop tests. The results are shown in the table below.

a) Calculate the mean reaction time for Student **2** and Student **3**.

	Reaction time (s)		
	Student 1	Student 2	Student 3
Test 1	0.09	0.16	0.20
Test 2	0.10	0.13	0.22
Test 3	0.43	0.15	0.19
Mean	0.21		

Student **2** = ... s

Student **3** = ... s

[2]

b) Identify the anomalous result in the table.

....
[1]

c) The students' reaction time without any caffeine was **not** measured. Explain why it should have been included in the investigation to assess the effect of each caffeinated drink.

....
....
....
[2]

d) Explain why the results of this investigation can't be used to **compare** the effect of the three different caffeinated drinks on reaction time.

....
....
[2]

e) An alternative version of the investigation was carried out. This time, the effect of a set quantity of caffeine on the reaction times of different individuals was investigated. Reaction times of three different students were measured, both before and after the consumption of caffeine.
Give **three** variables that should have been controlled in this investigation.

....
....
....
[3]

[Total 10 marks]

Topic B3 — Organism Level Systems

Hormones and Negative Feedback Systems

Warm-Up

The graph below shows the change in the level of a hormone controlled by a negative feedback response over time.
Use the words on the right to fill in the labels on the graph.

normal   low   stimulated
inhibited   high

- release of hormone ....
- .... level of hormone
- .... level of hormone detected
- .... level of hormone detected
- release of hormone ....

1 Hormones are chemical messengers that affect the behaviour of their target cells. Explain how hormones reach their target cells and cause them to respond.

Grade 6-7

....
....
....

[Total 3 marks]

2 Thyroxine and adrenaline are hormones that are released in the body.

Grade 6-7

a) Which statement best describes the role of thyroxine in the body?
- **A** It is involved in determining skin colour.
- **B** It regulates the metabolic rate.
- **C** It is produced in response to stress.
- **D** It decreases liver function.

Your answer ☐

[1]

b) Where is adrenaline released from?

....

[1]

c) Give an example of a situation that might trigger adrenaline release and describe the effect this might have on the body.

....
....
....

[3]

[Total 5 marks]

Topic B3 — Organism Level Systems

Hormones in Reproduction

1 The release of sex hormones begins at puberty. *Grade 4-6*

a) What is the name of the main female hormone, produced in the ovaries?

....
[1]

b) i) Name the hormone that stimulates sperm production in men.

....
[1]

ii) Where in the male body is this hormone produced?

....
[1]

[Total 3 marks]

2 The diagram shows how the levels of four hormones change during the menstrual cycle. *Grade 6-7*

a) During which time period marked on the diagram (**A**, **B**, **C** or **D**) does menstruation occur?

....
[1]

b) Add an arrow (↑) to the x-axis of the diagram, to show the time at which ovulation occurs.
[1]

c) Before ovulation can occur, an egg must mature. Name the hormone that causes this.

....
[1]

d) Name the hormone marked **X** on the diagram and explain its roles in the menstrual cycle.

....

....

....
[3]

[Total 6 marks]

Topic B3 — Organism Level Systems

Hormones for Fertility and Contraception

1 A couple want to have children but the woman has not yet become pregnant. Blood tests have shown that she has a low level of follicle-stimulating hormone (FSH). She is treated with a fertility drug.

Grade 6-7

a) Explain why a low level of FSH may be preventing the woman from becoming pregnant.

....

....
[2]

b) In addition to FSH, which other hormone may the fertility drug contain to help the woman become pregnant?

....
[1]
[Total 3 marks]

2 The mini-pill is a method of oral contraception. It contains progesterone and needs to be taken around the same time every day.

Grade 6-7

a) Name **three** other types of contraceptive that use **only** progesterone.

....

....
[3]

b) Like the mini-pill, the combined pill also contains progesterone. Name the other hormone that the combined pill contains.

....
[1]

c) Many women who take the mini-pill don't ovulate.

i) Explain why taking the mini-pill may prevent ovulation.

....

....
[2]

ii) It's not only the effect on ovulation that makes the mini-pill an effective contraceptive. Explain **two** other ways in which the mini-pill can prevent pregnancy.

....

....

....
[2]
[Total 8 marks]

Exam Practice Tip

For this stuff to make sense it's important to have learnt the menstrual cycle and all the different hormones involved.

Topic B3 — Organism Level Systems

More on Contraception

Warm-Up

Sort the methods of contraception into the correct columns in the table.

'natural' methods, condom, contraceptive injection, diaphragm, combined pill, intrauterine device (IUD), mini-pill, sterilisation, contraceptive patch

Hormonal	Non-hormonal

1 Fertility can be controlled by non-hormonal methods of contraception.

a) Name a barrier method of contraception that can be used by women.

....
[1]

b) How do barrier methods of contraception prevent pregnancy?

....
[1]

c) Which form of non-hormonal contraception is the least effective?

....
[1]

d) Sterilisation is a permanent method of contraception that can be carried out on both men and women. Explain how sterilisation of men and women prevents pregnancy.

....

....
[2]

e) i) Explain how intrauterine devices prevent pregnancy.

....

....
[2]

ii) Give **two** advantages of the intrauterine device over the female condom.

....

....
[2]

[Total 9 marks]

Topic B3 — Organism Level Systems

Controlling Blood Sugar Level

1 The concentration of glucose in the blood is controlled by hormones. *Grade 4-6*

a) Which gland in the human body monitors and controls blood glucose concentration?

    A pancreas
    B pituitary gland
    C thyroid
    D testis

Your answer ☐ *[1]*

b) Which hormone is produced when blood glucose concentration becomes too high?

.... *[1]*

c) What happens to excess glucose in the blood?

....

.... *[1]*

[Total 3 marks]

2 Diabetes exists in two different forms, Type 1 and Type 2. *Grade 6-7*

a) What causes Type 1 diabetes?

.... *[1]*

b) What can happen if Type 1 diabetes is left untreated?

.... *[1]*

c) Type 1 diabetes is treated with insulin therapy. This usually involves injecting insulin. Suggest **one** factor that might affect the amount of insulin injected by a patient.

.... *[1]*

d) What causes Type 2 diabetes?

.... *[1]*

e) Other than prescribing drugs, give **two** treatments recommended for Type 2 diabetes.

....

.... *[2]*

f) Give a risk factor for Type 2 diabetes.

.... *[1]*

[Total 7 marks]

Topic B3 — Organism Level Systems

3 In an experiment, the blood glucose concentration of a person without diabetes was recorded at regular intervals in a 90 minute time period. Fifteen minutes into the experiment, a glucose drink was given. The graph below shows the results of the experiment.

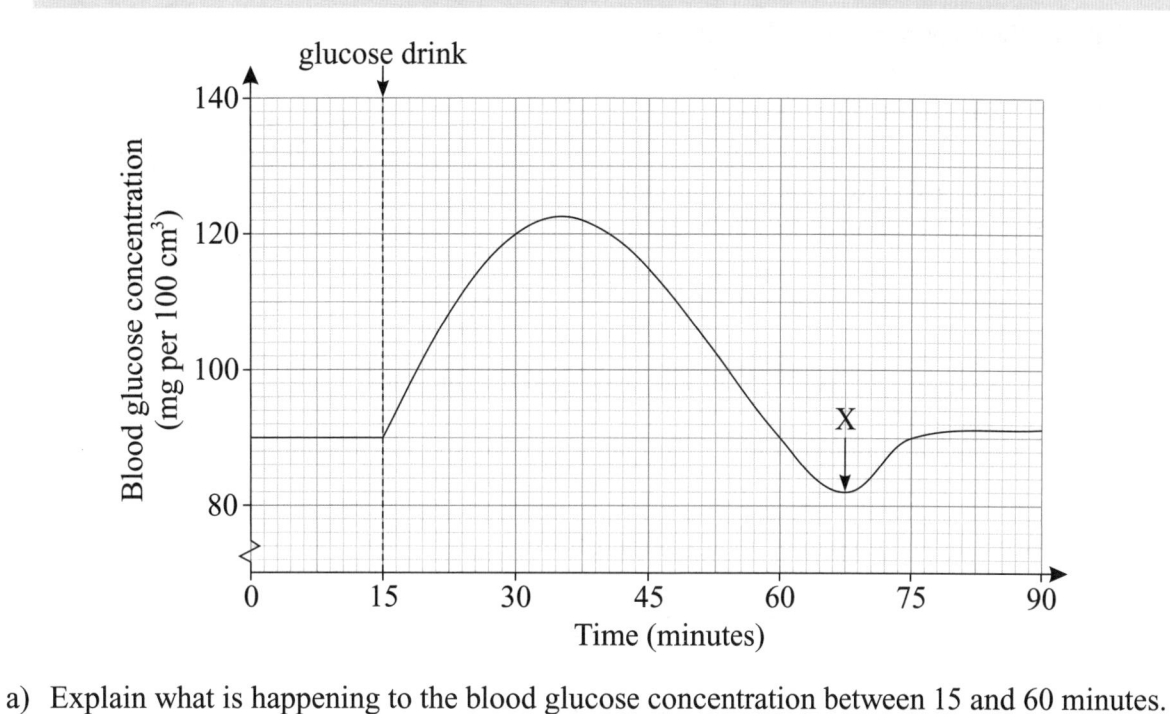

Grade 7-9

a) Explain what is happening to the blood glucose concentration between 15 and 60 minutes.

....
....
....
[3]

b) Name the hormone being released by the pancreas at point **X** on the graph.

....
[1]

c) Describe the effect that hormone **X** has on the blood glucose concentration.

....
[1]

d) Explain how hormone **X** causes this effect.

....
....
[1]

e) Suggest how the shape of the graph would differ if the person had Type 1 diabetes.

....
....
[1]

[Total 7 marks]

Exam Practice Tip

There are a few similar-sounding names when it comes to the control of blood glucose, so make sure you've got your head around which is which (and how to spell them). You won't get a mark if, for example, you write about 'glucogen'...

Topic B3 — Organism Level Systems

Topic B4 — Community Level Systems

The Carbon Cycle

1   The diagram shows part of the carbon cycle. The arrows indicate the transfer of carbon and carbon compounds within an ecosystem. *(Grade 6-7)*

a) Using the diagram, give **one** abiotic component of the ecosystem that carbon cycles through.

    ....
    [1]

b) Name the process occurring at the point labelled **Y** on the diagram.

    ....
    [1]

c) Name the process by which plants obtain carbon from the air.

    ....
    [1]

d) Explain how fossil fuels can contribute carbon to the atmosphere.

    ....
    [1]

e) Describe what is happening at the point labelled **X** on the diagram.

    ....
    ....
    ....
    ....
    [2]
    [Total 6 marks]

2   Many trees have fewer leaves in winter. Using your knowledge of the carbon cycle, suggest why this may contribute to an increase in the concentration of carbon dioxide in the atmosphere in winter. *(Grade 7-9)*

    ....
    ....
    ....
    ....
    [Total 2 marks]

Exam Practice Tip

There are lots of different ways that information about the carbon cycle can be shown, so don't be put off in the exam if you're presented with a cycle drawn differently to the way you're used to. Learn the cycle inside out and you'll be fine.

Topic B4 — Community Level Systems

The Nitrogen Cycle and the Water Cycle

1 Fresh water is constantly recycled through the water cycle. *(Grade 4-6)*

Complete the following sentences.

Heat from the Sun causes the .... of water from the land and sea.

Water is also transferred to the atmosphere from plants by the process of ....

As the warm water vapour rises, clouds form by the process of ....

Water falls from clouds in the form of rain, snow or hail, in a process known

as ....

[Total 4 marks]

2 All living things contain nitrogen. Nitrogen is constantly recycled in the nitrogen cycle. *(Grade 6-7)*

a) Nitrogen is needed for making proteins for growth. Give **two** ways that atmospheric nitrogen is converted into nitrogen compounds that plants can use.

....

....

....

....

....

[2]

b) Nitrogen compounds are taken in by animals when they eat plants or other animals. How are nitrogen compounds in animals returned to the soil?

....

....

....

....

[3]

[Total 5 marks]

3 Which of the following human activities might decrease the amount of nitrogen available to crops? *(Grade 6-7)*

    A   Applying horse manure to the soil.
    B   Using nitrogen-based fertilisers on the soil.
    C   Over watering of the crops, causing the soil to become waterlogged.
    D   Planting legumes in amongst the crops.

Your answer ☐

[Total 1 mark]

Topic B4 — Community Level Systems

Ecosystems and Interactions Between Organisms

Warm-Up

Environmental factors can be abiotic or biotic. In each box below, write either the letter 'A' if the environmental factor is abiotic, or the letter 'B' if the factor is biotic.

☐ Moisture level   ☐ Number of predators   ☐ pH of soil
☐ Food availability   ☐ Temperature   ☐ Light intensity

1 Ecosystems are organised into different levels.

Which of the following statements is the correct definition of a community?

A   A single organism.
B   All the organisms of different species living in a habitat.
C   All the organisms of one species in a habitat.
D   All the organisms living in a habitat along with all the non-living conditions.

Your answer ☐

[Total 1 mark]

2 Ants often live in the hollow thorns of a certain species of tree. The ants living in the trees feed on the trees' nectar. When herbivores try to graze on the trees, the ants bite them. Some ant species have also been shown to protect the trees from harmful bacteria.

Which of the following statements best describes the relationship between the ants and the trees?

A   The ants are parasites because they depend entirely on the trees to survive.
B   The relationship is mutualistic because both the ants and the trees benefit from it.
C   The relationship is parasitic because the host is harmed and doesn't benefit from it.
D   The relationship is mutualistic because the trees depend on the ants to survive.

Your answer ☐

[Total 1 mark]

3 Prickly acacia is a tree species native to many African and Asian countries. It was introduced to Australia many years ago. It has invaded large areas of land in the warmer parts of the country. The trees grow best in areas with a high average temperature and where there is plenty of water, such as along rivers or on flood plains where there is seasonal flooding.

a) Australia experienced particularly high rainfall in the 1950s and 1970s. Suggest how the prickly acacia population in Australia may have changed during these periods. Explain your answer.

....

....

[2]

Topic B4 — Community Level Systems

b) Global temperature is thought to be increasing. What may happen to the distribution of prickly acacia in Australia over the next few decades? Explain your answer.

....

....

....
[2]

c) When prickly acacia invade an area it can negatively impact the population of various grasses in that area. Suggest why this might be the case.

....

....
[1]
[Total 5 marks]

4   Data suggests that since the 1960s roe deer populations in the UK have increased dramatically. The natural predators of roe deer include lynx, wolves and bears, but these are all now extinct in the UK. Roe deer usually live in woodland but they have more recently been observed in fields and scrub land.

Grade 7-9

a) i) Explain the biotic factors that may have contributed to the roe deer's expanding habitat.

....

....

....

....
[3]

ii) Some people are campaigning for the reintroduction of lynx in certain areas of the UK. What effect might this have on the population of roe deer in those areas?

....

....
[2]

b) Ticks are tiny animals that sometimes live on roe deer and feed on their blood. What name is given to this type of relationship?

....
[1]
[Total 6 marks]

Exam Practice Tip
Don't panic if you don't recognise the species in an exam question — the same stuff about competition for resources and the effects of biotic and abiotic factors will still apply. Read any information you're given carefully and apply it logically. If conditions are ideal for the organism and there's not much competition, populations will start to increase and vice versa.

Topic B4 — Community Level Systems

Topic B5 — Genes, Inheritance and Selection

Genes and Variation

1 Genes are found on chromosomes.

What are chromosomes?

- **A** Enzymes used in the synthesis of proteins.
- **B** The bases that make up DNA.
- **C** Very long, coiled up molecules of DNA.
- **D** Proteins coded for by DNA.

Your answer ☐

[Total 1 mark]

2 Organisms have many different genes.

a) Explain the function of genes.

....

....
[2]

b) Explain the meaning of the term 'allele'.

....

....
[2]

[Total 4 marks]

3 Variation is the differences between individuals of the same species. It can be caused by differences in individual organisms' genotypes.

a) Describe what is meant by the following terms.

i) genotype

....

....
[1]

ii) phenotype

....

....
[1]

b) Apart from an organisms' genotype, state **one** other factor that can lead to variation between individuals of the same species.

....
[1]

[Total 3 marks]

Topic B5 — Genes, Inheritance and Selection

More on Variation and Genetic Variants

1 Mutations are rare events that can give rise to genetic variants.

a) What is a mutation?

....

....
[1]

b) Which of the following statements is **true**?

    A Most mutations have very little or no effect on the phenotype of an organism.
    B All mutations affect the phenotype of an organism.
    C Most mutations have a large effect on the phenotype of an organism.
    D Mutations only affect non-coding DNA sequences.

Your answer ☐
[1]
[Total 2 marks]

2 Many characteristics in humans show variation.

a) Give an example of a characteristic which shows continuous variation.

....
[1]

b) Explain your answer to part b).

....

....
[1]

c) Explain what is meant by discontinuous variation.

....

....
[1]
[Total 3 marks]

3 Proteins made in an organism's cells determine the characteristics of an organism, i.e. its phenotype. Using this information and your knowledge of mutations, explain how mutations can affect the phenotype of an organism.

....

....

....

....
[Total 3 marks]

Topic B5 — Genes, Inheritance and Selection

Sexual Reproduction and Meiosis

1 In sexual reproduction, a male gamete fuses with a female gamete. *(Grade 4-6)*

Which of the following statements is **true**?

- **A** Gametes contain twice as many chromosomes as normal body cells.
- **B** Gametes contain a quarter of the number of chromosomes in normal body cells.
- **C** Gametes contain three times as many chromosomes as normal body cells.
- **D** Gametes contain half the number of chromosomes in normal body cells.

Your answer ☐

[Total 1 mark]

2 Gametes are produced by meiosis. *(Grade 4-6)*

Which of the following statements is **true**?

- **A** Meiosis results in the production of two genetically identical gametes.
- **B** Meiosis results in the production of four genetically identical gametes.
- **C** Meiosis results in the production of two genetically different gametes.
- **D** Meiosis results in the production of four genetically different gametes.

Your answer ☐

[Total 1 mark]

3 The diagram below shows two cells. The cell on the left shows a diploid cell with duplicated DNA about to undergo meiosis. *(Grade 6-7)*

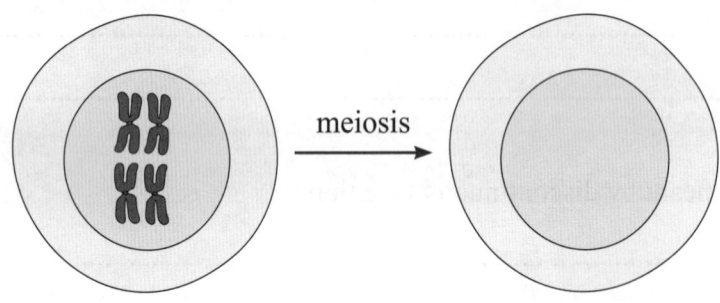

a) In the cell on the right, sketch the number of chromosomes that would be present after meiosis.
[1]

b) What term can be used to describe the number of chromosomes in the cell on the right?

....
[1]

c) How many cell divisions take place in meiosis?

....
[1]

[Total 3 marks]

Exam Practice Tip

It's pretty easy to get mitosis and meiosis mixed up because someone decided to give them such similar names. Remember, when you're talking about the production of gam**e**tes for sexual reproduction, it's m**e**iosis that you want.

Topic B5 — Genes, Inheritance and Selection

Sex Determination and Asexual Reproduction

1 Which of these statements about asexual reproduction is **false**? *Grade 4-6*

    A In asexual reproduction the offspring are genetically different from the parent.
    B Bacteria can reproduce asexually.
    C Asexual reproduction involves cell division by mitosis.
    D Some plants can reproduce asexually.

Your answer ☐

[Total 1 mark]

2 What is the chance that the offspring of human sexual reproduction will be male? *Grade 4-6*

    A 60%
    B 25%
    C 50%
    D 80%

Your answer ☐

[Total 1 mark]

3 Biological sex in humans is determined by the combination of the two sex chromosomes that an individual has. *Grade 6-7*

  a) Which of the following statements is **true**?

    A The presence of a Y chromosome results in male features.
    B The presence of two X chromosomes results in male features.
    C The presence of an X and a Y chromosome results in female features.
    D The presence of two Y chromosomes results in female features.

Your answer ☐

[1]

  b) A human egg and sperm cell fuse during fertilisation. Draw a genetic diagram to show the potential genotypes of the sex chromosomes in the resulting offspring.

[2]

[Total 3 marks]

Exam Practice Tip

Remember, if you're not sure exactly what the ratio of male to female offspring is, just draw a genetic diagram to work it out. Instead of putting different alleles in the diagram, just put the different sex chromosomes of each parent in.

Topic B5 — Genes, Inheritance and Selection

Genetic Diagrams

Warm-Up

Draw lines to match the words on the left to the correct definition on the right.

heterozygous — Having two alleles the same for a particular gene.

— The combination of alleles an organism has.

allele — The characteristics an organism has.

— Having two different alleles for a particular gene.

homozygous — A version of a gene.

1 Height in pea plants is controlled by a single gene. The allele for tall plants (T) is dominant over the allele for dwarf plants (t).

A student says that a pea plant must have the genotype TT to be tall. Is the student correct? Explain your answer.

....

....

....

[Total 3 marks]

2 The picture below shows a tabby cat. Tabby cats have a distinctive banding pattern on their fur. The banding is controlled by a single gene. The allele for banding (B) is dominant over the allele for solid colour fur (b).

a) State the **two** possible genotypes for a tabby cat.

1. ....

2. ....

[2]

b) A heterozygous tabby cat breeds with a cat which is not a tabby.

Complete the genetic diagram to predict the probability of one of the pair's offspring being a tabby cat.

probability of one of the offspring being a tabby = ...

[3]

[Total 5 marks]

Topic B5 — Genes, Inheritance and Selection

3 Hair length in dogs is mainly controlled by two alleles. Long hair is caused by a recessive allele (h) and short hair is caused by a dominant allele (H). *(Grade 6-7)*

a) Give the genotype for a long-haired dog.

....
[1]

b) A homozygous dominant dog was crossed with a homozygous recessive dog. They had 8 puppies. How many of those puppies would you expect to have long hair?
Construct a genetic diagram to explain your answer.

number of long-haired puppies = ...
[3]

c) A heterozygous dog was then crossed with a homozygous dominant dog. They had 8 puppies. How many puppies would you expect to have short hair?
Construct a genetic diagram to explain your answer.

number of short-haired puppies = ...
[3]
[Total 7 marks]

4 Fruit flies can either have normal wings or small, deformed wings. The gene for normal wings is dominant. In an experiment, a scientist wanted to produce a population of fruit flies made up of 75% flies with normal wings and 25% flies with small, deformed wings. *(Grade 7-9)*

Which of the following crosses would have the best chance of producing this population?

- **A** Male NN × Female Nn
- **B** Male NN × Female nn
- **C** Male nn × Female Nn
- **D** Male Nn × Female Nn

Your answer ☐

[Total 1 mark]

Topic B5 — Genes, Inheritance and Selection

Classification

Warm-Up

In classification, kingdoms can be subdivided into smaller groups. Write a number between 1 and 7 in each of the boxes below to put the groups in order of size, from largest (1) to smallest (7). The first one has been done for you.

☐ phylum   ☐ species   ☐ genus   ☐ order

[1] kingdom   ☐ family   ☐ class

1 The development of molecular phylogenetics has enabled us to discover new evolutionary relationships and clarify existing ones. The table below shows the percentage similarities between the DNA sequences of humans and a range of organisms.

Organism	A	B	C	D	E	F	G
% DNA sequence similarity to humans	18	87	44	26	92	96	54

a) Name the technique most likely used in molecular phylogenetics to gather this information.

....

[1]

b) Which organism in the table (**A - G**) is most closely related to humans? Use information from the table to explain your answer.

....

....

[2]

[Total 3 marks]

2 There are many thousands of different organisms on the planet. Scientists use classification systems to classify these organisms.

a) What is classification?

....

....

[2]

b) Which of these statements about artificial classification systems is **true**?

A   They use information about the common ancestors of organisms to classify them.
B   They are the preferred method of classification for today's scientists.
C   They rely on the use of detailed molecular techniques.
D   They use observable features to group organisms together.

Your answer ☐

[1]

[Total 3 marks]

Topic B5 — Genes, Inheritance and Selection

Evolution and Natural Selection

1 Scientists have discovered a species of wasp (species B) which they have evidence to suggest evolved from a closely related species (species A). The main difference between the two wasps is a difference in wing shape, which has been linked to variations in several alleles.

Grade 6-7

a) How do different alleles arise in a population?

....
[1]

b) The scientists think that the evolution of species B happened relatively quickly.
Give **one** factor which can affect the speed of evolution.

....
[1]

c) Describe how the scientists could test whether species A and B are truly separate species.

....

....
[1]

[Total 3 marks]

2 The photos below show two different hares. The hare on the left lives in a very cold climate. The hare on the right lives in a warm climate.

Grade 7-9

The hare on the right uses its large ears as a cooling mechanism. They allow lots of heat to leave the hare's body and regulate its temperature. The hare on the left has smaller ears.

Suggest how the species of hare on the left evolved to have smaller ears than hares that live in warmer climates.

....

....

....

....

....

....

....

[Total 5 marks]

Topic B5 — Genes, Inheritance and Selection

Evidence for Evolution

1 There is lots of good evidence for evolution. **Grade 6-7**

   a) Fossils are a source of evidence for evolution. What is a fossil?

   ....

   ....
   [1]

   The diagram below shows the bone structure of a modern human foot and incomplete fossils of the feet of two ancient ancestors of modern humans.

   Fossil A   Fossil B   Human foot

   b) Suggest the correct chronological order of the bone structures from the oldest to the most recent.

   ....
   [1]

   c) Explain how arranging fossils in chronological order can provide evidence for evolution.

   ....

   ....
   [2]

   d) Another source of evidence for evolution is the ability of bacteria to evolve and become resistant to antibiotics. The process occurs rapidly, so scientists are able to monitor the evolution as it is occurring. Explain how the evolution of antibiotic resistance occurs in bacteria.

   ....

   ....

   ....

   ....

   ....

   ....

   ....

   ....
   [5]

   [Total 9 marks]

Topic B5 — Genes, Inheritance and Selection

Topic B6 — Global Challenges

Investigating Distribution and Abundance

1 Which piece of equipment would be best for sampling the distribution of a species of grass? *(Grade 4-6)*

    A   pooter
    B   quadrat
    C   sweep net
    D   pitfall trap

Your answer ☐

[Total 1 mark]

PRACTICAL

2 A group of students investigated the distribution and abundance of organisms in a local park. *(Grade 6-7)*

a) What is meant by the term distribution?

....
[1]

b) One area of the park contains long grass. The students counted the number of individuals of three different flying insect species in five sample areas of the long grass. Their results are shown in the table below.

	Number of individuals counted				
	Sample area				
Organism	1	2	3	4	5
A	4	10	3	8	6
B	5	2	7	8	1
C	9	6	8	4	6

i) Suggest a piece of equipment they could have used to collect the organisms.

....
[1]

ii) Based on their results, which organism was the most abundant in the long grass? Give a reason for your answer.

....
....
[1]

c) In a different area of the park, the students collected ground insects using a pooter. Describe how a pooter could be used to compare insects in two sample areas.

....
....
....
....
[3]

[Total 6 marks]

Topic B6 — Global Challenges

54

PRACTICAL

3 Rebecca used a quadrat with an area of 0.5 m² to investigate the number of buttercups growing in a field. She counted the number of buttercups in the quadrat in ten randomly selected places. The table below shows her results.

Grade 6-7

Quadrat Number	Number of buttercups
1	15
2	13
3	16
4	23
5	26
6	23
7	13
8	12
9	16
10	13

a) i) Why is it important that the quadrats were placed randomly in the field?

....

[1]

ii) Describe a method that could have been used to randomly place the quadrats.

....

[1]

b) What is the modal number of buttercups in a quadrat in the table?

answer = ... buttercups
[1]

c) What is the median number of buttercups in the table?

answer = ... buttercups
[1]

d) Calculate the mean number of buttercups per 0.5 m² quadrat.

answer = ... buttercups per 0.5 m²
[1]

e) The total area of the field was 1750 m².
Estimate the number of buttercups in the whole of the field.

answer = ... buttercups
[3]

[Total 8 marks]

Topic B6 — Global Challenges

Using Keys and Factors Affecting Distribution

1 Samantha is using a key to identify some butterflies based on the markings on their wings. Part of the key is shown below.

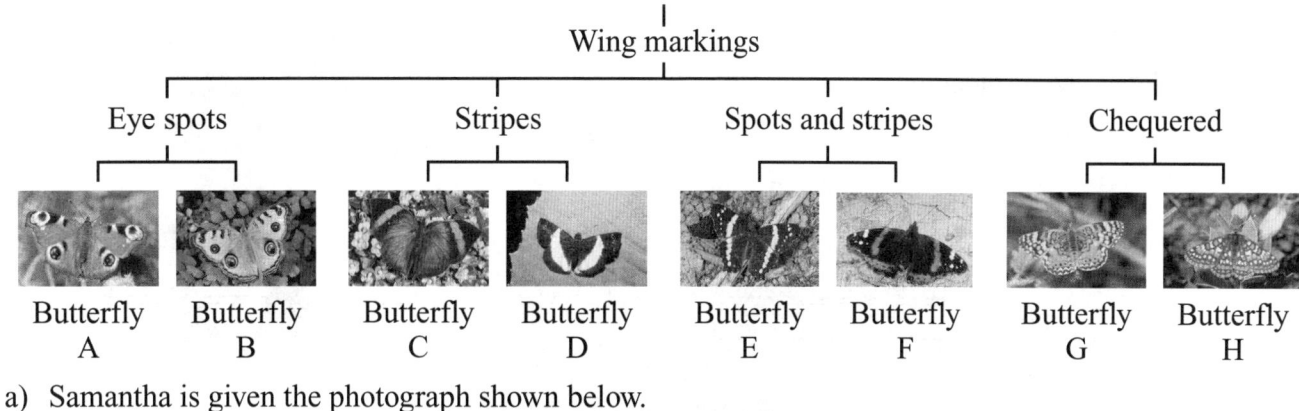

Wing markings
- Eye spots: Butterfly A, Butterfly B
- Stripes: Butterfly C, Butterfly D
- Spots and stripes: Butterfly E, Butterfly F
- Chequered: Butterfly G, Butterfly H

a) Samantha is given the photograph shown below.

i) Using the key, describe the wing markings shown on the butterfly in the photograph.

....

[1]

ii) Samantha uses the key to identify the butterfly species in the photograph — it is a Red Admiral butterfly. Which of the butterflies in the key is a Red Admiral butterfly?

....

[1]

b) Samantha is using the key to try and identify another butterfly. The butterfly has chequered wing markings but she can't work out if it is butterfly **G** or **H**, as they look very similar. Suggest **two** things that could help Samantha make a definite identification.

....

....

[2]

[Total 4 marks]

2 Students are investigating the distribution of different plant species using quadrats, in an area where soil pH varies considerably.

Explain why the students may want to measure the soil pH at the site where each quadrat is placed.

....

....

....

[Total 2 marks]

Topic B6 — Global Challenges

Using Transects

PRACTICAL

1. A transect was carried out from the edge of a small pond, across a grassy field and into a woodland. The distributions of four species of plant were recorded along the transect, along with the soil moisture and light levels. The diagram below shows the results.

Grade 6-7

Key: dandelion, daisy, short grass, long grass

pond — zone A — zone B — zone C — woodland

soil moisture level: high ⟶ low
light level: high ⟶ low

a) The grassy field is split up into three zones — **A**, **B** and **C**.
In the diagram, which zones contained only **one** species of plant?

....
[1]

b) Which of the four species of plant can grow in soils with both a high and low level of moisture, and at both low and high light intensities?

....
[1]

c) Suggest **two** reasons why long grass, daisies and dandelions all grow in **zone A**.

....
....
[2]

d) Children often play football on one zone of the grassy field. The trampling that occurs here makes it difficult for plants to become established. Suggest which zone might be used to play football. Explain your answer.

....
....
[2]

e) A transect can also be used to determine the abundance of species in an ecosystem. Explain how this transect could be used to determine the abundance of the four plant species.

....
....
....
[2]

[Total 8 marks]

Topic B6 — Global Challenges

Human Impacts on Ecosystems

1   Ferrets were introduced into New Zealand in the 1800s. There are now many ferrets living in a variety of different habitats across New Zealand. They can disrupt an ecosystem by feeding on native species.

     Which human activity is likely to have a **positive** impact on biodiversity in the ecosystems in which the ferrets live?

     A   Clearing large areas of the habitats in which the ferrets live.
     B   Setting out poisoned food sources across the habitat.
     C   Setting traps that will catch ferrets but not other types of animal.
     D   Removing the native species which the ferrets feed on.

     Your answer ☐

[Total 1 mark]

2   Chester Zoo is home to around 500 different animal species. Many of these species are endangered in the wild.

     a)   Explain how keeping endangered animals in a zoo can help to protect global biodiversity.

     ....
     ....
     ....

[2]

     b)   Chester Zoo also has a nature reserve on site. The nature reserve has designated pathways from which visitors can view local wildlife. Describe how the nature reserve protects local biodiversity.

     ....

[1]

[Total 3 marks]

3*   Explain, with reference to land use and hunting, how an increasing human population can have a negative impact on global biodiversity.

     ....
     ....
     ....
     ....
     ....
     ....
     ....

[Total 6 marks]

Topic B6 — Global Challenges

Maintaining Biodiversity

1 The Ngorongoro Conservation Area is a large protected area in Africa. The authority that manages it helps to protect biodiversity in the area as well as encourage ecotourism.

Grade 6-7

a) i) What is meant by the term ecotourism?

....

....
[2]

ii) How will ecotourism in the Ngorongoro Conservation Area help the local human population?

....
[1]

b) Apart from ecotourism, give **one** benefit to humans of places like the Ngorongoro Conservation Area, which help to protect ecosystems.

....
[1]

[Total 4 marks]

2 Fishing practices are leading to a decrease in many fish populations all over the world. Bluefin tuna is a species of fish that is now much rarer than it was in the 1960s, due to overfishing. International organisations have since set a limit on the number of bluefin tuna that can be caught within a given period of time.

Grade 6-7

a) Give **one** reason why controlling the fishing of bluefin tuna may be beneficial to humans.

....

....
[1]

b) Many bluefin tuna live in shoals which migrate through international waters that do not belong to any specific country. This means that fishing vessels from many different countries fish for bluefin tuna. Suggest **two** reasons why this might make it difficult to reduce the number of bluefin tuna caught by humans.

....

....

....

....
[2]

[Total 3 marks]

Exam Practice Tip
Maintaining biodiversity is generally a good thing — you should know about the positive effects it can have on ecosystems as well as the benefits it can have for humans, such as ecotourism. However, maintaining biodiversity is not always an easy task — make sure you're aware of some of the challenges involved.

Selective Breeding

1 Which of the following does **not** describe a potential use of selective breeding?

    A Producing bacteria with the human gene for insulin.
    B Producing pigs with a high meat yield.
    C Creating a new variety of a plant with larger flowers.
    D Producing a crop plant with high grain yield.

Your answer ☐

[Total 1 mark]

2 The diagram shows two cobs (**A** and **B**) which were produced from two different corn plants. Cob **B** is the result of selective breeding over many years.

a) Based on the diagram, suggest a desirable characteristic of corn plants.

....
[1]

b) Explain how this selective breeding process may help with food security.

....

....
[1]
[Total 2 marks]

3 Due to natural variation some dairy cows in a herd produce a higher yield of milk per day than others.

a) Explain how selective breeding can be used to produce a herd with high milk yields.

....

....

....

....
[3]

b) Suggest a reason why the emergence of an infectious disease, such as bovine tuberculosis, may be more of an issue for a herd of selectively bred cows than a herd that haven't been selectively bred.

....

....

....

....

....
[3]
[Total 6 marks]

Topic B6 — Global Challenges

Genetic Engineering

Warm-Up

Draw lines to connect each word or phrase on the left with the statement describing it on the right.

restriction enzyme	used to identify genetically engineered cells
resistance marker	cuts DNA open
ligase	transfers DNA into a cell
vector	sticks DNA ends together

1 Vectors are often used in genetic engineering. *Grade 4-6*

Which of these is an example of a vector used in genetic engineering?

A   a stem cell
B   a plasmid
C   a glucose molecule
D   a protein

Your answer ☐

[Total 1 marks]

2 Genetic engineering can be used to produce genetically modified corn plants. These plants are grown in many parts of the world due to their pest resistance. *Grade 6-7*

a) Explain what is meant by genetic engineering.

....

....
[1]

b) Apart from pest resistance, give another example of a beneficial characteristic that could be introduced into a crop by genetic engineering.

....
[1]

c) Give **two** reasons why some people may have concerns about the use of genetically modified crops in agriculture.

....

....

....

....
[2]

[Total 4 marks]

Topic B6 — Global Challenges

3 There are several stages involved in genetically engineering an organism. *(Grade 7-9)*

a) Outline how a desired gene would be isolated from an organism and then inserted into a vector.

....

....

....

....

[3]

b) Describe how antibiotic resistance markers can be used to identify bacterial cells that have been genetically engineered.

....

....

....

....

....

[4]
[Total 7 marks]

4 A scientist discovers that she is able to genetically modify hens to produce particular substances in the whites of their eggs. *(Grade 7-9)*

a) Suggest why the scientist's findings might be useful in treating nutrient deficiency diseases in certain countries.

....

....

[2]

b) Suggest **two** ethical objections that some people may have towards genetically engineering hens in this way.

....

....

....

....

[2]
[Total 4 marks]

Exam Practice Tip

Make sure you know plenty of arguments both for and against genetic engineering, as it's quite an important issue. And don't forget the basic principles of using vectors and enzymes to genetically modify an organism — the techniques may vary a little depending on whether it's an animal/plant etc., but the basic idea is still the same.

Topic B6 — Global Challenges

Health and Disease

1 Most plants and animals will experience disease during their lifetime. *(Grade 4-6)*

a) What is meant by the term disease?

....
[1]

Diseases can be communicable or non-communicable.

b) i) Describe the characteristics of communicable diseases.

....

....
[2]

ii) Describe the characteristics of non-communicable diseases.

....

....

....

....
[3]

[Total 6 marks]

2 There is often interaction between different diseases. *(Grade 6-7)*

a) Patients infected with HIV have an increased probability of developing tuberculosis. Explain why this is the case.

....

....

....
[2]

Girls between the ages of 12 and 13 are offered the HPV vaccination.

b) Explain why this vaccine protects them against cervical cancer.

....

....

....
[2]

[Total 4 marks]

Exam Practice Tip

Make sure that you understand the differences between communicable and non-communicable diseases. You might be given information on a disease you don't know about in the exam and asked to work out which category it fits into.

Topic B6 — Global Challenges

How Disease Spreads

Warm-Up

Draw lines to match up each word on the left to the correct description on the right.

Viruses — These pathogens are eukaryotic and usually single-celled. Many of the pathogens in this category are parasites.

Protists — Some of these pathogens are single-celled, while others have a body made up of hyphae.

Fungi — These pathogens are not cells. They replicate themselves inside the infected organism's cells.

Bacteria — These pathogens are prokaryotic, reproduce rapidly and produce toxins that damage your cells and tissues, making you feel ill.

1   Different types of pathogen can cause disease in plants. *(Grade 4-6)*

   a) What type of pathogen causes barley powdery mildew?
   A   a virus
   B   a bacterium
   C   a fungus
   D   a protist

   Your answer ☐

   [1]

   b) Tobacco mosaic virus (TMV) is a plant pathogen. How is it usually spread?
   A   in the air
   B   through the soil
   C   by direct contact
   D   by animals eating infected plants

   Your answer ☐

   [1]

   [Total 2 marks]

2   Infection with the bacteria *Agrobacterium tumefaciens* can cause disease in plants. *(Grade 6-7)*

   a) Name the plant disease caused by *Agrobacterium tumefaciens*.

   ....
   [1]

   b) Describe how infection with *Agrobacterium tumefaciens* affects plants.

   ....

   ....

   ....

   ....
   [3]

   [Total 4 marks]

Topic B6 — Global Challenges

3 The tobacco mosaic virus (TMV) is a widespread plant pathogen affecting many plant species. **Grade 6-7**

a) Describe the appearance of a plant with TMV.

....
[1]

b) Outline why a plant affected by TMV cannot grow properly.

....

....
[1]

The table shows the mean diameter and mass of fruits from 100 healthy plants and 100 plants infected with TMV.

	Healthy plants	Plants with TMV
Mean diameter of fruit (mm)	50	35
Mean mass of fruit (g)	95	65

c) Describe the effect of TMV on the diameter and mass of fruit produced in the infected plants compared to the healthy plants.

....

....

....
[2]

[Total 4 marks]

4 HIV is a virus that infects humans. **Grade 6-7**

a) HIV is spread via bodily fluids. Give **two** ways in which HIV may be transmitted between people.

....

....
[2]

b) Describe the effects of HIV on the body and explain why people with the virus can become less able to cope with other communicable diseases.

....

....

....

....
[4]

c) Other than via bodily fluids, give **two** other ways that communicable diseases can be transmitted.

....
[2]

[Total 8 marks]

Topic B6 — Global Challenges

Reducing and Preventing the Spread of Disease

1   Influenza is a common communicable disease. It is caused by a virus that can be spread by airborne droplets when an infected person coughs or sneezes.

   a) Give **two** ways in which the spread of influenza could be reduced or prevented.

   ....

   ....
   [2]

   b) Aspects of a person's lifestyle can increase the chance of them developing a communicable disease. Suggest and explain **two** social or economic factors that could also increase the chance of developing a communicable disease.

   ....

   ....

   ....

   ....
   [4]
   [Total 6 marks]

2   Crop plants are a vital food source for humans. Large scale infection of crop plants could risk the security of the human food supply. Chemical and biological control are two methods that are used to control the spread of disease in plants.

   a) Give **one** example of a chemical control method that could be used to control plant disease.

   ....
   [1]

   b) Apart from chemical and biological control methods, state and explain **two** other methods for controlling plant diseases.

   ....

   ....

   ....

   ....

   ....
   [4]
   [Total 5 marks]

Exam Practice Tip
There are quite a few different methods for controlling the spread of plant diseases and those for controlling animal diseases. Make sure you've got a good grasp of them — you might be asked to give examples in an exam.

Topic B6 — Global Challenges

The Human Immune System

1 The body has many features that protect it against pathogens. **Grade 4-6**

  a) Describe how the skin helps to defend the body against pathogens.

  ....

  ....
  [2]

  b) How do structures in the nose help to defend the body against the entry of pathogens?

  ....

  ....
  [1]
  [Total 3 marks]

2* Describe how the human body works to defend itself against pathogens that have entered the body. Include details of the body's internal defences and the role of the immune system. **Grade 7-9**

....

....

....

....

....

....

....

....

....

....

....
[Total 6 marks]

Exam Practice Tip
Think carefully about 6 mark questions like the one on this page. Don't just start scribbling everything you know about the topic. Stop and think first — work out what the question is asking you to write about, and then make sure you write enough points to bag yourself as many marks as possible. Good job you've got some practice on this page.

Topic B6 — Global Challenges

Vaccines and Medicines

Warm-Up

Use the words below to correctly fill in the gaps in the passage.
You don't have to use every word, but each word can only be used once.

> active   white   immune   antiviral   pathogenic
> antigens   inactive   memory   vaccines   red

When a person is vaccinated, they are exposed to dead, ... or weakened pathogens. These are harmless to the body, but carry ...., which trigger an .... response. .... blood cells produce antibodies to attack the pathogens. Some of these blood cells remain in the blood as .... cells.

1 Which of the following substances can be used to treat a bacterial infection? *(Grade 4-6)*

    A antibiotic
    B antiviral
    C antiseptic
    D antigen

Your answer ☐

[Total 1 mark]

2 A boy falls and cuts his leg while running. *(Grade 6-7)*

What type of medicine should he apply to his leg? Explain your answer.

....
....
....

[Total 3 marks]

3 A large proportion of a population is vaccinated against the pathogen which causes mumps. *(Grade 6-7)*

a) If the mumps pathogen enters the body of someone who has had the mumps vaccination, why would they be unlikely to become ill with mumps?

....

[1]

b) Explain how vaccinating a large proportion of a population against a disease can help protect people from catching the disease who haven't been vaccinated.

....
....
....

[2]

[Total 3 marks]

Topic B6 — Global Challenges

PRACTICAL: Investigating Antimicrobials

1 A scientist carried out an investigation into the effects of two different antibiotics (**A** and **B**) on two different cultures of the bacteria *Staphylococcus aureus* (culture **1** and **2**). Separate agar plates were inoculated with each bacterial culture. Three paper discs were then placed on the surface of each plate: one soaked in antibiotic **A**, one soaked in antibiotic **B** and one control disc soaked in sterile water. The agar plates were then incubated for two days to allow the bacteria to grow. The diagram below shows the results of the experiment.

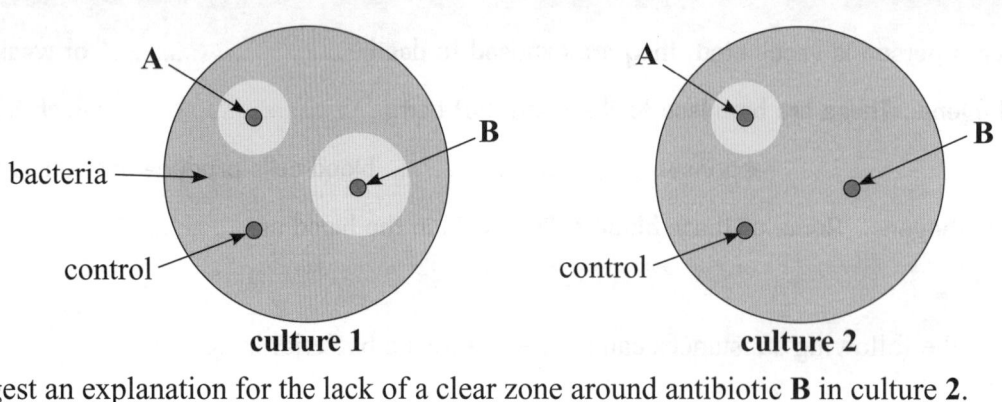

culture 1 **culture 2**

a) Suggest an explanation for the lack of a clear zone around antibiotic **B** in culture **2**.

....
....
[2]

b) Explain why the clear zone around antibiotic **B** in culture **1** is larger than the clear zone around antibiotic **A** in culture **1**.

....
....
[2]

c) Explain why a control disc was used.

....
....
[1]

Aseptic techniques were used when carrying out this investigation.

d) i) Why are aseptic techniques used?

....
[1]

ii) Give **two** aseptic techniques that should have been used during this investigation.

....
....
....
[2]

[Total 8 marks]

Topic B6 — Global Challenges

Comparing Antimicrobials — PRACTICAL

1   A scientist was investigating the effects of four different antibiotics (**A, B, C, D**) on the growth of a bacterial species. She soaked a separate paper disc in each antibiotic and placed them on the surface of an agar plate that had been inoculated with the bacteria. She also placed a control disc on the surface of the plate. The results are shown in the diagram below along with the diameter of each clear zone.

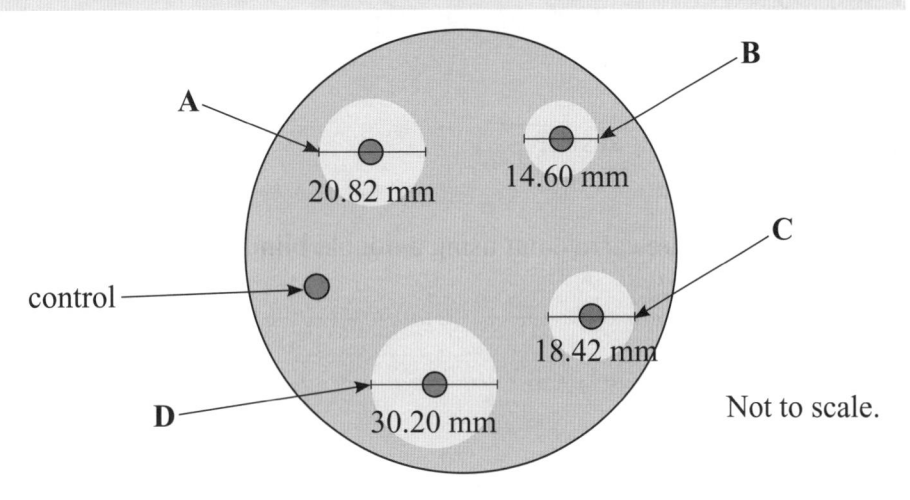

Grade 6-7

A — 20.82 mm
B — 14.60 mm
C — 18.42 mm
D — 30.20 mm
control

Not to scale.

a) Calculate the difference between the areas of the clear zones around antibiotic **B** and antibiotic **D**.
area = πr^2
$\pi = 3.14$

difference = ... mm²
[5]

b) The experiment was repeated three more times. The scientist noticed some variation in the diameter of the clear zone around antibiotic **C**. The table below shows the diameter of this clear zone on each of the four plates.

Plate	1	2	3	4
Diameter of clear zone **C** (mm)	18.42	6.85	17.98	18.75

i) Calculate the mean diameter of the clear zone around antibiotic **C** for all four plates.

mean diameter of clear zone **C** = ... mm
[1]

ii) Suggest an explanation for the result on plate **2**.

....
[1]

[Total 7 marks]

Exam Practice Tip
Make sure you don't get confused between the radius and the diameter when working out the area of a clear zone — the diameter is the width of the circle going through its centre point, and the radius is half the diameter.

Topic B6 — Global Challenges

Developing New Medicines

1 A group of patients are taking part in a double blind clinical trial. *(Grade 4-6)*

a) Which row (**A-D**) correctly shows which people know who is receiving a placebo?

	Patients	Doctor
A	✓	✓
B	✓	✗
C	✗	✓
D	✗	✗

Your answer ☐

[1]

b) Explain why clinical trials are carried out using a double blind method.

....

....

[1]

[Total 2 marks]

2 Before new drugs are tested on humans, they must successfully pass through a series of initial trials. *(Grade 6-7)*

a) i) What is the name given to this series of initial trials?

....

[1]

ii) Outline the phases that take place during these initial trials.

....

....

....

[3]

If a new drug successfully makes it through the initial trials, it is then tested on healthy individuals in clinical trials.

b) Explain why the drug is tested on healthy individuals before being tested on people suffering from the illness that it is designed to treat.

....

....

[1]

c) The clinical trial stage of drug testing usually takes place over a very long period of time. Explain why this is the case.

....

....

[2]

[Total 7 marks]

Topic B6 — Global Challenges

Non-Communicable Diseases

Warm-Up

For each of the following statements, circle whether the statement is **true** or **false**.

All non-communicable diseases are more common in developing countries.	true / false
Smoking is a risk factor for multiple diseases.	true / false
Risk factors are always more closely associated with low incomes than high incomes.	true / false

1 Non-communicable diseases are not spread by pathogens, instead they are associated with risk factors. *(Grade 4-6)*

a) Describe what is meant by a 'risk factor' for a disease.

....
.... *[1]*

b) Give **one** risk factor associated with liver disease.

.... *[1]*

c) Risk factors may be related to a person's lifestyle. Which of the following is **not** a lifestyle factor which may be associated with disease?

A a person's sleeping patterns
B the number of miles walked per week
C the presence of a particular combination of alleles in a person's genome
D the amount of calories consumed per day

Your answer ☐

[1]
[Total 3 marks]

2 Cigarettes contain tar, which is a substance containing carcinogens. Carcinogens can cause changes to occur within cells. *(Grade 6-7)*

a) Explain why smoking is a risk factor associated with cancer.

....
.... *[2]*

b) Apart from smoking, give **one** additional risk factor which may be associated with cancer.

.... *[1]*
[Total 3 marks]

Topic B6 — Global Challenges

72

3 Some non-communicable diseases are associated with nutrition. For example, kwashiorkor is associated with a lack of sufficient protein in the diet. It is mostly found in developing countries.

a) Suggest an explanation for the distribution of kwashiorkor at a global level.

....

....
[1]

b) Whether a person develops diabetes can be linked to their diet. Explain why an increased consumption of foods that are high in fat might lead to a higher incidence of type 2 diabetes.

....

....

....
[2]
[Total 3 marks]

4 A BMI (Body Mass Index) can be used to determine if a person is overweight or underweight. BMI is calculated by dividing a person's body mass by their height squared.

This table shows the weight descriptions associated with different BMI values.

Body Mass Index	Weight Description
below 18.5	underweight
18.5 - 24.9	normal
25 - 29.9	overweight
30 - 40	moderately obese
above 40	severely obese

This table shows the BMI values of five patients at a health centre.

Patient	BMI
A	19.2
B	26.1
C	25.3
D	23.8
E	30.6

a) Obesity is a risk factor for cardiovascular disease. Using the information in the tables, suggest and explain which patient (**A-E**) is most likely to be at risk of developing cardiovascular disease.

....

....
[2]

b) Explain why you can't judge whether or not a person will develop cardiovascular disease based on their BMI value alone.

....

....
[1]

c) Apart from obesity, give **two** additional lifestyle factors associated with cardiovascular disease.

....
[2]
[Total 5 marks]

Topic B6 — Global Challenges

Treating Cardiovascular Disease

Warm-Up

Use the correct words to fill in the gaps in the passage. Not all of them will be used.

pulmonary vein   blood vessels   asthma   atheromas   blood flow   cystic fibrosis
coronary arteries   toxins   fatty material   aorta   coronary heart disease

Cardiovascular disease is a term used to describe diseases of the .... and heart. .... is an example of a cardiovascular disease which is caused by narrowing of the .... due to the build-up of .... on the inside wall. These deposits harden to form ...., which can restrict .... to the heart.

1   Doctors were assessing the heart of a patient who had recently suffered from a heart attack. They noticed that one of the main arteries supplying the heart muscle was narrowed.

Grade 6-7

a) Give **two** pieces of lifestyle advice the doctors may give to the patient.

....

....
[2]

b) The doctors tell the patient he could have a surgical procedure to reduce the chance of having another heart attack.

i) Explain how a surgical procedure could improve the patient's condition.

....

....
[2]

ii) If the patient decides to go ahead with surgery, suggest **two** risks he should be made aware of.

....

....
[2]

c) Suggest **two** types of medication that the patient may be prescribed to improve his condition. Describe what each medication does.

....

....

....

....
[4]

[Total 10 marks]

Topic B6 — Global Challenges

Stem Cells in Medicine

1 Which of the following best describes stem cells?

    A   A stem cell is any type of cell.
    B   Stem cells can develop into different types of cell.
    C   Stem cells are only found in embryos.
    D   Stem cells are very dangerous.

Your answer ☐

[Total 1 mark]

2 Treatments using embryonic stem cells may be able to cure many diseases. However, the use of embryonic stem cells in research and medicine is a controversial subject. Many governments around the world strictly regulate how they are used by scientists.

   a) It is hoped that stem cell treatment could be used in the future to treat patients with spinal injuries. Explain why embryonic stem cells have the potential to be used in the treatment of a patient paralysed by damage to cells in their spinal cord.

     ....
     ....
[2]

   b) Lots of research is needed to overcome the challenges presented by using embryonic stem cells in medicine. Suggest a potential medical issue with the treatment suggested in part a).

     ....
     ....
[2]

   c) Scientists are currently investigating the possibility of using adult stem cells from the patient's own body in some stem cell treatments. Suggest how using cells from the patient's own body may increase the success of stem cell treatments.

     ....
[1]

   d) Give **one** reason why some people are against using embryonic stem cells.

     ....
     ....
     ....
[2]

[Total 7 marks]

Exam Practice Tip

Make sure you remember the differences between adult and embryonic stem cells. They each have their own characteristics, which you need to get clear in your head and learn so that you can get them down in the exam.

Topic B6 — Global Challenges

Using Genome Research in Medicine

1   The Human Genome Project was a major research programme that identified all the genes found in human DNA. *(Grade 7-9)*

   a)* Explain the potential importance of research into the human genome for medicine.

....

....

....

....

....

....

....

....

....

....

....

....

....

....

....

....

....
                                                                                                                     [6]

   b) There are ethical and practical issues associated with the application of gene technology in medicine. Describe **two** potential issues of using gene technology in medicine.

....

....

....

....

....
                                                                                                                     [2]

                                                                                                         [Total 8 marks]

Topic B6 — Global Challenges

Topic C1 — Particles

States of Matter

Warm-Up

Identify which of the following statements is false. Tick **one** box.

Particles in liquids are free to move past each other but tend to stick together. ☐

When cooled, a gas can condense and become a liquid. ☐

There is hardly any force of attraction between particles in gases. ☐

Particles in liquids are held in fixed positions by strong forces. ☐

---

1 A chemical can undergo a physical change when held at different temperatures. It can also undergo a chemical change when reacted with other substances.

Grade 4-6

Describe the differences between a physical change and a chemical change. Give your answer in terms of the end product.

....

....

....

....

[Total 2 marks]

---

2 The particle model helps to describe the different states of matter.

Grade 6-7

a) Give **two** limitations of the particle model.

....

....

[2]

b) Describe the differences between liquids and solids in terms of the movement of particles.

....

....

....

[2]

[Total 4 marks]

Topic C1 — Particles

The History of the Atom

1 Several theories of atomic structure have been proposed since the start of the 19th century.

a) Describe the 'plum-pudding model' developed by Thomson in 1897.

....

....

....

[2]

b) i) Rutherford carried out the gold foil experiment where positively charged particles were fired at an extremely thin sheet of gold. Describe what Rutherford observed in his experiment.

....

....

[1]

ii) Describe the atomic model that was proposed by Rutherford.

....

....

....

[3]

c) Explain how Bohr's model differs from Rutherford's theory, in terms of electrons.

....

....

....

[2]

d) Explain why our current model of atomic structure differs so much from the older theories.

....

....

....

[2]

e) Peer review is an important part of developing scientific theories. New theories are critically evaluated by other scientists before they are published or accepted. Why is the peer review process important?

....

....

[1]

[Total 11 marks]

Topic C1 — Particles

The Atom

1 Atoms are made up from protons, neutrons and electrons. *(Grade 4-6)*

a) The relative mass and charge for the three subatomic particles are displayed in the table below. Complete the table by filling in the correct names for these particles.

Particle	Relative Mass	Charge
....	1	+1
....	1	0
....	0.0005	−1

[1]

b) State the **two** subatomic particles which form the nucleus and use their charges to explain whether the overall charge of the nucleus is positive, negative or neutral.

....

....

....

[2]

[Total 3 marks]

2 The atomic radius is a measure of the size of an atom. It is approximately 10^{-10} m in length. *(Grade 6-7)*

a) Which of the following pairs is **closest** in length?

    A   Atomic radius and nuclear radius
    B   Atomic radius and simple molecules
    C   Atomic radius and bond length
    D   Nuclear radius and bond length

Your answer ☐

[1]

b) Explain how the movement of electrons determines the atomic radius of an atom.

....

....

....

[2]

[Total 3 marks]

Topic C1 — Particles

Atoms, Isotopes and Ions

1 The table below shows some information about certain atoms.

Name	Atomic Number	Mass Number
Carbon–12	6	12
Fluorine–19	9	19
Neon–20	10	20

a) What does the atomic number of carbon–12 show?

....
[1]

b) Calculate the number of neutrons found in one atom of neon–20.

Number of neutrons = ...
[1]

c) State the number of electrons found in one atom of fluorine–19.

....
[1]

[Total 3 marks]

2 Ions can have either a positive or a negative charge.

a) Describe what happens to an atom when it turns into a negative ion.

....
[1]

b) Calcium has an atomic number of 20. Calculate the number of electrons found in one Ca^{2+} ion.

Number of electrons = ...
[1]

[Total 2 marks]

3 Bromine has two main isotopes: Br–79 and Br–81.

a) Give the definition of an isotope.

....

....
[1]

b) Bromine has an atomic number of 35. Calculate the number of neutrons in both isotopes.

Br–79 : .... neutrons

Br–81 : .... neutrons
[1]

[Total 2 marks]

Topic C1 — Particles

Topic C2 — Elements, Compounds and Mixtures

The Periodic Table

1 Mendeleev was a scientist who developed an early version of the periodic table. Look at the diagram. It shows Mendeleev's Table of Elements.

H																
Li	Be											B	C	N	O	F
Na	Mg											Al	Si	P	S	Cl
K	Ca	*	Ti	V	Cr	Mn	Fe	Co	Ni	Cu	Zn	*	*	As	Se	Br
Rb	Sr	Y	Zr	Nb	Mo	*	Ru	Rh	Pd	Ag	Cd	In	Sn	Sb	Te	I
Cs	Ba	*	*	Ta	W	*	Os	Ir	Pt	Au	Hg	Tl	Pb	Bi		

Mendeleev's Table of Elements

a) Mendeleev left gaps in his table. Describe the reason why he did this.

....

....

....
[1]

b) Mendeleev used the gaps in his table to make predictions about the properties of elements that were still undiscovered at the time. Describe how the discovery of new elements in the years after Mendeleev published his table supported his decision to leave gaps.

....

....

....
[1]

c) Mendeleev tried to organise the elements in order of atomic mass. To get the arrangement he wanted, he then had to swap some of the elements round. Describe how the discovery of protons in the nuclei of atoms showed that Mendeleev was right to arrange the elements in the order that he did.

....

....

....

....
[2]

[Total 4 marks]

Topic C2 — Elements, Compounds and Mixtures

Electron Shells

1 The atomic number of neon is 10. *Grade 4-6*

How many electrons does neon have in its **outer shell**?

A 2
B 6
C 8
D 10

Your answer ☐

[Total 1 mark]

2 The atomic number of sulfur is 16. *Grade 6-7*

a) Write down the electronic structure of sulfur. ....
[1]

b) Draw a diagram to show how the electrons are arranged in a single sulfur atom.

[1]
[Total 2 marks]

3 Magnesium is found in group 2 and period 3 of the periodic table. *Grade 6-7*

Explain how you could use this information to **deduce** the electronic structure of magnesium. Give the electronic structure of magnesium as part of your answer.

....
....
....
....

[Total 4 marks]

Topic C2 — Elements, Compounds and Mixtures

Ionic Compounds

1 Sodium bromide, NaBr, is an ionic compound.

Sodium bromide conducts electricity when it is in solution, but **not** when it is a solid.
Explain why this is the case.

....

....

....

....

[Total 2 marks]

2 Potassium has the electronic structure 2.8.8.1.

a) What is the charge on a potassium ion?

....
[1]

b) What is the electronic structure of a potassium ion?

....
[1]
[Total 2 marks]

3 Calcium fluoride, CaF_2, is an ionic compound.

Draw a dot and cross diagram to show the bonding in calcium fluoride.
You should include the charges on the ions in your diagram.

[Total 3 marks]

Topic C2 — Elements, Compounds and Mixtures

4 Sodium, magnesium, sulfur and chlorine are all found in period 3 of the periodic table.
Sodium and chlorine form the ionic compound sodium chloride, NaCl.
Magnesium and sulfur form the ionic compound magnesium sulfide, MgS.

Grade 6-7

a) Magnesium forms 2+ ions.
Use this information to work out the charge on the sulfide ions in magnesium sulfide.
Explain your reasoning.

....

....

....
[2]

b) The melting point of sodium chloride is around 800 °C.
The melting point of magnesium sulfide is around 2000 °C.

i) Explain why ionic compounds generally have high melting points.

....

....

....
[2]

ii) The charges on the ions in sodium chloride are different from the charges on the ions in magnesium sulfide. Suggest how this difference leads to magnesium sulfide having a higher melting point than sodium chloride.

....

....

....

....

....
[3]
[Total 7 marks]

5 The elements strontium and barium both form ionic compounds.
Strontium and barium are both found in group 2 of the periodic table.
Strontium sits above barium in the group.

Grade 7-9

Predict whether barium is more reactive or less reactive than strontium.
Explain your answer in terms of loss of electrons.

....

....

....
[Total 3 marks]

Topic C2 — Elements, Compounds and Mixtures

Simple Molecules

1 Look at the diagrams. They show two different representations of the same molecule.

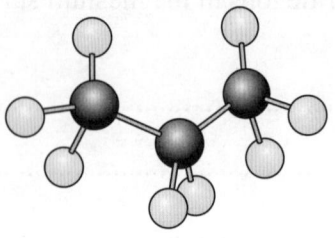

Diagram A

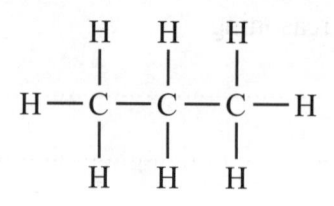

Diagram B

a) Name the two types of diagram used here.

i) Diagram **A** is a ....
[1]

ii) Diagram **B** is a ....
[1]

b) Suggest **one** limitation of the type of diagram shown in diagram **A**.

....

....

....
[1]
[Total 3 marks]

2 The atoms of many elements can form covalent bonds.

a) Describe how covalent bonds give atoms a more stable electronic structure.

....

....

....

....
[3]

b) Neon has the electronic structure 2.8.
Suggest why neon does not form covalent bonds.

....

....

....
[1]
[Total 4 marks]

Topic C2 — Elements, Compounds and Mixtures

3 Silicon has the electronic structure 2.8.4. *(Grade 6-7)*

Use this information to predict how many covalent bonds one atom of silicon will form in a simple molecule. Explain your answer.

....
....
....
....

[Total 2 marks]

4 Nitrogen has the electronic structure 2.5. Chlorine has the electronic structure 2.8.7. Nitrogen trichloride, NCl_3, is a covalent compound.
In each molecule of NCl_3, one nitrogen atom is covalently bonded to three chlorine atoms. *(Grade 6-7)*

Draw a dot and cross diagram to show the bonding in **one molecule** of nitrogen trichloride. You only need to include the outer shell electrons of each atom.

[Total 2 marks]

5 Hashim says: "Covalent bonds are very strong, so you need a lot of energy to separate the atoms in a covalent compound. This means simple molecular substances must have high melting and boiling points." *(Grade 6-7)*

Is Hashim correct? Explain your answer.

....
....
....
....
....

[Total 3 marks]

Exam Practice Tip
If you answered all these correctly, that's a pretty good sign that you know all about simple molecules and covalent bonding. But don't forget, that's only half the story — you need to be able to compare simple molecular substances with all the other types of structure covered in this section, such as ionic structures, polymers and giant covalent structure.

Topic C2 — Elements, Compounds and Mixtures

Giant Covalent Structures and Fullerenes

1 The diagrams below show two different types of carbon structure.

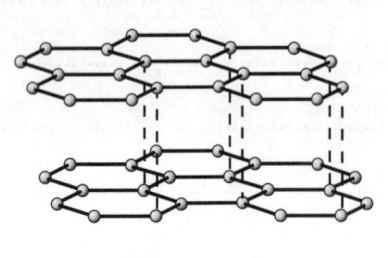

Diagram A

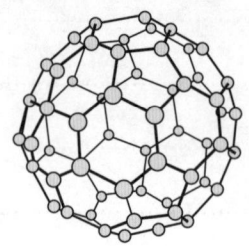

Diagram B

a) Name the two carbon structures shown.

   i) Diagram **A**: ....

   [1]

   ii) Diagram **B**: ....

   [1]

b) Both of the structures shown are able to conduct electricity.
   Explain why this is possible.

   ....

   ....

   ....

   [2]

c) Which of the two forms of carbon shown would you expect to have a **higher** melting point?
   Explain your answer.

   ....

   ....

   ....

   ....

   [3]

d) Name **one** other type of carbon structure, and draw a diagram below to show its bonding.

   Structure: ....

   [2]

   [Total 9 marks]

Polymers

Warm-Up

The sentences below are about polymers. Use the words below to correctly fill in the gaps in the passage. Each word can only be used once.

Polymers are .... molecules. They are formed from .... molecules called ....

Polymers are often referred to as ....

Polymers contain .... bonds, but often behave very differently from simple .... substances.

long covalent molecular plastics monomers small

1* Look at the information below. It describes some properties of two polymers, Y and Z.

Polymer Y
- contains carbon and hydrogen atoms only
- high melting point
- rigid
- does not stretch

Polymer Z
- contains carbon and hydrogen atoms only
- low melting point
- flexible
- easily stretched

Suggest and explain the reasons for the differences in the properties of the two polymers. Give your answer in terms of the nature and arrangement of their chemical bonds.

....
....
....
....
....
....
....
....
....

[Total 6 marks]

Topic C2 — Elements, Compounds and Mixtures

Properties of Materials

1 Look at the table. It lists several compounds containing elements from group 7 of the periodic table.

Grade 6-7

Name of compound	Formula	Structure
iodine monochloride	ICl	simple molecular
potassium chloride	KCl	ionic
sodium fluoride	NaF	ionic
fluoroethane	C_2H_5F	simple molecular
poly(fluoroethene)	$(C_2H_3F)_n$	polymer

a) Which other compound in the table would you expect to be **most similar** to fluoroethane, in terms of its melting and boiling point? Explain your answer.

....

....
[2]

b) Bromine is another element in group 7. Under certain conditions, some compounds of bromine can conduct electricity. Other compounds of bromine exist which never conduct electricity.

Explain how it is possible for different bromine compounds to have different electrical properties.

....

....

....
[2]
[Total 4 marks]

2 The element phosphorus exists in several different forms.
Two of the forms of phosphorus are known as white phosphorus and black phosphorus.
White phosphorus is made of molecules of four phosphorus atoms.
Black phosphorus has a giant covalent structure similar to graphite.

Grade 6-7

Marcus predicts that black phosphorus and white phosphorus will have similar melting points, since they both contain only phosphorus atoms. Do you agree with Marcus? Explain your answer.

....

....

....

....

....
[Total 5 marks]

Topic C2 — Elements, Compounds and Mixtures

Metals

Warm-Up

Which of the following are typical properties of a metal? Circle the correct answers.

good conductor of heat   brittle   high melting point   low density   malleable

low boiling point   poor conductor of electricity   crystal structure when solid

---

1 Which of the following **best** describes the properties of **most** metal oxides? *Grade 4-6*

	State at room temperature	Result when added to water
A	solid	forms basic solution
B	solid	forms acidic solution
C	liquid	forms basic solution
D	liquid	forms acidic solution

Your answer ☐

[Total 1 mark]

---

2 Many properties of solid metals are due to their structure. *Grade 6-7*

a) Draw and label a diagram to show the structure of a solid metal.

[3]

b) i) Explain how this structure means metals usually have high melting points.

....

....

....

[2]

ii) Explain how this structure allows solid metals to conduct electricity.

....

....

....

[2]

[Total 7 marks]

Topic C2 — Elements, Compounds and Mixtures

States, Structure and Bonding

1 Methane (CH$_4$) has a melting point of –182 °C and a boiling point of –161 °C.
Water (H$_2$O) has a melting point of 0 °C and a boiling point of 100 °C.
Methane and water are both simple molecular compounds.

Based on this information, which compound has the **stronger** intermolecular forces?

- A methane
- B water
- C both the same strength
- D can't tell from this information

Your answer ☐

[Total 1 mark]

2 Look at the table. It shows some properties of four elements.

Name	Melting point / °C	Boiling point / °C	Appearance solid	Appearance liquid	Appearance gas
fluorine	–220	–188	colourless	bright yellow	pale yellow
mercury	–39	357	silvery metallic	silvery metallic	n/a
bromine	–7	59	red-brown metallic	red-brown	red-brown
rubidium	39	688	silvery-white metallic	silvery-white metallic	n/a

During an experiment, samples of each of these four elements were placed in separate test tubes.
All four test tubes were then gradually cooled together, from 25 °C to –200 °C.

Describe what you would expect to observe as the experiment progressed.
In your answer you should describe what will happen to each sample.

....
....
....
....
....
....
....

[Total 4 marks]

Topic C2 — Elements, Compounds and Mixtures

3 Look at the table. It shows some properties of six substances.

Substance	Melting point / °C	Boiling point / °C	Conducts electricity?
1	−190	−165	no
2	1500	2840	yes
3	761	1584	only if molten or in solution
4	1690	2815	no
5	−73	65	no
6	688	1367	only if molten or in solution

a) Leonie says: "Substances 2 and 4 have similar melting points, so they probably have a similar structure." Is she likely to be correct? Explain your answer.

....

....

....
[1]

b) Jing says "Substances 3 and 6 are ionic compounds." Is she likely to be correct? Explain your answer.

....

....

....
[1]

c) i) Which substance is a gas at room temperature? ....
[1]

ii) What does this suggest about the structure of this substance? Explain your answer.

....

....

....
[2]

[Total 5 marks]

Exam Practice Tip
These questions are about comparing properties of different substances. You can use everything you know about the properties of different structures to help identify unknown substances or to choose the right material for a particular job.

Topic C2 — Elements, Compounds and Mixtures

Purity

1 Misty-Marie is doing a chemistry experiment.
The instructions say she needs to use pure water.
Stanley offers her a bottle labelled '100% Pure Spring Water'.

Suggest why Stanley's water is unlikely to be suitable for Misty-Marie's experiment.

....

....

....

....

[Total 2 marks]

2 A scientist is comparing two samples of the same compound.
One sample is pure, but the other contains a number of impurities.
The compound is a solid at room temperature.

The scientist decides to work out which is the pure sample by heating both samples and recording their melting points. Explain how she will be able to tell which is the pure sample, even if she does not know the melting point of the pure compound.

....

....

....

[Total 2 marks]

3 The melting point of ammonium nitrate, NH_4NO_3, is 170 °C.
The melting point of citric acid, $C_6H_8O_7$, is 156 °C.

An unidentified substance is found to have a melting point of 163 °C.
Which of the following **best** describes what this tells you about the unidentified substance?

   A   The substance could be impure ammonium nitrate, but isn't impure citric acid.
   B   The substance could be impure citric acid, but isn't impure ammonium nitrate.
   C   The substance could be either impure ammonium nitrate or impure citric acid.
   D   The substance could be a mixture of equal parts ammonium nitrate powder and citric acid powder.

Your answer ☐

[Total 1 mark]

Topic C2 — Elements, Compounds and Mixtures

Purification Techniques

1 Look at the diagram.
It shows a set of equipment you could use for separating a mixture in the lab.

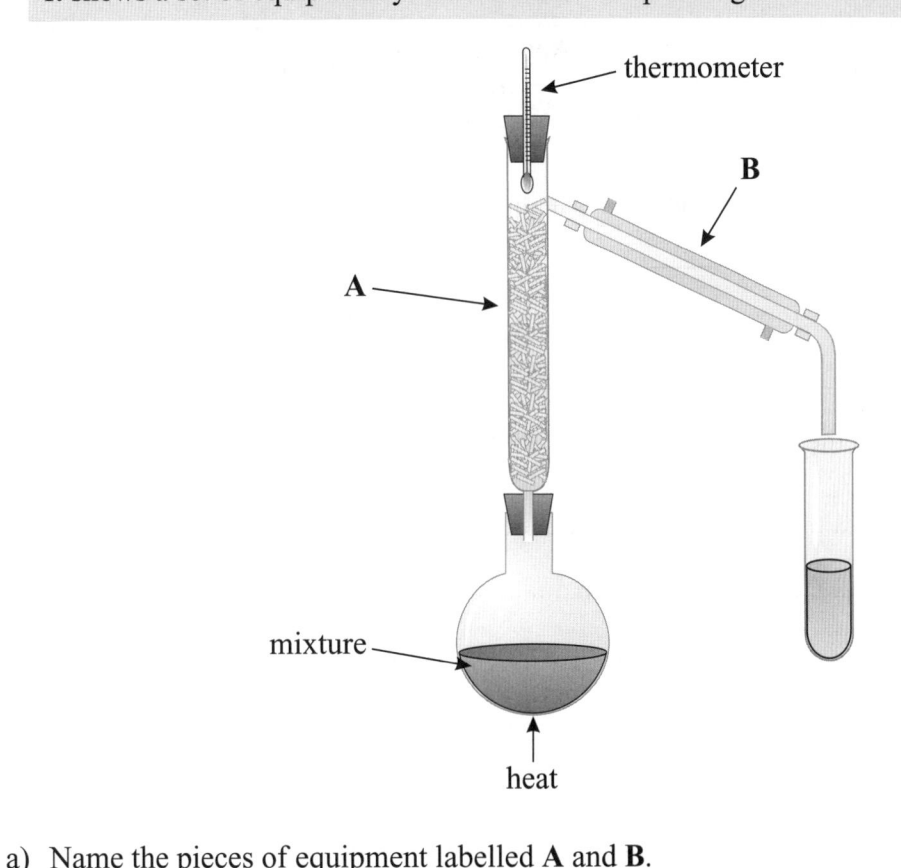

a) Name the pieces of equipment labelled **A** and **B**.

   i) **A**: ....
   [1]

   ii) **B**: ....
   [1]

b) i) What is the name of the separation method this equipment would be used for?

   ....
   [1]

   ii) Describe what type of mixture you would use this method to separate.

   ....
   ....
   [2]

   iii) Reuben is using this method to separate a mixture.
   His mixture contains a flammable liquid.
   Suggest a suitable piece of equipment that he could use to heat the mixture.

   ....
   [1]

   [Total 6 marks]

Topic C2 — Elements, Compounds and Mixtures

2* A student wants to separate the components of a mixture.
The mixture is a white powder composed of barium sulfate, BaSO₄, and potassium iodide, KI.
Look at the table. It shows some information about the two compounds in the mixture.

Name	Melting point / °C	Boiling point / °C	Appearance at room temperature	Soluble in water?
barium sulfate	1580	1600	white solid	no
potassium iodide	681	1330	white solid	yes

Describe in detail a method the student could use to obtain pure samples of both compounds.

....

[Total 6 marks]

Topic C2 — Elements, Compounds and Mixtures

3 Sodium chloride dissolves in water, but not in ethanol.
Sodium chloride has a melting point of 801 °C and a boiling point of 1413 °C.
Ethanol has a melting point of –114 °C and a boiling point of 78 °C.

a) Suggest a purification method which would separate a mixture of sodium chloride and ethanol, but **not** a mixture of sodium chloride and water. Explain your answer.

....

....

....

....
[3]

b) Suggest a purification method you could use **either** to separate a mixture of sodium chloride and water **or** to separate a mixture of sodium chloride and ethanol. Explain your answer.

....

....
[2]
[Total 5 marks]

4 Look at the table. It lists the melting and boiling points of three compounds.

Name	Formula	Melting point / °C	Boiling point / °C
cyclopentane	C_5H_{10}	–94	49
cyclohexane	C_6H_{12}	6	81
ethyl ethanoate	$C_4H_8O_2$	–84	77

Suggest why a mixture of cyclohexane and ethyl ethanoate might be more difficult to separate than a mixture of cyclohexane and cyclopentane.

....

....

....

....
[Total 2 marks]

Topic C2 — Elements, Compounds and Mixtures

Chromatography

1 Which of the following **best** describes the mobile phase and stationary phase used in gas chromatography?

	Mobile phase	Stationary phase
A	viscous liquid	heated tube
B	unreactive gas	heated tube
C	viscous liquid	unreactive gas
D	unreactive gas	viscous liquid

Your answer ☐

[Total 1 mark]

2 The diagram below shows the chromatogram produced by analysing an unidentified substance using gas chromatography.

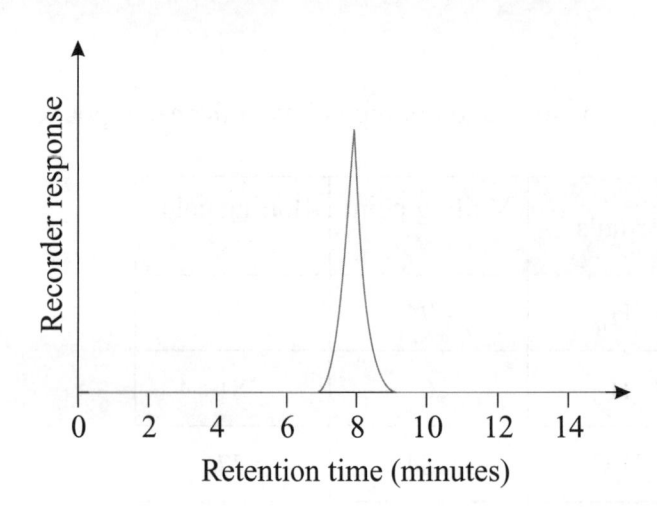

a) Explain why this chromatogram suggests that the unidentified substance is a pure chemical.

....

....
[1]

b) In gas chromatography, what is meant by the term 'retention time'?

....

....
[1]

[Total 2 marks]

Topic C2 — Elements, Compounds and Mixtures

3 Olivia analysed an unknown mixture of liquids using paper chromatography. The chromatogram she produced is shown below.

PRACTICAL

Grade 6-7

a) How many component liquids does this chromatogram suggest are in the mixture? Explain your answer.

....

....
[1]

b) Calculate the R_f value of spot **B**. Use a ruler to help you.

R_f = ...
[2]

c) Olivia is given a list of five chemicals.
She is told that her mixture contains some combination of chemicals from the list.
Explain how Olivia could use pure samples of the chemicals on the list to identify the components of the mixture using paper chromatography.

....

....

....

....
[2]
[Total 5 marks]

Exam Practice Tip
There are a couple of quite different methods here — paper chromatography might be easier to get your head around, especially if you've done it in class, but you need to know the details of gas chromatography too. Make sure you know what 'mobile phase' and 'stationary phase' mean, and what the different phases are for each type of chromatography.

Topic C2 — Elements, Compounds and Mixtures

Relative Masses

1 Which of the following compounds has a relative formula mass of 62.3?

    A   sodium chloride, NaCl
    B   potassium bromide, KBr
    C   magnesium fluoride, MgF$_2$
    D   sodium bromide, NaBr

Your answer ☐

[Total 1 mark]

2 The formula of the compound zinc cyanide is Zn(CN)$_2$.

Find the relative formula mass of zinc cyanide.

relative formula mass = ...
[Total 2 marks]

3 The formula of the compound barium nitrate is Ba(NO$_3$)$_2$.

Find the relative formula mass of barium nitrate.

relative formula mass = ...
[Total 2 marks]

4 An oxide of an element, X, has the formula X$_2$O$_3$.
The relative formula mass of X$_2$O$_3$ is 159.6.

Calculate the relative atomic mass of element X.

relative atomic mass = ...
[Total 3 marks]

Topic C2 — Elements, Compounds and Mixtures

Molecular and Empirical Formulas

Warm-Up

The molecular formula of the compound pentanoic acid can be written $CH_3(CH_2)_3COOH$.

How many oxygen atoms are there in one molecule of pentanoic acid?

How many carbon atoms are there?

How many nitrogen atoms?

How many hydrogen atoms?

---

1 The compound butane-1,4-diamine has the molecular formula $C_4H_{12}N_2$. Which of the following is the empirical formula of butane-1,4-diamine?

- A C_2H_5N
- B $C_2H_6N_2$
- C CH_3N
- D C_2H_6N

Your answer ☐

[Total 1 mark]

2 Look at the diagram. It shows the displayed formula of the compound dithionic acid.

$$H-O-S(=O)(=O)-S(=O)(=O)-O-H$$

a) What is the molecular formula of this compound?
Give your answer in the form $H_aS_bO_c$, where a, b and c are whole numbers.

....

[1]

b) What is the empirical formula of this compound?

....

[1]

[Total 2 marks]

Topic C2 — Elements, Compounds and Mixtures

3 Decaborane is a compound with the molecular formula $B_{10}H_{14}$.

What is the empirical formula of decaborane?

....
[Total 1 mark]

4 Compound R has the empirical formula $C_6H_5O_2$.
Each molecule of compound R contains 10 hydrogen atoms.

What is the molecular formula of compound R?

....
[Total 2 marks]

5 Oct-1-ene is a compound with the molecular formula C_8H_{16}.
Emmy says the empirical formula of oct-1-ene is C_2H_4.

Is Emmy correct? Explain your answer.

....
....
....
[Total 1 mark]

6 Compound Q has the empirical formula C_2HF.
The relative formula mass of compound Q is 132.0.

What is the molecular formula of compound Q?

....
[Total 3 marks]

Topic C2 — Elements, Compounds and Mixtures

Topic C3 — Chemical Reactions

Conservation of Mass

1 During an experiment, a student burns 4.7 g of iron metal in air to form 6.7 g of a solid oxide of iron. The student claims that increase in mass has come from extra atoms being created during the reaction. Do you agree with the student? Explain your answer.

....

....

....

[Total 1 mark]

2 A student is investigating a reaction between zinc and hydrochloric acid. The reaction produces hydrogen gas and a solution of zinc chloride. The student's experimental set-up is shown in the diagram below.

a) How would you expect the mass of the conical flask and its contents to change over the course of the reaction? Explain your answer.

....

....

....

[2]

b) The student repeats the reaction, but this time attaches a gas syringe to the top of the flask. How would you expect the mass of the apparatus and its contents to change over the course of the reaction? Explain your answer.

....

....

....

....

[2]

[Total 4 marks]

Topic C3 — Chemical Reactions

Chemical Formulas

Warm-Up

Sort the elements below into the table to show the charges on the ion that they generally form. You might want to use the periodic table on the inside back cover to help you with this question.

iodine barium sodium selenium magnesium
lithium calcium sulfur chlorine

Charge on Ion			
+2	+1	−1	−2

---

1 Radium is in Group 2 of the periodic table.

What ion would you expect radium to form?
A Ra^{2+}
B Ra^{+}
C Ra^{2-}
D Ra^{-}

Your answer ☐

[Total 1 mark]

---

2 In an ionic compound containing just iron and chlorine, the ratio between the number of iron ions and the number of chloride ions is 1 : 3.

What is the charge on the iron ion present in the compound?

Charge on iron ion = ...
[Total 1 mark]

---

3 During a reaction, an ionic compound containing magnesium and nitrate ions is produced.

Which of the following chemical formulas correctly shows the compound formed?
A Mg_3NO_2
B Mg_2NO_3
C $Mg(NO_3)_2$
D $MgNO_3$

Your answer ☐

[Total 1 mark]

Topic C3 — Chemical Reactions

Chemical Equations

1 Hydrogen gas is an important reactant, used in the Haber Process. It can be made, at high temperatures, using the following reaction.

$$CH_4 + H_2O \rightarrow CO + 3H_2$$

Which of the following word equations correctly describes this reaction?

A methane + steam → carbon dioxide + hydrogen
B ethane + steam → carbon dioxide + hydrogen
C methane + steam → carbon monoxide + hydrogen
D methane + steam → carbon + oxygen + hydrogen

Your answer ☐

[Total 1 mark]

2 Calcium carbonate chips were reacted with nitric acid at room temperature. The products of the reaction were water, a gas and a salt solution.

Complete the reaction equation by adding state symbols to describe the reaction.

$$CaCO_3(\text{..........}) + 2HNO_3(\text{..........}) \rightarrow Ca(NO_3)_2(\text{..........}) + H_2O(\text{..........}) + CO_2(\text{..........})$$

[Total 2 marks]

3 Sodium metal can react with oxygen molecules in the air to form sodium oxide (Na_2O).

Write a balanced equation for this reaction.

....

[Total 2 marks]

4 Silver chloride, AgCl, can be made by reacting silver nitrate, $AgNO_3$, and sodium chloride, NaCl, together in a precipitation reaction.

$$AgNO_{3\,(aq)} + NaCl_{(aq)} \rightarrow AgCl_{(s)} + NaNO_{3\,(aq)}$$

a) How can you tell from the reaction equation that this is a precipitation reaction?

....

[1]

b) Write a balanced ionic equation for the reaction above.

....

[2]

[Total 3 marks]

Topic C3 — Chemical Reactions

5 In a chemical reaction, sulfuric acid and aluminium metal react to form hydrogen gas and a salt solution of aluminium sulfate.

Ben has written this equation for the reaction:

$$Al_{(s)} + H_2SO_{4\,(aq)} \rightarrow Al_2(SO_4)_{3\,(aq)} + H_{2\,(g)}$$

a) Explain what is meant by the symbol '(aq)' in the chemical equation.

....
[1]

b) Ben's equation is not balanced. Write a balanced chemical equation for this reaction.

....
[2]

c) Given that all the solutions involved in this reaction are colourless, use the chemical equation to say what would you expect to see happen during the reaction. Explain your answer.

....

....
[2]
[Total 5 marks]

6 Balance the following symbol equation to show how sulfur reacts with nitric acid.

$$S + HNO_3 \rightarrow H_2SO_4 + NO_2 + H_2O$$

....
[Total 2 marks]

7 Use the half equations below to construct a full equation to show the reaction between aqueous bromine and solid potassium to form potassium bromide, a soluble salt.

Magnesium half-equation: $K_{(s)} \rightarrow K^+_{(aq)} + e^-$
Bromine half-equation: $Br_{2\,(aq)} + 2e^- \rightarrow 2Br^-_{(aq)}$

....
[Total 2 marks]

Topic C3 — Chemical Reactions

8 Zinc reacts with tin sulfate solution as part of a redox reaction. The full reaction equation is shown below.

$$Zn_{(s)} + SnSO_{4\,(aq)} \rightarrow ZnSO_{4\,(aq)} + Sn_{(s)}$$

a) Write the ionic equation for the reaction above.

....
[2]

b) Use your ionic equation to write balanced half-equations for the oxidation of zinc and the reduction of tin in the reaction above. Use e⁻ to represent an electron.

Zinc half equation: ....

Tin half equation: ....
[2]
[Total 4 marks]

9 A student is carrying out a reaction in a lab that involves reacting a solution containing silver ions, Ag^+, with solid copper.

a) Write the balanced ionic equation for the reaction, using the half equations below.

Copper half equation: $Cu_{(s)} \rightarrow Cu^{2+}_{(aq)} + 2e^-$

Silver half equation: $Ag^+_{(aq)} + e^- \rightarrow Ag_{(s)}$

....
[2]

b) Given that the only other ions present in the reaction are nitrate ions (NO_3^-), write a full balanced equation for the reaction.

....
[2]
[Total 4 marks]

Exam Practice Tip
Chemical equations are the bread and butter of chemistry, so being able to balance them is a skill you simply can't do without. You'll be needing to balance chemical equations and half equations for loads, and I mean loads, of questions, so if that's not enough reason to practise 'em I don't know what is.

Topic C3 — Chemical Reactions

Moles

1 What is the approximate number of atoms in 1 mole of carbon atoms?

    A 7.23×10^{23} atoms
    B 7.23×10^{24} atoms
    C 6.022×10^{-23} atoms
    D 6.022×10^{23} atoms

Your answer ☐

[Total 1 mark]

2 A pharmacist is synthesising aspirin, $C_9H_8O_4$, as part of a drugs trial.
After the experiment, the pharmacist calculates that she has made 12.4 moles of aspirin.
What mass of aspirin has she made?

.... g
[Total 2 marks]

3 How many atoms are there in 7 moles of ammonia, NH_3?
Give your answer to 3 significant figures.

.... atoms
[Total 2 marks]

4 The table below contains information about various atoms. Complete the table.
Where appropriate, give any answers to 2 significant figures and in standard form.

Element	Atomic Number	Mass Number	Mass of 1 atom (g)
Hydrogen	1	1	....
Nitrogen	7	....	2.3×10^{-23}
Aluminium	13	27	....
Argon	....	40	6.6×10^{-23}
Titanium	22	48	....

[Total 5 marks]

Topic C3 — Chemical Reactions

5 A sample of an unknown element contains 1.2044 × 10²⁵ atoms. *(Grade 7-9)*

a) How many moles of atoms of the element are in the sample?

....
[1]

b) Given that the atoms have a mean mass of 9.27 × 10⁻²³ g, what is the identity of the element?

....
[2]
[Total 3 marks]

6 A student is investigating an unidentified acid, which is made up of oxygen, sulfur and hydrogen atoms. *(Grade 7-9)*

a) Given that 3.5 moles of the acid has a mass of 343.35 g, what is the relative formula mass of the acid?

....
[1]

b) The percentage mass of the acid made up of oxygen atoms is 65%.
To the nearest whole number, how many moles of oxygen atoms are in one mole of the acid?

....
[2]

c) In one mole of the acid, there is one mole of sulfur atoms.
Deduce the chemical formula of the acid.

....
[3]
[Total 6 marks]

Topic C3 — Chemical Reactions

Calculating Masses

Warm-Up

Complete the following sentences by filling in the blanks with the words on the right.

1) If the amount of limiting reactant in a reaction is decreased, then the amount of product made will ....

2) If the amount of limiting reactant in a reaction is increased, then the amount of product made will ....

3) If the amount of an excess reactant is increased, then the amount of product made will ....

not change

decrease

increase

1 James is investigating the reactivity of some metals. As part of his investigation, he places a piece of magnesium metal in a flask containing an excess of hydrochloric acid and monitors the reaction. The reaction produces hydrogen gas and a metal salt solution.

a) Which of the reactants is the limiting reactant?

....
[1]

b) James repeats the experiment but changes the starting quantities of magnesium and acid. He lets the reaction proceed to completion, and notes that once the reaction has finished, the reaction vessel contains a small amount of grey metal and a colourless solution.

In this second experiment, which of the reactants is the limiting reactant? Explain your answer.

....

....

....
[2]
[Total 3 marks]

2 An industrial process converts the alkene ethene into ethanol, according to the reaction below.

$$C_2H_4 + H_2O \rightarrow CH_3CH_2OH$$

What mass of ethanol can be made from 53.2 g of ethene, given that water is in excess?

.... g
[Total 2 marks]

Topic C3 — Chemical Reactions

3 The following equation shows the complete combustion of ethane in air. *(Grade 7-9)*

$$2C_2H_6 + 7O_2 \rightarrow 4CO_2 + 6H_2O$$

a) Given that 128 g of oxygen were burnt in the reaction, what mass of water was produced? Give your answer to an appropriate number of significant figures.

.... g
[3]

b) A company burns ethane to generate power for an industrial process.

As part of a carbon-reducing scheme, the company can only produce a maximum 4.4 tonnes of carbon dioxide per day (where 1 tonne = 1 000 000 g). What is the maximum amount of ethane that the company can burn each day so as not to exceed the limit of carbon dioxide?

.... tonnes
[2]

[Total 5 marks]

4 Urea, $(NH_2)_2CO$, is a compound that can be synthesised industrially using the following reaction. *(Grade 7-9)*

$$2NH_3 + CO_2 \rightarrow (NH_2)_2CO + H_2O$$

a) A company makes 120.6 tonnes of urea each day (where 1 tonne = 1 000 000 g). What mass of carbon dioxide is required to make this mass?

.... tonnes
[2]

b) Usually the reaction happens in an excess of ammonia. However, a leak in the reaction vessel means the mass of ammonia entering the reaction chamber each day is reduced to 59.5 tonnes.

What is the decrease, in tonnes, in the amount of urea produced per day?

.... tonnes
[3]

[Total 5 marks]

Topic C3 — Chemical Reactions

More Mole Calculations

1 An unknown hydrocarbon, **A**, completely combusts in oxygen to produce just water and carbon dioxide. *(Grade 6-7)*

a) Given that four moles of carbon dioxide and four moles of water are produced during the combustion of 1 mole of **A**, suggest the chemical formula of hydrocarbon **A**.

....
[2]

b) Write a balanced chemical equation for the complete combustion of **A**.

....
[1]
[Total 3 marks]

2 Viola reacts an element, **X**, with oxygen. The result of the reaction is a single product, an oxide of element **X**. *(Grade 7-9)*

a) Given that 200 g of **X** burn to produce 280 g of X oxide, what mass of oxygen gas was used in the reaction?

.... g
[1]

b) Given that the relative atomic mass of **X** is 40, write a balanced equation for the reaction of **X** with oxygen in the air. You should represent **X** oxide as X_aO_b, where a and b are integers.

....
[4]
[Total 5 marks]

Topic C3 — Chemical Reactions

3 A student reacts an unknown acid, H₂X, with sodium hydroxide, NaOH. A neutralisation reaction takes place.
The products are a salt and one other product, Y.

Grade 7-9

a) i) What is the chemical formula of Y?

....
[1]

ii) Write a balanced equation for this reaction.

....
[2]

b) The total mass of the reactants was 228.2 g and 156.2 g of the salt was produced.

i) Calculate the number of moles of Y produced.

.... moles
[2]

ii) What mass of sodium hydroxide was used during this reaction?

.... g
[2]

iii) Find the relative molecular mass of the unknown acid.

....
[3]

iv) The student knows the acid is either chromic acid, (H₂CrO₄), hydrogen sulfide (H₂S) or sulfuric acid (H₂SO₄). Deduce which of these is the correct identity of acid H₂X.

....
[1]

[Total 11 marks]

Exam Practice Tip

If a question involves dealing with moles of unknown masses, you can bet your bottom dollar that you're going to need to be able to use the equations that link moles, mass and relative formula/atomic masses with ease. Writing out this formula triangle that links these variables before you start these sorts of calculation questions is always a good idea — it will help you to see what you can work out from what you're given.

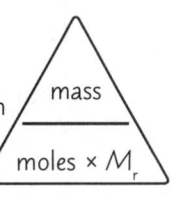

Topic C3 — Chemical Reactions

Concentration

Warm-Up

Circle the formula triangle below which is **correct**.

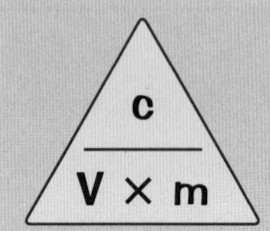

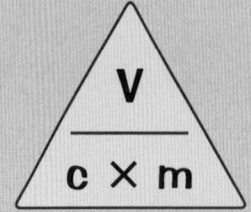

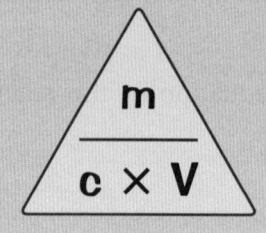

$\dfrac{c}{V \times m}$ $\dfrac{V}{c \times m}$ $\dfrac{m}{c \times V}$

m = mass
c = concentration
V = Volume

1 A student makes a saline solution by dissolving 36 g of sodium chloride in 0.40 dm³ of water. What is the concentration of the solution?

    A   90 g/dm³
    B   14.4 g/dm³
    C   14 400 g/dm³
    D   0.090 g/dm³

Your answer ☐

[Total 1 mark]

2 A student makes up a volume of a standard solution of copper sulfate, **X**, with a concentration of 75.0 g/dm³. He does this by dissolving copper sulfate in 220 cm³ of water.

a) Calculate the mass of copper sulfate that was used to make the solution.

Mass = ... g
[1]

b) Calculate the concentration of the standard solution, **X**, in mol/dm³.
Give your answer to 2 significant figures. Relative formula mass (M_r): $CuSO_4$ = 159.6

Concentration = ... mol/dm³
[1]

c) Which of the following statements is **true**?

    A   **X** will become more concentrated if more water is added to the solution.
    B   Dissolving 56 g of copper sulfate in 220 cm³ of water will make a solution more concentrated than **X**.
    C   Adding an additional 10 g of the solute to **X** will make the solution less concentrated.
    D   The concentration of **X** will halve if an additional 10 cm³ of water are added to the solution.

Your answer ☐

[1]
[Total 3 marks]

Topic C3 — Chemical Reactions

3 A student dissolves 56 g of potassium chloride in 400 cm³ of water.

a) Calculate the concentration of the resultant potassium chloride solution in g/dm³.

Concentration = ... g/dm³
[1]

b) The student wants to make a solution with the same concentration using only 300 cm³ of water. Calculate the mass of potassium chloride that the student will need to add to this volume of water.

Mass = ... g
[1]
[Total 2 marks]

4 A lab technician is making up some solutions for students to use in some of their classes.

a) The technician makes a standard solution of sodium hydroxide for a titration experiment. She makes 600 cm³ of the solution at a concentration of 5.00 mol/dm³.

Calculate the mass of sodium hydroxide used to make the solution.
Give your answer to 3 significant figures. Relative formula mass (M_r): NaOH = 40.0

Mass = ... g
[2]

b) i) The technician also makes a standard solution of sodium carbonate. The solution has a concentration of 80.0 g/dm³ and was made by adding 36.0 g of sodium carbonate to a volume of water. Calculate the volume of water, in cm³, that she used to make the solution.

Volume of water = ... cm³
[2]

ii) For a separate experiment, the technician needs a sodium carbonate solution with a concentration of 40.0 g/dm³.
What can she do to her 80.0 g/dm³ solution to make it this concentration?

....
[1]
[Total 5 marks]

Exam Practice Tip

Make sure you pay close attention to the units used in the question. You might need to convert some values before you can carry out any calculations, e.g. converting volumes from cm³ to dm³ by dividing by 1000. You might also need to convert some values at the end, e.g. if they ask for the concentration of the solution in mol/dm³ instead of in g/dm³.

Topic C3 — Chemical Reactions

Endothermic and Exothermic Reactions

1 Which of the following energy changes could be the result of an exothermic reaction?

	Energy of products	Temperature of surroundings
A	Greater than reactants	Increases
B	Less than reactants	Increases
C	Greater than reactants	Decreases
D	Less than reactants	Decreases

Your answer ☐

[Total 1 mark]

2 The reaction between ethanoic acid and sodium carbonate is an endothermic reaction.

Sketch and label a reaction profile for this reaction on the axes below.

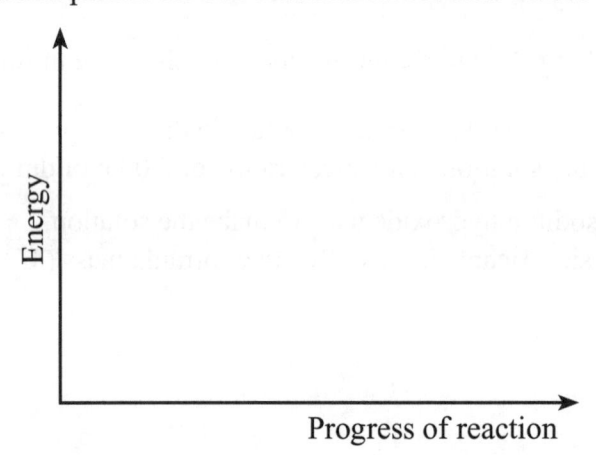

[Total 2 marks]

3 The diagram below shows the reaction profile for a chemical reaction.

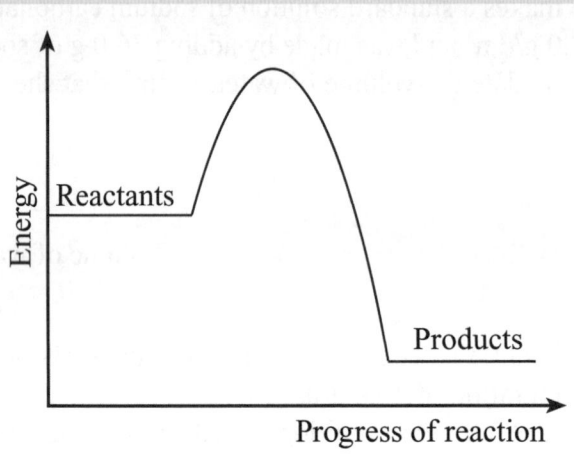

a) Mark the activation energy on the reaction profile.

[1]

b) Does this reaction profile show an endothermic or an exothermic reaction? Explain your answer.

....

....

[1]

[Total 2 marks]

Topic C3 — Chemical Reactions

Bond Energies

1 Which of the following statements is **true**?

    A During exothermic reactions, the energy taken to break the bonds in the reactants is greater than the energy released by making the bonds in the products.

    B During endothermic reactions, the energy released by breaking bonds in the reactants is less than the energy taken to make the bonds in the products.

    C During exothermic reactions, the energy taken to break the bonds in the reactants is less than the energy released by making the bonds in the products.

    D During endothermic reactions, the energy taken to break the bonds in the reactants is less than the energy released by making the bonds in the products.

Your answer ☐

[Total 1 mark]

2 Look at the table below. It shows the bond energies of some bonds.

Bond	Bond energy (kJ/mol)
C — H	413
C — O	358
H — O	463
C = C	614
C — C	347

a) Use the table to work out the energy change of the following reaction between ethene and water.

$$H_2C=CH_2 + H_2O \rightarrow H_3C-CH_2-OH$$

.... kJ/mol

[3]

b) Use your answer to a) to deduce whether the reaction between ethene and water is endothermic or exothermic. Explain your answer.

....

....

[2]

[Total 5 marks]

Topic C3 — Chemical Reactions

116

3 The energy change of the following reaction is –119 kJ/mol. *Grade 7-9*

$$H-\underset{H}{\overset{H}{\underset{|}{C}}}-\underset{H}{\overset{H}{\underset{|}{C}}}-H \;+\; Cl-Cl \;\rightarrow\; H-\underset{H}{\overset{H}{\underset{|}{C}}}-\underset{H}{\overset{Cl}{\underset{|}{C}}}-H \;+\; H-Cl$$

a) Is the reaction endothermic or exothermic?

....

[1]

b) Use this information, as well as the data in the table, to work out the approximate bond energy of a H—Cl bond.

Bond	Bond energy (kJ/mol)
C — H	413
C — C	347
C — Cl	339
Cl — Cl	239

.... kJ/mol

[3]

c) Use your answer from b) to rank the bonds from the table, and the H—Cl bond in order of strength, from weakest to strongest.

....

[1]

[Total 5 marks]

Exam Practice Tip

In questions involving calculating energy changes from bond energies (or vice versa), it can be really useful to draw out the displayed formulas of any chemicals you're dealing with (unless you're given them in the question o' course). Displayed formulas show all the atoms and all the bonds between them, and make it easy to see what bonds have broken and what new bonds have been made during a chemical reaction.

Topic C3 — Chemical Reactions

Acids and Bases

Warm-Up

Circle the statements below that are **true**.

As H⁺ concentration increases, pH decreases.

Acids contain lots of OH⁻ ions.

Neutral substances have a pH of 8.

Alkalis turn Universal indicator blue/purple.

Acids have pHs of less than 7.

Alkalis are soluble bases.

1 Which of the following equations shows a neutralisation reaction? *(Grade 4-6)*

A $HNO_3 + LiOH \rightarrow LiNO_3 + H_2O$
B $Mg + H_2O \rightarrow MgO + H_2$
C $Na_2O + H_2O \rightarrow 2NaOH$
D $C_4H_{10} + 6½O_2 \rightarrow 4CO_2 + 5H_2O$

Your answer ☐

[Total 1 mark]

2 Gemma and Srdjan are measuring the pHs of some common household substances using Universal indicator. *(Grade 4-6)*

a) They add a few drops of Universal indicator to some vinegar.
Given that vinegar is acidic, what colour would you expect the Universal indicator to turn?

....
[1]

b) They add a few drops of Universal indicator to a flask containing some kitchen cleaner.
A blue solution forms. Suggest a pH for the kitchen cleaner.

....
[1]

c) Gemma and Srdjan add Universal indicator to a sample of bleach. It produces a purple colour. Gemma thinks it has a pH of 12 while Srdjan thinks it has a pH of 11.

Suggest an alternative piece of equipment they could use that would give them a more accurate reading for the pH value.

....
[1]

[Total 3 marks]

3 Write an ionic equation to show the reaction of any acid and alkali. Include state symbols. *(Grade 6-7)*

....
[Total 2 marks]

Topic C3 — Chemical Reactions

118

4 Which one of the following statements about pH probes is **false**?

    A pH probes give a numerical value for the pH of a solution.
    B Before using a pH probe, you should calibrate it by setting it to measure pH 7 in a sample of pure water.
    C You should wash a pH probe with a weak acid in between readings.
    D pH probes measure pH electronically.

Your answer ☐

[Total 1 mark]

5 Pedro carries out an acid-base titration by adding a base to an acid. He measures the pH of the solution throughout the experiment, and uses the results to draw the titration curve, shown on the right.

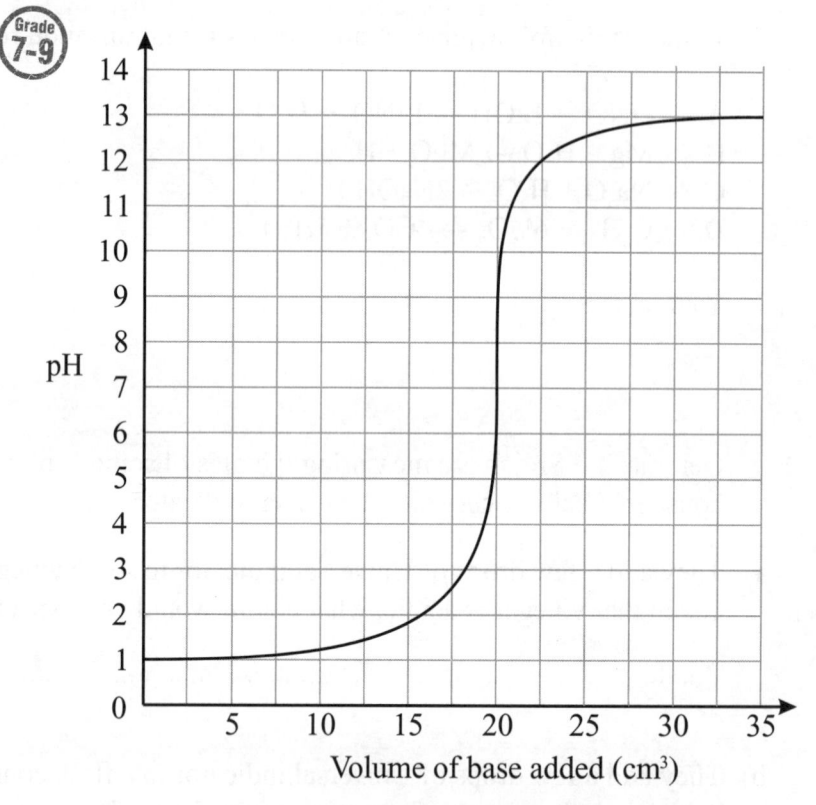

a) What was the starting pH of the acid?

....
[1]

b) Mark, with an asterisk (*), the end point of the titration on the curve on the graph.
[1]

c) How much base was needed to completely neutralise the volume of acid used in the titration?

.... cm³
[1]

d) At the end point, how does the concentration of **hydrogen** ions compare with the concentration of **hydroxide** ions?

....
[1]

[Total 4 marks]

Topic C3 — Chemical Reactions

Strong and Weak Acids

1 Methanoic acid, HCOOH, is a **weak acid**. *(Grade 6-7)*

a) Explain what is meant by the term 'weak acid'.

....

....
[1]

b) Write a chemical equation to show how methanoic acid acts as a weak acid.

....
[2]

[Total 3 marks]

2 Tamal has two beakers, each containing a sample of a different acid. *(Grade 6-7)*
The acid in beaker X is **stronger** than the acid in beaker Y.
The acid in beaker Y is **more concentrated** than the acid in beaker X.

Which of the following options could describe the contents of the two beakers?

	Beaker X	Beaker Y
A	0.002 mol/dm³ HCl	4.0 mol/dm³ CH$_3$COOH
B	4.0 mol/dm³ HCl	0.002 mol/dm³ CH$_3$COOH
C	0.002 mol/dm³ CH$_3$COOH	4.0 mol/dm³ HCl
D	4.0 mol/dm³ CH$_3$COOH	0.002 mol/dm³ HCl

Your answer ☐

[Total 1 mark]

3 Jackie is carrying out an experiment to measure how the pH of a strong acid is affected by its concentration. *(Grade 7-9)*

a) Jackie takes a sample of an acidic solution, A, made by dissolving a solid acid in deionised water.
He wants to make his sample of the acid more concentrated.
Which of the following things could he do?

A Add a more dilute solution of the acid to the sample.
B Add more water to the sample.
C Add more solution the same as A to the sample.
D Dissolve more solid acid in the sample.

Your answer ☐

[1]

b) At a certain dilution, the hydrogen ion concentration is 0.001 mol/dm³ and the acid has a pH of 3.
Jackie increases the concentration of hydrogen ions in the sample to 0.1 mol/dm³.
What is the new pH of the acid?

....
[1]

[Total 2 marks]

Topic C3 — Chemical Reactions

Reactions of Acids

1 June allows a metal carbonate and an acid to react together in a flask. Which of the following chemicals are not produced?

A carbon dioxide
B a salt
C water
D hydrogen

Your answer ☐

[Total 1 mark]

2 Complete the table to show the chemical formulas of the salts created in the reactions involving the following acids.

	Hydrochloric acid (HCl)	Nitric acid (HNO_3)	Sulfuric acid (H_2SO_4)
Zinc metal (Zn)	$ZnCl_2$	....	$ZnSO_4$
Calcium carbonate ($CaCO_3$)	$CaCl_2$	$Ca(NO_3)_2$	....
Sodium hydroxide (NaOH)	NaCl	$NaNO_3$	....
Potassium carbonate (K_2CO_3)	....	KNO_3	K_2SO_4

[Total 4 marks]

3 Andy is making a sample of potassium sulfate, K_2SO_4, by reacting potassium hydroxide, KOH, and sulfuric acid, H_2SO_4, together. **PRACTICAL**

a) Potassium sulfate is a soluble salt. Explain what is meant by the term soluble in this context.

....
[1]

b) Write a balanced chemical equation for this reaction.

....
[2]

c) Andy uses a titration method to add a potassium hydroxide solution to the acid until he reaches the end point, which is shown by a change in colour of an indicator in the solution. He then crystallises the solution to obtain the salt. Will this produce a pure sample of the salt? Explain your answer.

....
....
[1]

[Total 4 marks]

Topic C3 — Chemical Reactions

4 Pauline mixes zinc carbonate, $ZnCO_3$, with hydrochloric acid, HCl, and notes that the mixture starts to bubble as a gas is given off.

a) What is the name of the gas that is responsible for the bubbles in the reaction?

....

[1]

b) Write a balanced chemical equation for the reaction between hydrochloric acid and zinc carbonate.

....

[2]

c) What is the name of the salt produced by the reaction?

....

[1]

[Total 4 marks]

5 Sodium sulfate is a soluble salt that can be made by the reaction between sulfuric acid, H_2SO_4, and sodium hydroxide, NaOH solution.

a) Write a balanced chemical equation for the reaction between sulfuric acid and sodium hydroxide.

....

[2]

b)* Outline how you could prepare a pure sample of sodium sulfate in the lab from sulfuric acid and sodium hydroxide. **PRACTICAL**

....

....

....

....

....

....

....

....

....

[6]

[Total 8 marks]

Exam Practice Tip

If you're asked to predict what will form in a reaction involving an acid, it can help to write out a balanced chemical equation. That way, you can see exactly what atoms you're dealing with in the reactants, and make sure they're all accounted for in the products. It may sound like a bit of an effort, but it will make sure you don't miss out anything.

Topic C3 — Chemical Reactions

Making Salts

1 Insoluble salts can be made by precipitation reactions.
Which of the following equations describes a precipitation reaction?

A $CuO_{(s)} + 2HCl_{(aq)} \rightarrow CuCl_{2\,(aq)} + H_2O_{(l)}$

B $HCl_{(aq)} + NaOH_{(aq)} \rightarrow NaCl_{(aq)} + H_2O_{(l)}$

C $2HNO_{3\,(aq)} + ZnCO_{3\,(s)} \rightarrow Zn(NO_3)_{2\,(aq)} + H_2O_{(l)} + CO_{2\,(g)}$

D $Pb(NO_3)_{2\,(aq)} + 2NaCl_{(aq)} \rightarrow PbCl_{2\,(s)} + 2NaNO_{3\,(aq)}$

Your answer ☐

[Total 1 mark]

2 Jeremy is making a sample of silver chloride, an insoluble salt, using an acid and a salt solution.

a) Suggest an acid that Jeremy could use to make silver chloride.

....
[1]

b) Once Jeremy has made the salt, he pours the whole solid and salt solution into a filter funnel, as shown below.

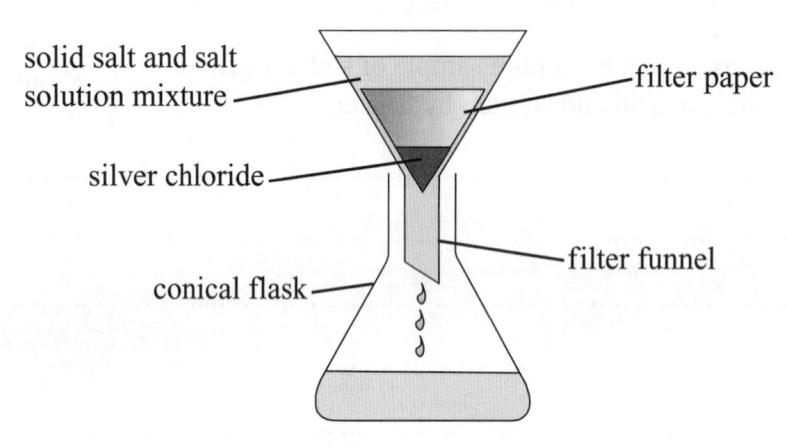

(Diagram: filter funnel containing solid salt and salt solution mixture, with silver chloride on filter paper, above a conical flask)

What has Jeremy done wrong? Explain how this will affect the mass of solid salt that he collects from the solution.

....
....
....
[2]

c) After Jeremy has isolated the salt, he washes it with deionised water.
Explain why he uses deionised water as opposed to tap water.

....
....
[1]

[Total 4 marks]

Topic C3 — Chemical Reactions

3 The following steps describe how you would produce a pure sample of magnesium sulfate, MgSO₄, from solid magnesium hydroxide and sulfuric acid.

 1   Slowly heat the solution to evaporate off some of the water.
 2   Filter the solid off and dry it in a desiccator.
 3   Filter out the excess solid using a filter funnel and filter paper.
 4   Add magnesium hydroxide to a flask containing sulfuric acid until no more of the metal hydroxide reacts (at this point, the excess solid will just sink to the bottom of the flask).
 5   Leave the solution to crystallise.

a) Which is the correct order that these steps should be carried out in?

   A   4, 1, 3, 2, 5
   B   1, 4, 2, 5, 2
   C   4, 3, 1, 5, 2
   D   3, 1, 2, 5, 4

   Your answer ☐

   [1]

b) Write a balanced symbol equation, including state symbols, that describes the reaction between magnesium hydroxide, Mg(OH)₂, and sulfuric acid, H₂SO₄.

   ....

   [3]
   [Total 4 marks]

4 Davina reacts iron nitrate, Fe(NO₃)₃, and sodium hydroxide, NaOH, together to make an insoluble salt containing iron.

a) Write down the chemical formula of the insoluble salt.

   ....

   [1]

b) The following steps outline the method Davina used to make the insoluble salt.

   1. Mix equal quantities of iron nitrate and sodium hydroxide.
   2. Once a precipitate has started to form, filter the solution to remove the solid.
   3. Heat the solid with a Bunsen burner to dry it.

   Suggest **two** improvements that you could make to Davina's method to ensure that all the insoluble salt is extracted and that the final sample is pure.

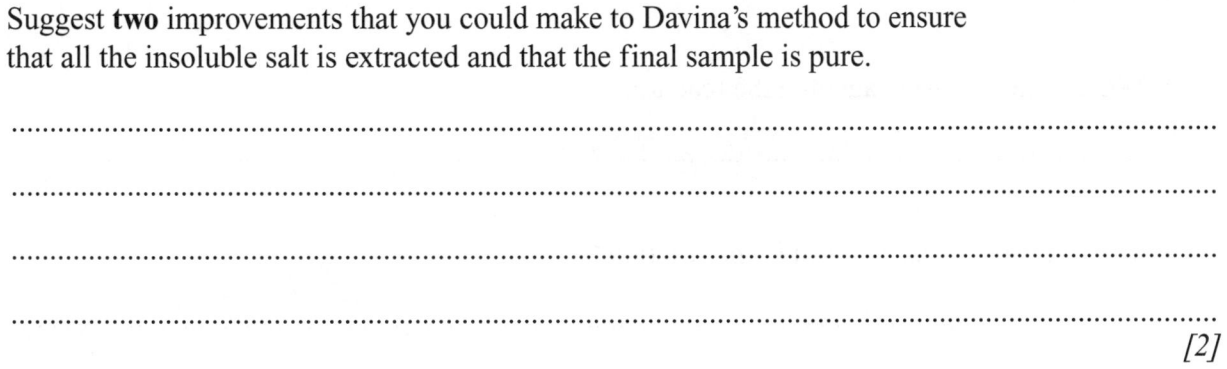

   ....
   ....
   ....
   ....

   [2]
   [Total 3 marks]

Topic C3 — Chemical Reactions

Oxidation and Reduction

1 The combustion of hydrocarbons can be described as an oxidation reaction. Explain why.

....

....

[Total 1 mark]

2 Which of the following statements is **false**?

    A Oxidation is the gain of oxygen.
    B Reduction and oxidation happen at the same time.
    C Reduction is the loss of electrons.
    D Reducing agents donate electrons.

Your answer ☐

[Total 1 mark]

3 In a redox reaction, aluminium atoms are oxidised to Al^{3+} ions.

  a) Write a balanced half equation to show this reaction. Use e⁻ to represent an electron.

....
[1]

  b) In the redox reaction, would aluminium act as an oxidising agent or a reducing agent?

....
[1]

[Total 2 marks]

4 The following ionic equation shows a redox reaction involving hydrogen ions and zinc.

$$Zn + 2H^+ \rightarrow Zn^{2+} + H_2$$

  a) Write balanced half equations to show how electrons are transferred in this reaction.
    Use e⁻ to represent an electron.

    i) Zinc half equation: ....
[1]

    ii) Hydrogen half equation: ....
[1]

  b) What is the oxidising agent in the reaction?

....
[1]

  c) Which element was oxidised in the reaction?

....
[1]

[Total 4 marks]

Topic C3 — Chemical Reactions

Electrolysis

Warm-Up

Fill in the labels on the diagram, using the words below, to show the different parts of the electrochemical cell.

wires   cathode   electrolyte   power supply   anode

1 As part of an industrial process, a sample of sodium chloride, NaCl, was electrolysed. *Grade 4-6*

a) Before the sodium chloride is electrolysed, it either has to be molten or dissolved in solution. Explain why this is necessary.

....

....
[2]

b) Given that inert electrodes were used and the sodium chloride was molten, what would be formed at:

i) the anode? ....
[1]

ii) the cathode? ....
[1]
[Total 4 marks]

2 The two half equations below show the reactions happening at the anode and the cathode during an electrolysis experiment. *Grade 6-7*

$Pb^{2+} + 2e^- \rightarrow Pb$
$2I^- \rightarrow I_2 + 2e^-$

a) Give the chemical formula of the electrolyte, given that it's a molten metal compound.

....
[1]

b) What would you expect to happen at the cathode?

....
[1]
[Total 2 marks]

Topic C3 — Chemical Reactions

3 Zoe sets up an electrochemical cell. A diagram of her set up is shown below.

Grade 6-7

PRACTICAL

- wires
- beaker
- inert electrodes
- electrolyte

What **two** things are wrong with Zoe's set-up?

....

....

[Total 2 marks]

4 Matthew carries out an electrolysis experiment using inert electrodes. The electrolyte he uses is a solution of potassium nitrate.

Grade 6-7

a) Matthew predicts that potassium will be discharged at the cathode. Given that potassium is more reactive than hydrogen, do you agree with Matthew? Explain your answer.

....

....

[2]

b) Describe what you would expect to see happening at the anode. Explain your answer.

....

....

[2]

[Total 4 marks]

5 Electrolysis is carried out on a solution of copper(II) chloride, $CuCl_2$, using inert electrodes.

Grade 6-7

a) Which of the following ions is **not** present in the solution?
- A H^+
- B H_2O^-
- C Cu^{2+}
- D Cl^-

Your answer ☐

[1]

b) What would you expect to see happen at:

i) the anode? ....

ii) the cathode? ....

[2]

[Total 3 marks]

Topic C3 — Chemical Reactions

Electrolysis of Copper Sulfate

1 The following question is about the electrolysis of copper sulfate solution using platinum electrodes.

a) Platinum electrodes are an example of an inert electrode. Explain what is meant, in this context, by the term 'inert'.

....
[1]

b) Assuming the copper sulfate is pure, list the four ions that are present in solution during the electrolysis of copper sulfate solution using inert electrodes.

....
[2]

c) Write balanced half equations to show the reactions that occur at:

i) the anode ....

ii) the cathode ....
[2]
[Total 5 marks]

2 Lucy has two identical strips of copper. She uses them as electrodes in the electrochemical cell shown on the right.

a) She places the electrochemical cell on a mass balance and turns on the power supply. She leaves the power supply on for 30 minutes, and monitors the mass of the cell throughout the reaction. How would you expect the mass of the cell to change over the 30 minutes?

....
[1]

b) After 30 minutes, Lucy turns the power supply off and disconnects the electrodes. How would you expect the appearances of each electrode to have changed throughout the electrolysis? Explain your answer.

....

....

....
[3]
[Total 4 marks]

Topic C3 — Chemical Reactions

3 Which of the following statements best describes what occurs during the electrolysis of copper sulfate with copper electrodes?

  A   Copper atoms are transferred from the cathode to the anode.
  B   Sulfate ions are discharged at the anode.
  C   Copper atoms are oxidised to Cu^{3+} ions.
  D   Copper ions are reduced to copper atoms at the cathode.

  Your answer ☐

[Total 1 mark]

4 Valentino is investigating the electrolysis of copper sulfate. He sets up two cells. In cell A he uses platinum electrodes. In cell B, he uses copper electrodes. The cells are identical in all other respects.

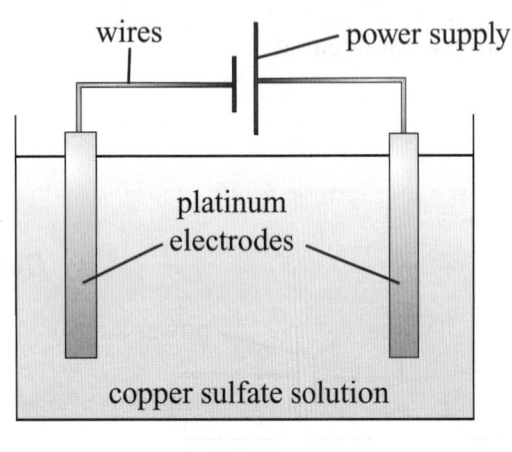

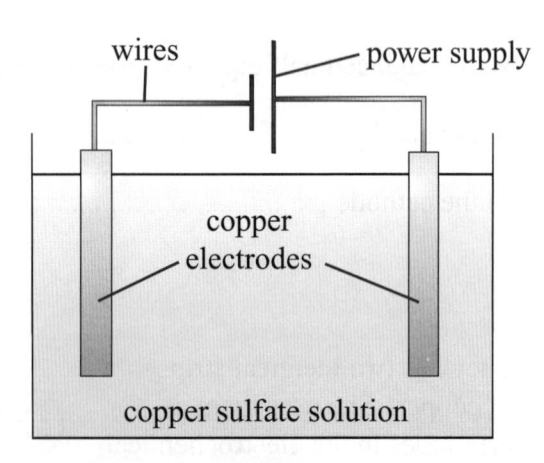

Both cells are turned on and left for 5 hours. Given that the masses of the two cells were the same at the start of the electrolysis, how would you expect them to compare after the 5 hours? Explain your answer. Use appropriate half equations to justify your answer.

....
....
....
....
....
....
....

[Total 5 marks]

Exam Practice Tip

When dealing with electrolysis questions (like the ones on the last four pages), read the question carefully, and then read it again. The products of electrolysis depends on loads of things — whether your electrolyte is molten or aqueous, what your electrodes are made of and what ions are present in your electrolyte. So, make sure you know exactly what set-up you're dealing with before you jump in with an answer. You have been warned...

Tests for Gases

1 Amelia is testing for gases.

The diagram below shows a gas being tested.

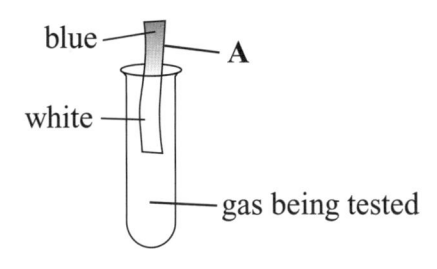

a) Identify the item labelled **A** in the diagram.

....
[1]

b Suggest which gas was present in the test tube.

....
[1]
[Total 2 marks]

2 Vicky performs an experiment that produces a colourless gas. Vicky does not know what the gas is, so she collects it and tests it in order to identify it.

a) Suggest why Vicky should perform the experiment in a fume cupboard.

....
[1]

b) Describe how Vicky could test the gas to see if it was carbon dioxide.

....

....
[2]

c) When Vicky placed a lighted splint into a sample of the gas, it was **not** accompanied by a popping sound. What does this tell you about the gas she had collected?

....
[1]

d) When Vicky placed a glowing splint into a sample of the gas, the splint relighted. Identify the gas that was produced by her experiment.

....
[1]
[Total 5 marks]

Topic C3 — Chemical Reactions

130 Topic C4 — Predicting and Identifying Reactions and Products

Group 1 — Alkali Metals

1   The Group 1 elements are metals with relatively low melting and boiling points. They react readily to form ionic compounds. Their ions usually have a charge of 1+. *(Grade 6-7)*

a) Explain why the elements in Group 1 usually form 1+ ions.

....

....
[2]

b) The table below shows information about the melting and boiling points of the first three Group 1 elements.

Element	Melting point (°C)	Boiling point (°C)
Lithium	181	1342
Sodium	....	883
Potassium	63	759

Use the information in the table to predict the melting point of sodium.
Put your answer in the table.
[1]

[Total 3 marks]

2   A teacher adds a small piece of sodium to cold water. The sodium floats around on the surface, fizzing fairly vigorously, and melts as it reacts. *(Grade 6-7)*

a) Name the **two** products of this reaction.

....
[2]

b) Describe what you would expect to see if a small piece of potassium was added to cold water.

....

....

....

....
[4]

c) It is safe to demonstrate the reaction between potassium and water in a school laboratory, but it is **not** safe to demonstrate the reaction between rubidium and water. Explain why.

....

....
[1]

[Total 7 marks]

Topic C4 — Predicting and Identifying Reactions and Products

Group 7 — Halogens

Warm-Up

The sentences below are about the elements in Group 7 of the periodic table. Choose from the words on the right to fill the gaps. Use each word only once.

The five known Group 7 elements, or halogens, are fluorine, chlorine, bromine, ... and astatine. They have similar chemical properties, because they all have .... electrons in their outer shell. The halogens exist as .... molecules, where two halogen atoms share a pair of electrons in a .... bond. A halogen atom can also form a stable ion by gaining one electron — these ions are called .... ions.

diatomic

seven

halide

iodine

covalent

1 The melting and boiling points of the halogens **increase** as you move down Group 7.

a) State which element in Group 7 will have the **lowest** boiling point.

....
[1]

b) At room temperature and pressure, chlorine is a gas, bromine is a liquid and iodine is a solid. Use this information to predict the physical state of the element astatine at room temperature.

....
[1]

[Total 2 marks]

2 The halogens can react with alkali metals to form metal halide salts.

a) Name the metal halide salt that will be formed when the following pairs of elements react.

i) Bromine and sodium.

....
[1]

ii) Iodine and potassium.

....
[1]

b) When chlorine gas reacts with lithium, the salt lithium chloride, LiCl, is formed. Construct the balanced symbol equation for this reaction.

....
[2]

[Total 4 marks]

Topic C4 — Predicting and Identifying Reactions and Products

3 Josie investigated the reactions that occur when chlorine, bromine or iodine are added to different sodium halide solutions. The table below shows her results.

Grade 6-7

	Sodium chloride solution (NaCl$_{(aq)}$, colourless)	Sodium bromide solution (NaBr$_{(aq)}$, colourless)	Sodium iodide solution (NaI$_{(aq)}$, colourless)
Add chlorine water (Cl$_{2\,(aq)}$, colourless)	no reaction	solution turns orange	solution turns brown
Add bromine water (Br$_{2\,(aq)}$, orange)	no reaction	....	solution turns brown
Add iodine water (I$_{2\,(aq)}$, brown)	no reaction	no reaction	no reaction

a) Use your knowledge of the reactivity trend of the halogens to fill in the missing result in the table.

[1]

b) Explain why there was no reaction when Josie added iodine water to sodium bromide solution.

....

....
[2]

c) Construct a balanced symbol equation for the reaction that happened when Josie added chlorine water to sodium bromide solution.

....
[2]
[Total 5 marks]

4 There is a trend in the reactivity of the Group 7 elements.

Grade 7-9

a) State the trend in reactivity as you go down Group 7.

....
[1]

b) Explain the trend you have described in part a). Give your answer in terms of electronic structure.

....

....

....

....
[3]
[Total 4 marks]

Topic C4 — Predicting and Identifying Reactions and Products

Group 0 — Noble Gases

1 Which of these statements is **true** for the noble gases?

    A   They are colourful gases.
    B   They have only 1 electron in their outer shells.
    C   They are monatomic.
    D   They react with alkali metals to form salts.

Your answer ☐

[Total 1 mark]

2 The noble gases are inert gases that make up Group 0 of the periodic table.

a) 'Inert' means 'very unreactive'. Explain why the elements in Group 0 are inert.

....
....
....

[2]

b) The table below shows some information about the first four noble gases.

Element	Symbol	Melting point (°C)	Boiling point (°C)	Density (kg/m^3)
Helium	He	−272	−269	0.2
Neon	Ne	−249	−246	0.9
Argon	Ar	−189	−186	1.8
Krypton	Kr	−157	−153	3.7

i) The element below krypton in Group 0 is xenon.
Use the information in the table to predict what the density of xenon will be.

....

[1]

ii) Would you expect the melting point of xenon to be higher or lower than the melting point of krypton? Explain your answer.

....
....

[1]
[Total 4 marks]

Exam Practice Tip

Make sure you get lots of practice at questions like 2 b), where you're given information about some of the elements in a group and asked to use it to predict something about another element in the group — they need careful thinking through. Remember, you could get asked to do this sort of thing for elements in Group 1, Group 7 or Group 0.

Topic C4 — Predicting and Identifying Reactions and Products

Reactivity of Metals

1 Amal performed some experiments to investigate the reactivity of metals.

a) First, Amal placed pieces of four different metals into dilute hydrochloric acid.
The diagram below shows what the four experiments looked like after 1 minute.

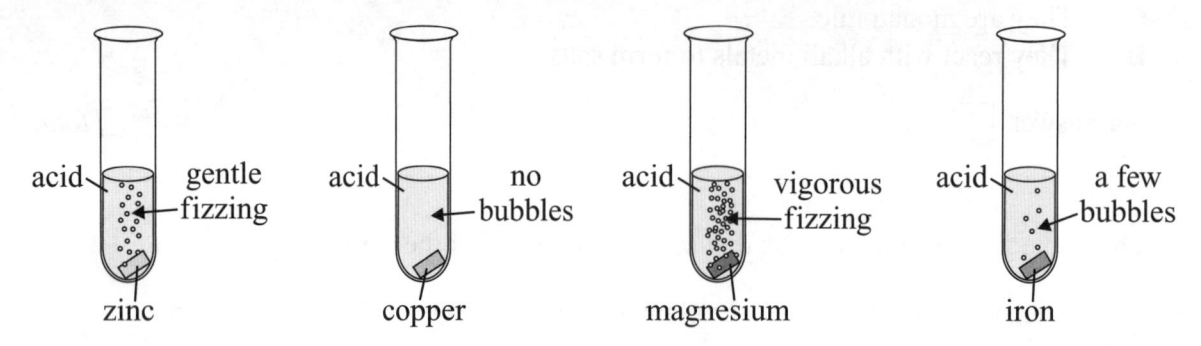

- zinc — gentle fizzing
- copper — no bubbles
- magnesium — vigorous fizzing
- iron — a few bubbles

Use the information in the diagram to put these metals in order of reactivity.

Most reactive: ....

....

....

Least reactive: ....

[2]

b) Next, Amal was given samples of three mystery metals, marked **X**, **Y** and **Z**. She put small pieces of each of the metals in cold water. If there was no reaction with cold water, she tested the metal to see if it would react with steam. Her results are shown in the table below.

Metal	Any reaction with cold water?	Any reaction with steam?
X	Reacts vigorously. Hydrogen gas is produced.	
Y	no reaction	Reacts vigorously. Metal is coated with a white solid. Hydrogen gas is produced.
Z	no reaction	no reaction

i) Metal **Y** was zinc. It reacted with the steam to produce hydrogen gas and a white solid. Name the white solid that was produced by this reaction.

....

[1]

ii) One of the other metals Amal was given was sodium.
Suggest whether sodium was metal **X** or metal **Z**. Give a reason for your answer.

....

....

[1]

[Total 4 marks]

Topic C4 — Predicting and Identifying Reactions and Products

2 Which of the statements below about metal reactivity is **incorrect**?

    A   The easier it is for a metal atom to form a positive ion, the less reactive it will be.
    B   A metal will displace a less reactive metal from a salt solution.
    C   In a reactivity series, you will find a reactive metal above a less reactive metal.
    D   The more reactive a metal is, the faster its reaction with dilute acid will be.

Your answer ☐   *[Total 1 mark]*

3 Shaun adds small pieces of some metals to metal salt solutions and leaves them for 1 hour. He records whether or not any reaction has taken place. His table of results is shown below.

	Magnesium	**Silver**	**Aluminium**	**Lead**
Magnesium chloride	no reaction	no reaction	no reaction	no reaction
Silver nitrate	magnesium nitrate and silver formed	no reaction	aluminium nitrate and silver formed	lead nitrate and silver formed
Aluminium chloride	magnesium chloride and aluminium formed	no reaction	no reaction	no reaction
Lead nitrate	magnesium nitrate and lead formed	no reaction	aluminium nitrate and lead formed	no reaction

a) Shaun says "My results show that lead is more reactive than silver."
Do you agree? Explain your answer.

....

....

[1]

b) Construct a balanced symbol equation for the reaction between magnesium and aluminium chloride, $AlCl_3$.

....

[2]

c) Nickel is above lead in the reactivity series. Nickel is a shiny grey metal and nickel nitrate is green in solution. Lead is a dull grey metal and lead nitrate is colourless in solution. Suggest what Shaun would observe if he added nickel to lead nitrate solution.

....

....

....

[2]
[Total 5 marks]

Exam Practice Tip

It sounds a bit obvious, but the main thing to remember when you're answering questions on this topic is that the more reactive a metal is, the more likely it will be to react and form a compound. So the more reactive a metal is, the more vigorously it will react with water and acids, and a reactive metal will push a less reactive metal out of a salt solution...

Topic C4 — Predicting and Identifying Reactions and Products

Topic C5 — Monitoring and Controlling Chemical Reactions

Reaction Rates

1 A student reacts sulfuric acid with calcium carbonate to form calcium sulfate, water and carbon dioxide gas. *Grade 6-7* **PRACTICAL**

a) Outline a method the student could follow to monitor the rate of this reaction.

....

....

....

....
[3]

b) The graph below shows his results. On the graph below, sketch a curve that shows the rate of reaction that would be seen if the experiment was carried out at a higher temperature.

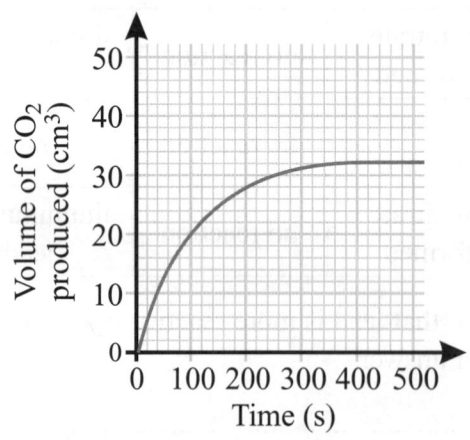

[1]

c) The scientist carries out the same reaction using different quantities of reactants. Reaction **X** used 0.500 g of calcium carbonate and an excess of 0.100 mol/dm³ sulfuric acid. Which of the sets of conditions below could have resulted in reaction **Y**?

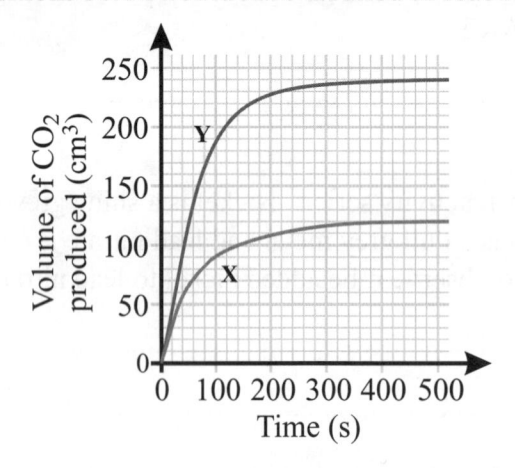

A 0.250 g of calcium carbonate and an excess of 0.100 mol/dm³ sulfuric acid.
B 1.00 g of calcium carbonate and an excess of 0.100 mol/dm³ sulfuric acid.
C 0.250 g of calcium carbonate and an excess of 0.200 mol/dm³ sulfuric acid.
D 1.00 g of calcium carbonate and an excess of 0.200 mol/dm³ sulfuric acid.

Your answer ☐

[1]

[Total 5 marks]

2 Shabnam reacted magnesium ribbons with hydrochloric acid. As the reaction proceeded, hydrogen gas was produced.

Grade 7-9   PRACTICAL

a) Shabnam decides to measure the loss of mass over the course of the reaction.
   Draw a labelled diagram to show the apparatus Shabnam could use to follow the rate of this reaction.

[2]

b) Shabnam carried out two different reactions, **M** and **N**, using two different concentrations of hydrochloric acid in order to see how concentration affects the rate of reaction.

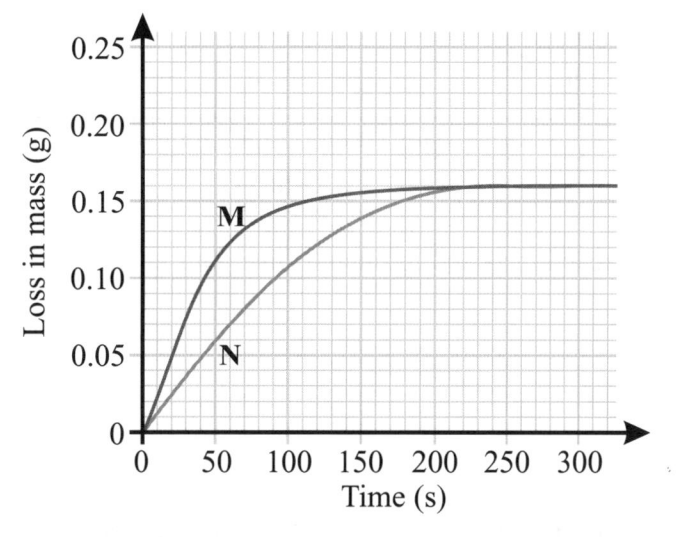

Reaction **N** used a lower concentration of hydrochloric acid.
Using the graph, calculate the rate of reaction N between 0 and 50 seconds.

Rate = ... g/s
[2]

c) Shabnam then reacted magnesium and hydrochloric acid under four temperature conditions, **A**, **B**, **C** and **D**, whilst keeping all other variables the same. Her results are displayed in the following table. Complete the table by calculating the relative rate of each of the reactions.

Temperature	A	B	C	D
Time taken for reaction to stop (s)	243	371	286	435
Relative rate (1/s)	....	....	....	....

[2]

d) Using your results, put the temperatures, A, B, C and D, in order of increasing temperature.

....
[1]

[Total 7 marks]

Topic C5 — Monitoring and Controlling Chemical Reactions

3 A student wanted to calculate the rate of reaction between nitric acid and zinc. He carried out two experiments under the same conditions, but in one he used zinc ribbons and in the other he used zinc powder.

a) The graph below shows the rate of reaction for both experiments, labelled **Q** and **R**.

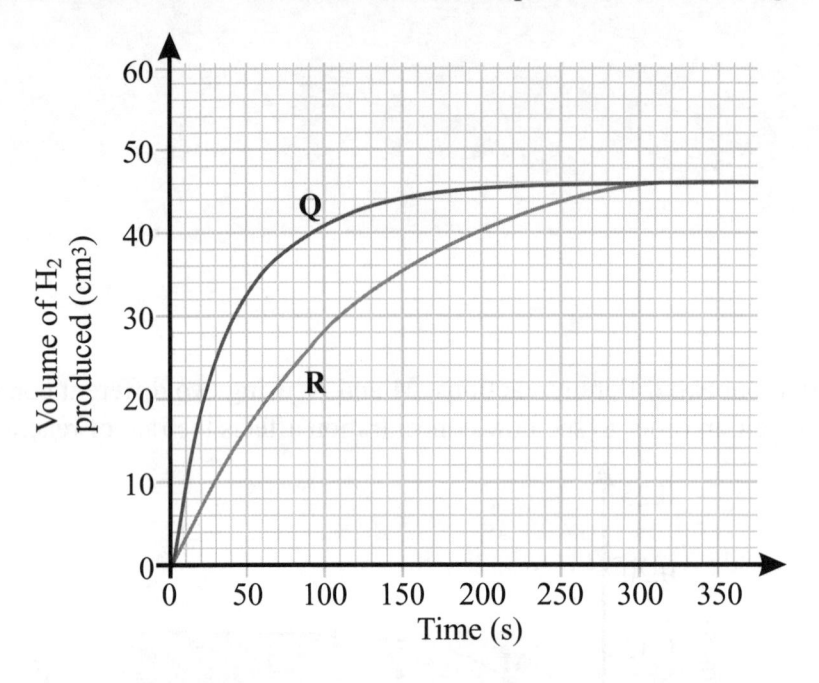

i) Calculate the rate of reaction **Q** at 3 minutes. Give your answer to 3 significant figures.

Rate = ... cm³/s
[2]

ii) Calculate the rate of reaction **R** at 4 minutes. Give your answer to 3 significant figures.

Rate = ... cm³/s
[2]

b) Determine which reaction, **Q** or **R**, used the powdered zinc. Explain your answer.

....

....

....
[2]

[Total 6 marks]

Exam Practice Tip
Drawing a tangent at a specific point on a curve can be quite tricky. You need to make sure that it has the same gradient of the curve at that specific point. Drawing a tangent too different from the correct gradient could make a big difference to your final answer, so take your time and try moving your ruler around a bit first to find the best position.

Topic C5 — Monitoring and Controlling Chemical Reactions

Collision Theory

1 The Sabatier reaction can be used industrially to make methane from carbon dioxide and hydrogen in the following reaction:
$$CO_{2(g)} + 4H_{2(g)} \rightarrow CH_{4(g)} + 2H_2O_{(g)}$$

a) How could the pressure be altered to **increase** the rate of the reaction?

....
[1]

b) Use the collision theory to explain how this pressure change causes the rate to increase.

....

....

....
[2]
[Total 3 marks]

2 Horatio and Sharon are carrying out an experiment. They each react 50 cm³ of 0.30 mol/dm³ sodium thiosulfate with 5.0 cm³ of 2.0 mol/dm³ hydrochloric acid.

a) Horatio carries out his reaction at room temperature. Sharon heats her reactants to 45 °C and carries out the reaction in a 45 °C water bath. Horatio thinks that his reaction will have taken place much more quickly than Sharon's reaction. Is Horatio correct? Explain your answer.

....

....

....

....

....
[3]

b) i) Sharon repeats her experiment using different concentrations of hydrochloric acid. Which of the following concentrations of hydrochloric acid would result in the **slowest** rate of reaction?

    A   0.350 mol/dm³ hydrochloric acid
    B   1.250 mol/dm³ hydrochloric acid
    C   2.100 mol/dm³ hydrochloric acid
    D   0.550 mol/dm³ hydrochloric acid

Your answer ☐
[1]

ii) Explain your answer.

....

....
[2]
[Total 6 marks]

Topic C5 — Monitoring and Controlling Chemical Reactions

Catalysts

1 Identify which of the following catalysts is an example of an enzyme. *(Grade 4-6)*

    A Iron: a catalyst used in the Haber process.
    B Manganese(IV) oxide: a catalyst used in the decomposition of hydrogen peroxide.
    C RuBisCO: a catalyst used in photosynthesis.
    D Vanadium pentoxide: a catalyst used in the Contact process.

Your answer ☐

[Total 1 mark]

2 Zola is observing the decomposition of hydrogen peroxide. The reaction is very slow. Meredith tells her to repeat the experiment with manganese(IV) oxide powder, and the rate of reaction increases. Zola hypothesises that the manganese(IV) oxide is a catalyst. *(Grade 6-7)*

a) Describe how Zola can determine whether or not the manganese(IV) oxide is a catalyst.

....
....
....
....
[2]

b) Zola determines that the manganese(IV) oxide acted as a catalyst.
Explain how a catalyst works to increases the rate of reaction.

....
....
....
[2]

c) The reaction profile for the catalysed and uncatalysed reaction is shown below. Identify what each of the labels, A–D, show.

A: ....
B: ....
C: ....
D: ....

[4]

[Total 8 marks]

Topic C5 — Monitoring and Controlling Chemical Reactions

Dynamic Equilibrium

Warm-Up

Choose from the words in the box below to complete the paragraph.

| increases | change | the same rate | different rates | decreases | not change |

In a reaction, as the concentration of reactants fall, the rate of the forward reaction ....
and as the concentration of the products rises, the rate of the backward reaction ....
When both the forward and backward reaction are going at ...., they are at
equilibrium. At this point, the concentration of the reactants and products will ....

1 Dynamic equilibria can only be achieved in reversible reactions. The position of equilibria can be affected by different factors. *(Grade 4-6)*

a) Give the definition of a reversible reaction.

....

....
[1]

b) During a certain reversible reaction, the equilibrium lies to the left. How should the concentration of the reactants be altered in order to increase the rate of product formation?

....
[1]

[Total 2 marks]

2 Methanol can be manufactured industrially from a gas mixture of mainly carbon monoxide and hydrogen in the following reaction: $CO_{(g)} + 2H_{2(g)} \rightleftharpoons CH_3OH_{(g)}$. This occurs over a Cu-ZnO-Al$_2$O$_3$ catalyst, under conditions of 250 °C and 50–100 atm. The forward reaction is exothermic. *(Grade 6-7)*

a) Under a certain set of conditions, the equilibrium lies to the right. Describe what this means, in terms of the concentration of products and reactants.

....

....
[1]

b) Identify which of the following statements is **false**.

   A   A decrease in the concentration of CO shifts the position of equilibrium to the left.
   B   Increasing the pressure to 200 atm shifts the position of equilibrium to the right.
   C   Increasing the temperature to 470 °C shifts the position of equilibrium to the left.
   D   The Cu-ZnO-Al$_2$O$_3$ catalyst shifts the position of equilibrium to the right.

Your answer ☐

[1]

[Total 2 marks]

Topic C5 — Monitoring and Controlling Chemical Reactions

3 Nitrogen dioxide forms an equilibrium mixture with dinitrogen tetroxide in the following reaction: $2NO_{2(g)} \rightleftharpoons N_2O_{4(g)}$. The forward reaction is exothermic.

a) Which of the following conditions would result in the greatest shift of the equilibrium to the **left**?

- **A** High temperature and high pressure.
- **B** High temperature and low pressure.
- **C** Low temperature and high pressure.
- **D** Low temperature and low pressure.

Your answer ☐

[1]

b) In terms of equilibrium, explain why it is important for the reaction vessel to be completely sealed.

....

....

[1]

[Total 2 marks]

4 An exothermic reaction between potassium thiocyanate and iron(III) nitrate in solution forms an equilibrium mixture: $Fe^{3+}_{(aq)} + SCN^-_{(aq)} \rightleftharpoons [Fe(SCN)]^{2+}_{(aq)}$. Fe^{3+} is orange, SCN^- is colourless and $[Fe(SCN)]^{2+}$ (iron thiocyanate) is red.

a) Russell has a solution of iron thiocyanate. He divides the solution equally between four test tubes. The table below shows the treatment given to each of the test tubes. Complete the table by determining the colour of the solution in each condition.

Test Tube	Condition	Colour of solution
A	Control	Red
B	Addition of $[Fe(SCN)]^{2+}$	....
C	Hot water bath	....
D	Ice bath	....

[3]

b) Explain your answer for test tube **C**.

....

....

....

....

[2]

c) Amara says, to increase the yield of the reaction, they should increase the pressure of the reaction. Russell disagrees. Which student do you agree with? Explain your answer.

....

....

[1]

[Total 6 marks]

Topic C5 — Monitoring and Controlling Chemical Reactions

Topic C6 — Global Challenges

Extracting Metals from their Ores

1 The method used to extract metals from their ores can be determined using the reactivity series. The reactivity series of some elements is shown below. *(Grade 6-7)*

Potassium	K	Most Reactive
Calcium	Ca	
Aluminium	Al	
Carbon	C	
Zinc	Zn	
Tin	Sn	
Copper	Cu	Least Reactive

a) Give the definition of a metal ore.

....

....
[1]

b) Describe how tin is extracted from its ore in industry.

....

....
[1]

c) State **one** other metal from the reactivity series above that can be extracted in the same way as tin.

....
[1]
[Total 3 marks]

2 Iron is extracted from its ore, iron oxide (Fe_2O_3), in a blast furnace using carbon. *(Grade 7-9)*

a) Write a balanced equation for this reaction.

....
[2]

b) A certain batch of iron ore that contains impurities of zinc oxide and calcium oxide is reacted in a blast furnace. After the reaction is complete, any metal produced by the reaction was removed. Any unreacted ore was left in the reaction vessel.

The iron metal product was tested for purity and was found to contain traces of another metal. Suggest an identity for the other metal and explain why it's present.

....

....

....

....
[2]
[Total 4 marks]

Topic C6 — Global Challenges

More on Extracting Metals

1 A manufacturing company wants to extract a metal for use as a component in a car. After consideration, they decide to use either aluminium or iron.

a) Using the reactivity series below, determine which metal would be more expensive to extract from its ore. Explain your answer.

Aluminium	Al	Most Reactive
Carbon	C	↓
Iron	Fe	Least Reactive

....
....
....
....
....

[4]

b) The company also needs copper wires for the cars' electrical systems. They extract copper from its ore using carbon in a blast furnace.

State why the copper needs to undergo purification before it can be used for electrical wires and name the process used to purify it.

....
....

[2]

[Total 6 marks]

2 The increasing demand and the limited supply of metal-rich ores means that scientists are now developing new ways to extract metal from low-grade ores.

a) Describe how phytoextraction is used to extract some metals from their ores.

....
....
....
....
....

[4]

b) Give **one** advantage and **one** disadvantage of using phytoextraction to extract metals from their ores.

....
....

[2]

[Total 6 marks]

Life-Cycle Assessments

Warm-Up

A company is developing a new product. Identify the factors that they should consider when producing a life-cycle assessment. Tick **two** boxes.

Colour of the product ☐	Demand for the product ☐
Recyclability of the product ☐	Attractiveness of the product ☐
Source of raw materials ☐	Profitability of the product ☐

1   A furniture company is designing a new range of chairs for children. They need to decide whether the chair will be made out of polypropene or timber.

Material	Source	Relative Energy Cost to Make/Extract	Recyclability
Timber	Trees	1	Recyclable
Polypropene	Crude oil	15	Recyclable

a) The company carries out a life-cycle assessment of both possible products. Describe the purpose of a life-cycle assessment.

....

....
[1]

b) Using the table above, explain which material would be the **best** choice to make the chair from, in terms of sustainability. Explain your answer.

....

....

....

....

....
[3]

c) Suggest **two** further factors, that aren't discussed in the table, that the company should consider in their life-cycle assessment, when deciding whether to make the chairs from timber or polypropene.

....

....
[2]

[Total 6 marks]

Topic C6 — Global Challenges

2 A toy company is carrying out a life-cycle assessment of four prototype toys. The table below displays some of the data from their assessments.

Grade 7-9

Toy	CO$_2$ emissions (kg)	Solvent use (dm^3)	Consumption of non-renewable energy (MJ)
A	16.2	3981	267.84
B	14.8	2672	212.26
C	14.9	3876	159.82
D	12.4	2112	174.56

a) Using the data in the table, explain which toy, A, B, C or D, the company should produce.

....

....

....

....

....

....

[4]

b) Toy A contains components made from iron. Iron is found naturally as iron oxide in the ground. Give **two** disadvantages associated with extracting iron.

....

....

[2]

c) All of the toys contain components that cannot be recycled, so the company suggests that at the end of their life spans, the toys should be disposed of in landfill. Explain why the use of landfill as a form of disposal is **unsustainable**.

....

[1]

d) Several of the toys are sold in plastic packaging. Which of the options below describes the best way to dispose of this packaging, in terms of sustainability?

- **A** Dispose of the waste in nearby rivers.
- **B** Bury the waste in landfill.
- **C** Recycle the waste into different products.
- **D** Incinerate the waste.

Your answer ☐

[1]

[Total 8 marks]

Exam Practice Tip

You may be given data and asked to figure out which product has the biggest or smallest environmental impact. It's likely that there won't be an obvious answer at first glance — some products may have really low CO$_2$ emissions but may pollute lots of water. You'll have to look at <u>all</u> the factors and decide which product is the best or worst overall.

Topic C6 — Global Challenges

Recycling Materials

1 Rachel is sorting some rubbish that has accumulated around her house. *Grade 6-7*

a) Rachel has three pieces of rubbish made from three different materials, A, B and C. Some data about the materials is in the table below.

Material	Availability of resource	Energy to recycle	Energy to extract
A	Abundant	High	Low
B	Limited	Low	High
C	Limited	Medium	High

Which material from the table above is the **best** to recycle? Explain your answer.

....

....

....

....

[2]

b) Rachel is able to recycle plastic bottles at her local recycling centre. Given that many parts of the manufacturing process involve using fractions of crude oil, explain why it is important to recycle plastics.

....

....

[1]

c) i) Rachel has a drinks carton that is made from a paper box with a plastic coating and an aluminium cap. Suggest why it might **not** be economical to recycle the drinks carton.

....

....

[1]

ii) Rachel decides to recycle the drinks carton since it contains non-renewable materials. Which materials in the drinks carton come from **non-renewable** sources?

    A   Paper, plastic and aluminium.
    B   Paper and plastic.
    C   Aluminium only.
    D   Plastic and aluminium.

Your answer ☐

[1]

iii) Give **one** use for the recycled paper from the drinks carton.

....

[1]

[Total 6 marks]

Topic C6 — Global Challenges

Crude Oil

Warm-Up

Use a line to match each of the following fractions of crude oil with one of their main uses.

Naphtha		Fuel for aircraft
Diesel		Raw material in industrial processes
Kerosene		Fuel for lorries

1 Crude oil is our main source of hydrocarbons. *Grade 4-6*

a) Describe how crude oil is formed.

....
....
....
[2]

b) Crude oil is a mixture of a variety of hydrocarbons. Give the general formula of the homologous series which makes up a majority of these hydrocarbons.

....
[1]

[Total 3 marks]

2 Today's society is crucially dependent on crude oil as a source of energy, however, a variety of alternative energy sources are being developed by scientists. *Grade 6-7*

a) Give **two** reasons why the Earth's usage of fossil fuels is increasing.

....
....
[2]

b) Name **two** alternative sources of energy.

....
[2]

c) Why it is important that scientists develop alternative energy sources?

....
....
[1]

[Total 5 marks]

Topic C6 — Global Challenges

3 Crude oil can be separated using the process of fractional distillation. The length of the hydrocarbon chains is fundamental to this process.

a) Outline the process of fractional distillation.

....

....

....

....

....

....
[4]

b) i) Name the fraction of crude oil which contains the **shortest** hydrocarbon chains.

....
[1]

ii) Name **one** other fraction that is produced by the fractional distillation of crude oil.

....
[1]

c) The table below shows the boiling points of some molecules that are present in fractions produced when crude oil is fractionated.

Hydrocarbon	Chemical formula	Boiling point (°C)
Heptane	C_7H_{16}	98
Triacontane	$C_{30}H_{62}$	343

i) Which hydrocarbon would you expect to be collected **further down** the column?

....
[1]

ii) Explain your answer, with reference to the intermolecular bonding present between the hydrocarbons.

....

....

....

....

....
[5]

[Total 12 marks]

Topic C6 — Global Challenges

Cracking

1 Cracking involves splitting long-chain hydrocarbons into smaller molecules.

a) Explain why cracking is important.

....

....
[2]

b) Name the catalyst used for cracking in industry.

....
[1]

c) Two products were formed by cracking a hydrocarbon. The chemical formulas for the two products were $C_{15}H_{32}$ and C_5H_{10}. Give the chemical formula for the original hydrocarbon.

....
[1]

[Total 4 marks]

2 Hydrocarbon fractions, produced by the fractional distillation of crude oil, are important chemicals used in many industrial processes. The graph below shows the approximate percentage of each fraction produced by an oil refinery, and the demand for each fraction.

a) The demand for diesel is greater than the supply.
Name **two** other fractions whose demand is greater than their supply.

....
[2]

b) Suggest what could be done to ensure that the supply of diesel matches the demand.

....

....
[1]

[Total 3 marks]

Topic C6 — Global Challenges

The Atmosphere

1 Which of the following gases was **not** present in the early atmosphere?

    A   water vapour
    B   ammonia
    C   ozone
    D   methane

Your answer ☐

[Total 1 mark]

2 Scientists have looked at the composition of other planets to provide evidence for what the early atmosphere on Earth was like. The table below shows the compositions of the atmospheres on Mars and Earth.

	Percentage composition (%)					
	H_2O	Ne	CO_2	N_2	O_2	Ar
Mars	0.030	trace	95	2.7	0.13	1.6
Earth	0–4.0	0.0018	0.036	78	21	0.93

   a) i) Scientists believe Earth's early atmosphere was similar to the atmosphere on Mars. Using the table, suggest which gas made up the majority of Earth's early atmosphere.

....

[1]

      ii) Explain **two** ways in which this gas was removed from Earth's atmosphere as it evolved.

....

....

[2]

   b) Explain how oxygen built up in Earth's atmosphere and suggest why there is hardly any oxygen present in the atmosphere on Mars.

....

....

....

[2]

   c) i) Which gas is present in the **highest** concentration in the Earth's atmosphere today?

....

[1]

      ii) Explain how and why this gas built up in the Earth's atmosphere.

....

....

....

[3]

[Total 9 marks]

Topic C6 — Global Challenges

The Greenhouse Effect and Global Warming

Warm-Up

Identify the statements below that describe things that a family can do to reduce their carbon dioxide emissions. Tick **two** boxes.

Leaving lights on all day	☐	Using a tumble drier	☐
Walking to school	☐	Installing solar panels at home	☐
Turning the heating up	☐	Using air conditioning	☐

1 Which statement about alternative fuels is **false**?

    A Ethanol can be mixed with petrol to produce a better fuel.
    B Ethanol is made by the fermentation of plants.
    C Biodiesel and ethanol are carbon neutral.
    D Biodiesel is cheap to produce.

Your answer ☐

[Total 1 mark]

2 Many scientists believe that the increased levels of greenhouse gases, such as carbon dioxide, has resulted in global warming.

  a) Give the definition of a greenhouse gas.

....

....
[1]

  b) Apart from carbon dioxide, list **two** further greenhouse gases.

....
[2]

  c) Elvis states that any greenhouse effect is dangerous as it could cause global warming.
     Is Elvis correct? Explain your answer.

....

....

....
[1]

  d) Global warming is a type of climate change.
     Give **two** environmental consequences associated with global warming.

....

....
[2]

[Total 6 marks]

Topic C6 — Global Challenges

3 Scientists believe that the increased burning of fossil fuels has contributed to global warming and this has caused glaciers to melt, thus resulting in rising sea levels.

The graph below shows CO_2 emissions by fossil fuels in the UK and the changes in sea levels between 1993 and 2013.

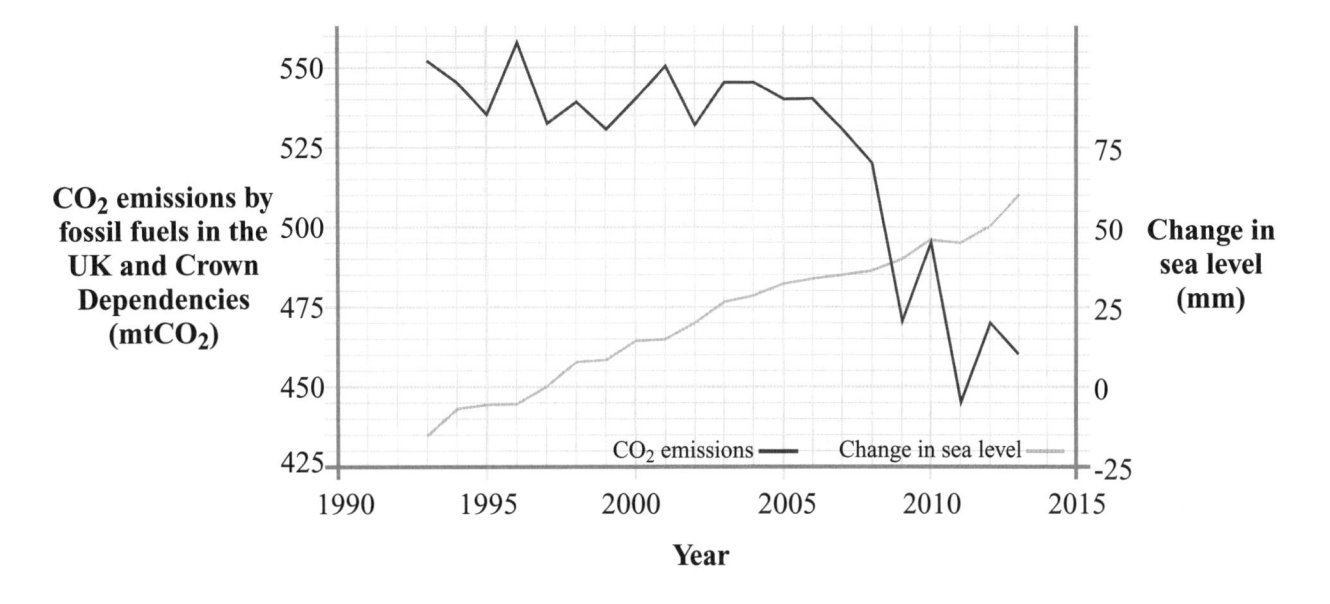

CO₂ emissions by fossil fuels in the UK and Crown Dependencies (mtCO₂) vs **Change in sea level (mm)** plotted against Year.

a)* Look at the graph. Explain whether the evidence shown by this graph supports a link between anthropogenic activity and climate change, and discuss any uncertainty associated with the conclusion you can draw from this data.

....

[6]

b) Many governments are trying to decrease their countries' CO_2 emissions.
Give **two** ways that the government in the UK is trying to reduce carbon dioxide emissions.

....

[2]

[Total 8 marks]

Exam Practice Tip
If you're given some data about climate change to analyse, you need to think very carefully about what the data does and doesn't show, without making any assumptions. For example, if you're given data for one country, you can't assume that any patterns will be true globally. You'd need more data to be able to draw a conclusion about the whole planet.

Topic C6 — Global Challenges

Pollutants

1 Carbon monoxide is a gas that is toxic to humans.

a) Explain why carbon monoxide is toxic.

....
....
....
[2]

b) How is carbon monoxide produced?

- **A** By incomplete combustion in car engines.
- **B** By complete combustion in car engines.
- **C** By nitrogen and oxygen reacting together due to the heat of combustion reactions.
- **D** By reactions between carbon and oxygen in car engines.

Your answer ☐

[1]

[Total 3 marks]

2 The table below shows the concentration of pollutants in two cities, **A** and **B**.

City	Concentration of Pollutants (µg/m³)			
	Nitrogen dioxide	Ozone	Particulate carbon	Sulfur dioxide
A	13.2	53.6	65.1	8.9
B	106.4	84.5	13.2	68.2

a) In one city, the buildings have become covered with a black powder.
Suggest which city this has happened in and why it has occurred.

....
....
[2]

b) Give **two** risks to human health associated with high levels of ground level ozone.

....
....
[2]

c) Limestone buildings in one of the cities have become damaged as a result of chemical weathering. Which of the cities, **A** or **B**, is this likely to have occurred in? Explain your answer using evidence from the table.

....
....
....
[2]

[Total 6 marks]

Topic C6 — Global Challenges

Water Treatment

1 Fresh water in the UK comes from different sources and is used for drinking, domestic use and industrial processes. Identify which of the following statements is **incorrect**.

    A Water can be used as a cheap raw material in industry.
    B Water in the UK can be obtained from treated waste water.
    C Water can be used as a coolant for industrial processes.
    D Water can be sourced from groundwater, which comes from lakes and rivers.

Your answer ☐

[Total 1 mark]

2 A purification plant uses multiple steps to purify water.

  a) The purification plant uses aluminium sulfate during the sedimentation step. How does the aluminium sulfate contribute to the purification process?

....
....
[1]

  b) The purification process ends with chlorination. Explain what happens during this process.

....
....
[1]

[Total 2 marks]

3 The way that countries source their water is dependent on a variety of factors. The table below shows the average annual rainfall in the UK and Kuwait.

Country	Average annual rainfall (mm)
UK	1129
Kuwait	120

  a) One of these countries gets large quantities of its water by distilling sea water. Suggest which country and explain your answer.

....
....
....
[2]

  b) Give **one** disadvantage of using this process to purify large quantities of drinking water.

....
[1]

[Total 3 marks]

Topic C6 — Global Challenges

The History of the Atom and Atomic Structure

Warm-Up

Use the words below to correctly fill in the gaps in the passage.
You don't have to use every word, but each word can only be used once.

An atom is made up of .... surrounded by ....

An atom is mostly made up of .... The diameter of an atom is about

.... and the diameter of a nucleus is about ....

| empty space | 1×10^{15} m | neutrons | electrons |
| protons | 1×10^{-10} m | a nucleus | 1×10^{-15} m |

---

1 A lithium nucleus contains 3 protons and 3 neutrons. Which row of the table correctly shows the relative mass and relative charge of the lithium nucleus?

	Mass	Charge
A	6	−3
B	3	+6
C	6	+3
D	3	−6

Your answer ☐

[Total 1 mark]

2 The theory of the structure of atoms has changed over time.

a) Describe the experiment carried out by Rutherford, Geiger and Marsden, and explain how it disproved Thomson's model.

....
....
....
....
....

[3]

b) How are electrons arranged around atoms in Bohr's model of the atom?

....

[1]

[Total 4 marks]

Topic P1 — Matter

Density

PRACTICAL

1 Rachael has a mass balance, a measuring beaker and some acetic acid. *Grade 4-6*

a) Describe an experiment that Rachael can carry out to calculate the density of acetic acid, using the equipment listed.

....

....

....

....

....
[4]

b) The density of acetic acid is 1.05 g/cm³. What would be the mass of 200 cm³ of acetic acid?

A   210 g
B   190 g
C   0.005 kg
D   190 kg

Your answer ☐
[1]
[Total 5 marks]

2 The titanium bar shown in the diagram has a mass of 90.0 kg. *Grade 7-9*

area = 0.050 m²
length = 0.40 m

Calculate the density of titanium in **g/cm³**. Show your working.

Density = ... g/cm³
[Total 4 marks]

Exam Practice Tip

Always show your working, whether you're asked to or not, and include any equations you've used and how you've rearranged them. It'll help you check your working and you could still get some marks even if your final answer is wrong.

Topic P1 — Matter

Particle Theory and States of Matter

1 The three states of matter are solid, liquid and gas. *(Grade 4-6)*

a) Which sentence is **correct** about the density of the different states of the same substance?

- A   A liquid is usually less dense than a gas.
- B   A liquid is usually more dense than a solid.
- C   A solid is usually more dense than a gas.
- D   A solid, liquid and gas usually have the same density.

Your answer ☐

[1]

b) What is the name of the process that occurs when a solid changes directly to a gas?

....
[1]

[Total 2 marks]

2 Joe leaves a closed plastic bottle with some water in it on a windowsill on a hot day. In the afternoon, he notices that the volume of liquid water has decreased. *(Grade 6-7)*

a) Explain in terms of the particles in the water, why the volume of liquid water in the bottle has decreased during the day.

....

....

....

....
[3]

b) Explain what happens to the total mass of the bottle and its contents during the day.

....

....

....
[2]

c) The next morning, Joe notices that the water is back to the same level as the previous morning. How does this show that a physical change, and **not** a chemical change, has taken place?

....

....
[2]

[Total 7 marks]

Topic P1 — Matter

Specific Heat Capacity

PRACTICAL

1* A student carries out an experiment to find the specific heat capacity of aluminium. The diagram shows her setup. Describe how the student should carry out the experiment, including how she should make the experiment more accurate.

Grade 4-6

....
....
....
....
....
....
....
....

[Total 6 marks]

2 A pan of water is heated on a hob. The specific heat capacity of water is 4200 J/kg°C.

Grade 6-7

a) Define the term specific heat capacity.

....
....

[1]

b) The hob transfers 302 400 J of energy to 1.2 kg of water in the pan. If the initial temperature of the water is 24°C, calculate the temperature of the water after it has been heated. Use the formula:
change in thermal energy = mass × specific heat capacity × change in temperature.

Temperature = ... °C

[2]

[Total 3 marks]

Exam Practice Tip

Different substances have different specific heat capacities, e.g. water has a higher specific heat capacity than alcohol. You don't need to remember any specific heat capacity values though, you'll be given them in the exam if you need them.

Topic P1 — Matter

Specific Latent Heat

Warm-Up

The graph shows temperature against time of a substance that is being heated.
Use the words below to correctly label the graph.
You don't have to use every word, but each word can only be used once.

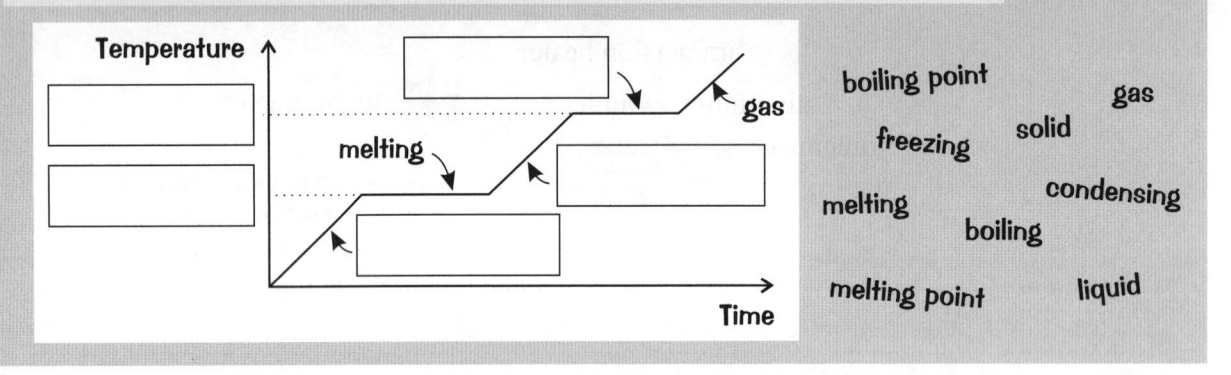

boiling point, gas, freezing, solid, melting, condensing, boiling, melting point, liquid

1 The table shows the mass and specific latent heat of vaporisation of substances A-D. Which substance requires the **most energy** to completely boil it (without changing its temperature)?

Grade 4-6

Substance	Mass / kg	Specific latent heat of vaporisation / J/kg
A	1	1.5
B	1	1.0
C	2	1.5
D	2	2.0

Your answer ☐

[Total 1 mark]

2 A car is parked on a street overnight. During the night, the temperature drops low enough for 1400 g of water to condense on the car. When the temperature is low enough, the water freezes.

Grade 6-7

a) If 462 J of energy is released from the water as it freezes, calculate the specific latent heat of fusion of water. Use the formula:
thermal energy for a change in state = mass × specific latent heat. Show your working.

Specific latent heat of fusion = ... J/kg
[3]

b) What happens to the temperature of this water as it freezes?

....
[1]
[Total 4 marks]

Topic P1 — Matter

Pressure of Gases

Warm-Up

Circle the correct words or phrases below so that the sentences are correct.

A gas exerts a force on a container due to <u>collisions / radioactivity</u>. The particles are always moving in <u>the same direction / random directions</u>. When the particles collide with the walls of the container, they exert <u>magnetism / a force</u> on it. This creates a <u>magnetic force / net force</u> on the inside surface of the container walls.

1 A tyre is pumped up to its maximum volume. *(Grade 4-6)*

a) Explain what would happen to the tyre pressure if more air were pumped in, but its volume remained the same.

....
....
....
[3]

b) At its maximum volume, why would the tyre pressure be higher on a hot day compared to a cold day?

....
....
....
....
[3]

[Total 6 marks]

2 Each container has the same mass of gas inside. In which container is the pressure the **highest**? *(Grade 7-9)*

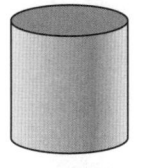

A — Volume = 0.04 m³, Temperature = 10°C

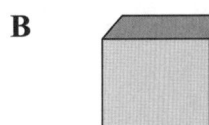

B — Volume = 0.04 m³, Temperature = 20°C

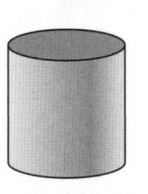

C — Volume = 40 000 cm³, Temperature = 10°C

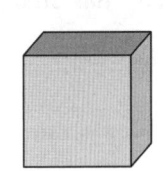

D — Volume = 40 000 cm³, Temperature = 30°C

Your answer ☐

[Total 1 mark]

Topic P1 — Matter

Speed and Velocity

Warm-Up

Put the following quantities under the correct heading to show if they're scalar or vector quantities.

acceleration   speed   velocity   distance   displacement

Scalar	Vector

1 Nick is walking at a constant speed of 1.5 m/s.

a) How far has he walked in 120 s? Give the unit.

Distance = ... Unit ....
[3]

b) Nick then starts jogging. He jogs 5100 m in 34 minutes. What is Nick's average jogging speed?

Speed = ... m/s
[3]

[Total 6 marks]

2 Suma is driving **east** at 50 km/hr.

a) What is Suma's speed in m/s?

A   180 m/s
B   13.9 m/s
C   18 m/s
D   1.39 m/s

Your answer ☐
[1]

b) The road turns so Suma is now driving **north** at 50 km/hr.
Explain why her velocity has changed but her speed hasn't.

....
....
....
[2]

[Total 3 marks]

Acceleration

1 Trigger the dog sets off running from rest and reaches a speed of 3.2 m/s in 8.0 s. *(Grade 6-7)*

a) Find Trigger's acceleration. Give the unit.

Acceleration = ... Unit ....
[3]

b) She keeps running with this acceleration for a further 6.0 s. Calculate Trigger's final speed. Show your working.

Speed = ... m/s
[3]

c) Trigger continues to run at this final speed in circular loops around the garden. Which statement is **correct**?

A Trigger is accelerating, but her velocity is constant.
B Trigger is accelerating and her velocity is changing.
C Trigger is not accelerating, but her velocity is constant.
D Trigger is not accelerating and her velocity is changing.

Your answer ☐
[1]
[Total 7 marks]

2 A boat is travelling at a constant velocity of 5.0 m/s. It then starts to accelerate with a constant acceleration of 0.25 m/s² for a distance of 1.2×10^3 m. *(Grade 6-7)*

a) Find the final velocity of the boat. Use the formula:
(final velocity)² − (initial velocity)² = 2 × acceleration × distance.

Velocity = ... m/s
[2]

b) Calculate the time it takes for the boat to travel this distance.

Time = ... s
[3]
[Total 5 marks]

Exam Practice Tip
Remember that displacement, velocity and acceleration are all vector quantities, which means they have both a magnitude and a direction. Whereas distance and speed are scalar quantities, and so they only have a magnitude (no direction).

Topic P2 — Forces

PRACTICAL — Investigating Motion

1 Alice wants to carry out an experiment to investigate the motion of a trolley down a ramp. Her textbook suggests setting up her apparatus as shown in the diagram.

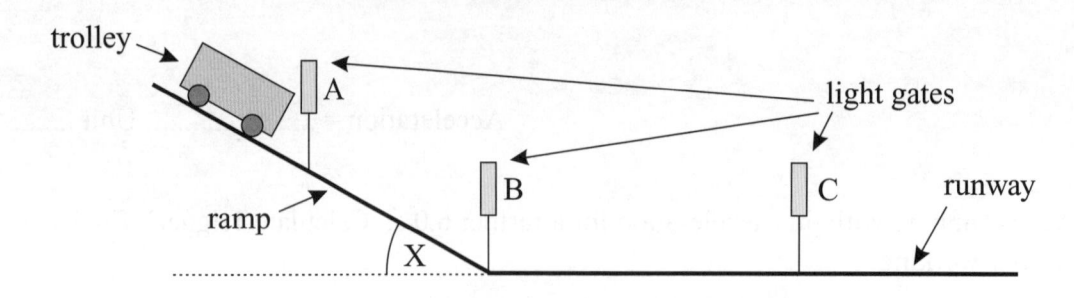

Grade 4-6

a)* Describe how Alice could use this apparatus to find the **acceleration** of the trolley down the ramp.

[6]

b) Alice wants to calculate the average speed of the trolley on the runway. But she can't find any light gates, so she decides to use a stopwatch instead.

i) What measurements would Alice need to make to determine the average speed of the trolley on the **runway** now? Explain your answer.

[3]

ii) Give **one** disadvantage of using a stopwatch instead of light gates.

[1]

c) What would happen to the speed of the trolley on the runway if the angle labelled X in the diagram was **increased**?

[1]

[Total 11 marks]

Topic P2 — Forces

Distance-Time Graphs

1 Simon walks to work. He starts off at a steady speed, before stopping for a quick drink of water. He then travels at a steady speed again, but faster than before.

Sketch a line on the axes below to show the distance-time graph for Simon's walk to work.

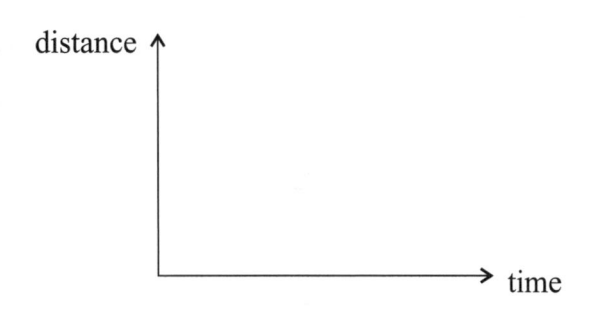

[Total 3 marks]

2 The graph shows the distance-time graph for a car journey.

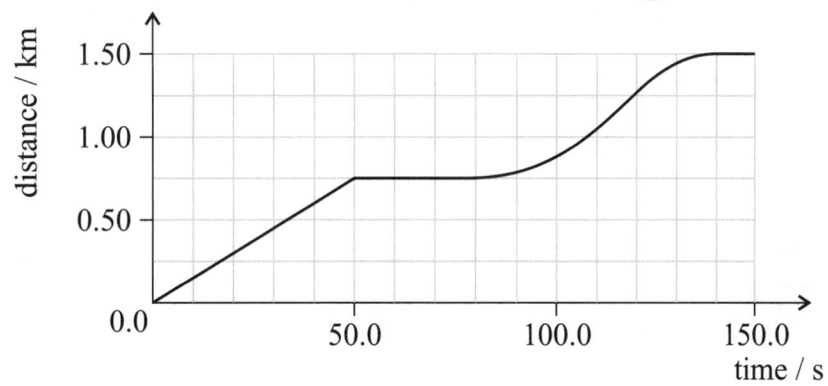

a) Describe the car journey using data from the graph.

....
....
....
....
....

[4]

b) i) Calculate the car's average speed between 80.0 s and 140.0 s.
Give your answer in m/s.

Speed = ... m/s
[3]

ii) Calculate the car's speed at 100.0 s.

Speed = ... m/s
[3]

[Total 10 marks]

Topic P2 — Forces

Velocity-Time Graphs

Warm-Up

Use two of the phrases from the list below to correctly label the velocity-time graph.

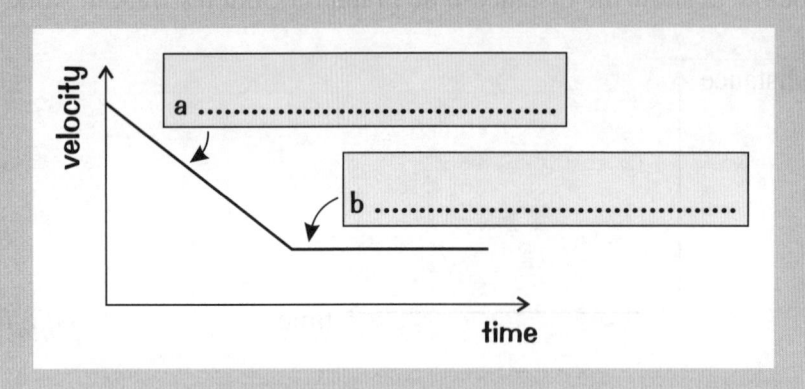

a ....
b ....

decreasing deceleration
steady speed
decreasing acceleration
constant acceleration
constant deceleration

1 Velocity-time graphs can be used to show the motion of an object.

Which quantity is represented by the area under a velocity-time graph?

A   speed
B   acceleration
C   distance
D   deceleration

Your answer ☐

[Total 1 mark]

2 A bear runs with a constant acceleration for 10 s before running at a constant velocity of 8 m/s for a further 10 s. Which of the following velocity-time graphs shows this?

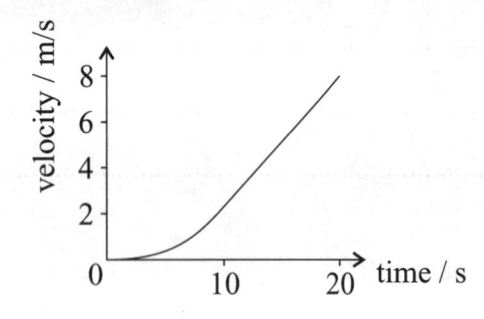

A, B, 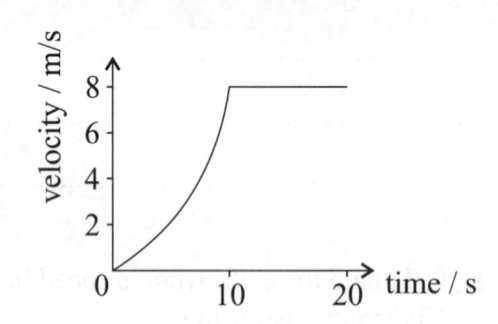 C, 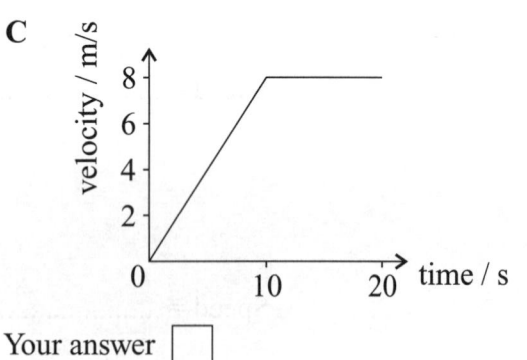 D graphs

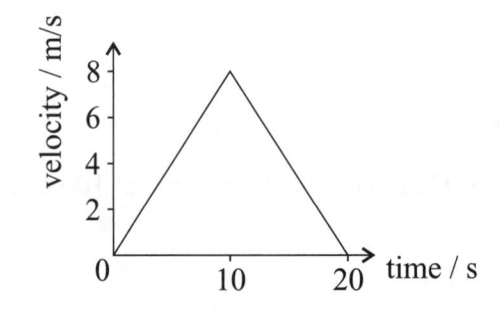

Your answer ☐

[Total 1 mark]

Topic P2 — Forces

3   A lorry is driving along a straight road. The table shows the acceleration of the lorry during different time periods and the lorry's velocity at the end of each time period.

Time period (hours)	Acceleration	Final velocity (mph)
0.00 - 0.10	Constant	20.0
0.10 - 0.20	Increasing	24.0
0.20 - 0.30	Increasing	40.0
0.30 - 0.40	0	40.0
0.40 - 0.50	Constant	60.0
0.50 - 0.60	Constant	0.0

a) Complete the velocity-time graph for the lorry's journey.
The first 0.30 hours have been done for you.

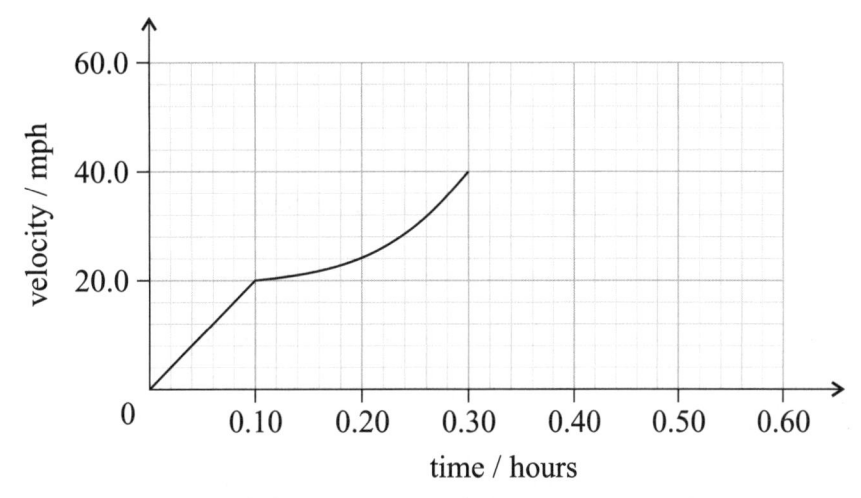

[3]

b) How far does the lorry travel in the first 0.30 hours?

Distance = ... miles
[3]

c) Calculate the acceleration (in m/s²) of the lorry at 0.20 hours. 1 mile = 1600 m.
Give your answer to **2** significant figures.

Acceleration = ... m/s²
[5]

[Total 11 marks]

Exam Practice Tip
A velocity-time graph doesn't just tell you what the velocity of an object is, it can also be used to find the distance travelled by the object and its acceleration throughout its journey. That's a lot of information on one graph.

Topic P2 — Forces

Forces and Free Body Force Diagrams

1 The diagram shows a free body force diagram for a truck. *Grade 4-6*

a) What is the magnitude and direction of the resultant force?

- 300 000 N (up)
- 10 000 N (left)
- 20 000 N (right)
- 300 000 N (down)

A 10 000 N to the left
B 20 000 N to the left
C 30 000 N to the right
D 10 000 N to the right

Your answer ☐

[1]

b) What do we mean by the resultant force acting on an object?

....

....
[2]

[Total 3 marks]

2 A toy car is at rest on a table. A free body force diagram of the car is shown. *Grade 6-7*

(Diagram: Toy car on Table, arrow A pointing up, arrow B pointing down)

a) Name the forces that are labelled A and B in the diagram.

A = ... B = ...
[2]

b) Describe the resultant force acting on the car.

....
[1]

c) Someone pushes the car, so it starts to move towards the left.

   i) Draw and label arrows on the diagram to show the new forces acting on the car.
   [3]

   ii) Describe the resultant force acting on the toy car now.

   ....
   [1]

[Total 7 marks]

Topic P2 — Forces

Scale Diagrams and Forces

1 Which of the following sentences is **correct** for an object that is in equilibrium?

    A   All the forces acting on the object cancel each other out.
    B   All the forces acting on the object must act in the same direction.
    C   All the forces acting on the object must be the same size.
    D   There is only one force acting on the object.

Your answer ☐

[Total 1 mark]

2 Which of the following shows the correct way to resolve a force (solid line) into its horizontal and vertical component forces (dotted lines).

    A   **B**   **C**   **D**

Your answer ☐

[Total 1 mark]

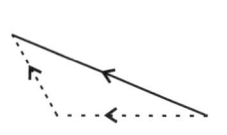

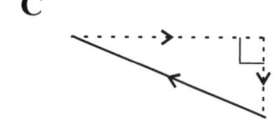

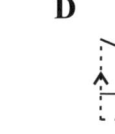

3 A light aircraft is flying north-east in a straight line. The aircraft's engine provides a force of 600 N north. A strong wind is blowing in an easterly direction and provides a force of 800 N on the aircraft.

Draw a scale drawing on the grid below. Find the magnitude of the resultant force on the aircraft.

Resultant force = ... N

[Total 3 marks]

Topic P2 — Forces

4   A toy dog on wheels can be pulled along with a piece of string. The string is at an angle to the ground, but the toy dog moves forwards along the ground at a steady speed. A scale diagram of this is shown below.

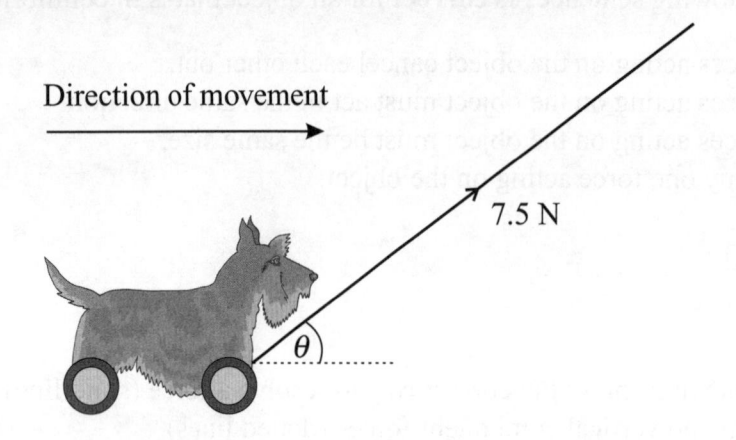

Direction of movement

7.5 N

θ

a) i) Using the diagram, find the force acting on the toy dog in the direction of its movement.

Force = ... N
[3]

ii) What is the magnitude of the frictional force acting on the dog?

A   4.5 N
B   6 N
C   1.5 N
D   7.5 N

Your answer ☐
[1]

b) The normal contact force acting on the toy dog from the ground is 1.5 N. Find the weight of the toy dog.

Weight = ... N
[3]

The toy dog is now pulled along so that the angle, θ, increases but the magnitude of the force stays the same.

c) Explain what will happen to the speed of the dog.

....

....

....
[3]
[Total 10 marks]

Topic P2 — Forces

Newton's First and Second Laws of Motion

Warm-Up

Use the words below to correctly fill in the gaps in the passage.
You don't have to use every word, but each word can only be used once.

Newton's First Law of motion says that an object will remain stationary or moving at
.... if there is .... resultant force acting on it.

If there is .... resultant force acting, it will ....

a constant velocity   accelerate   a zero
a non-zero   remain stationary   an increasing speed

---

1 A rocket is moving at a constant velocity in space (a vacuum). In order to change its velocity, it turns on its thrusters, accelerates to the desired velocity and then turns them off again. *(Grade 4-6)*

a) The mass of the rocket is 110 000 kg and it accelerates at 5.0 m/s². What force is provided by the thrusters?

A   550 000 N
B   55 000 N
C   22 000 N
D   220 000 N

Your answer [ ]

[1]

b) After the rocket has turned off its thrusters, the rocket continues moving at a constant velocity. Use Newton's First Law to explain why.

....

....

....

[2]
[Total 3 marks]

---

2 A sailboat has a mass of 60 kg and is accelerating at 0.4 m/s². The wind acting on the sail provides a force of 44 N. The drag from the water acts in the opposite direction. *(Grade 6-7)*

Calculate the force of the drag acting on the boat. Show your working.

Force = ... N
[Total 3 marks]

Topic P2 — Forces

3   Meena has been using the apparatus below to investigate the effect of force on the acceleration of a trolley. The trolley is on a frictionless, flat surface.

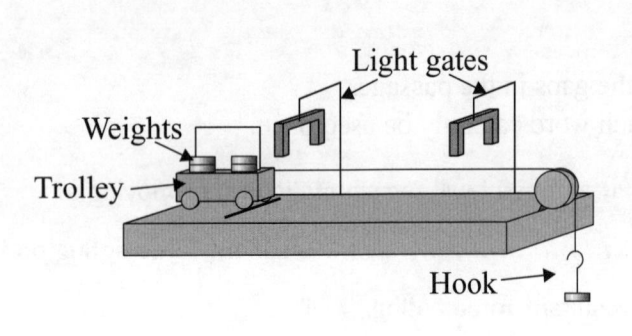

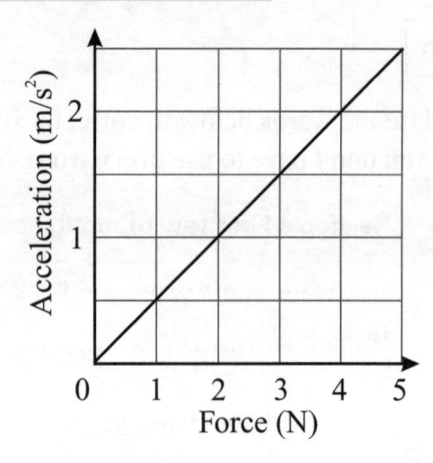

When the hook is allowed to fall, the trolley accelerates. Meena records the force acting on the trolley and calculates its acceleration. Meena repeats this process, each time moving a 1 N weight from the trolley to the hook. She draws a graph of mean acceleration against force for the trolley.

a) Which **two** measurements must Meena record in order to calculate the acceleration of the trolley?

....

....
[2]

b) Give **one** conclusion you can draw from Meena's graph.

....
[1]

c) Calculate the mass of the system.

Mass = ... kg
[3]

[Total 6 marks]

4   A car of mass 1.5×10^3 kg accelerates uniformly from rest. It reaches 23 m/s in 7.0 s.

Calculate the force needed to cause this acceleration.
Give your answer to **2** significant figures.

Force = ... N
[Total 4 marks]

Topic P2 — Forces

Friction and Terminal Velocity

1 Which of the following graphs shows an object that is reaching terminal velocity?

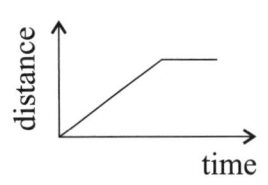

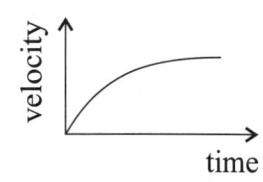

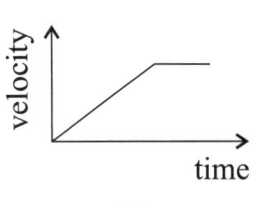

A: distance vs time (rising then flat)
B: velocity vs time (curve rising to plateau)
C: velocity vs time (rising then flat)
D: distance vs time (curve rising to plateau)

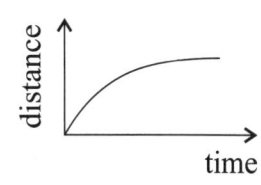

Your answer ☐

[Total 1 mark]

2 Which statement describes the forces acting when an object is travelling at terminal velocity?

- **A** driving force > friction force
- **B** driving force < friction force
- **C** driving force = friction force
- **D** driving force ∝ friction force

Your answer ☐

[Total 1 mark]

3* A student drops a large book and a cricket ball that both have the same weight from a tall building. Explain why both objects eventually reach terminal velocity. Compare the magnitude of each object's terminal velocity.

....
....
....
....
....
....
....

[Total 6 marks]

Exam Practice Tip
Remember that the acceleration of a falling object on Earth is always changing because of the air resistance acting on it. That means you won't be able to use any of those equations for uniform acceleration (unless you ignore air resistance).

Topic P2 — Forces

Inertia and Newton's Third Law of Motion

1 The inertia of an object is dependent on its mass. *Grade 4-6*

a) What do we mean by the term inertia?

....
[1]

b) A ball is rolling freely along a table. There is a frictional force of 0.50 mN acting on the ball, so that it's decelerating at 0.0025 m/s². Calculate the mass of the ball.

Mass = ... kg
[3]
[Total 4 marks]

2 Dave is at rest on his skateboard (combined mass of 80 kg). He pushes a wall with a force of 24 N. You can assume there is no friction between the skateboard and the ground. *Grade 6-7*

a) Explain why Dave would move away from the wall.

....

....

....
[2]

b) Dave's brother goes on the skateboard and pushes away from the wall with the same force. His mass combined with the skateboard is 40 kg. What is the difference in their accelerations?

    A   0.3 m/s²
    B   0.6 m/s²
    C   1.6 m/s²
    D   3.3 m/s²

Your answer ☐
[1]
[Total 3 marks]

3 A plate in equilibrium is sat on a table. Explain why $W_E = R_T$. *Grade 7-9*

R_P = normal contact force of table pushing up on plate
R_T = normal contact force of plate pushing down on table
W_P = gravitational force of Earth pulling down on plate
W_E = gravitational force of plate pulling up on Earth

....

....

....

....
[Total 4 marks]

Topic P2 — Forces

Momentum and Conservation of Momentum

Warm-Up

Circle the correct words or phrases below so that the sentences are correct.

In a collision where <u>no other / two other</u> external forces act,

momentum is <u>increased / conserved</u>.

This means that the momentum before <u>equals / is double</u> the momentum after.

When a <u>zero / non-zero</u> resultant force acts on an object for a certain

amount of time, it causes a change in momentum.

---

1 A vehicle is moving east with a velocity of 15 m/s and momentum 46 000 kg m/s. *(Grade 4-6)*

a) Calculate the mass of the vehicle.
Give your answer to **3** significant figures.

Mass = ... kg
[3]

b) A vehicle of half the mass is driving west at the same speed.
What is the momentum of this vehicle?

- **A** −46 000 kg m/s
- **B** 46 000 kg m/s
- **C** −23 000 kg m/s
- **D** 23 000 kg m/s

Your answer ☐

[1]
[Total 4 marks]

2 A full trailer is pulled by a car travelling north at 20 mph. The car stops and the trailer is unloaded, which halves the mass of the trailer. The car travels back south at 40 mph. *(Grade 6-7)*

How will the trailer's momentum have changed compared to when it was travelling north?

	Momentum magnitude	Momentum sign
A	Doubles	Changes from positive to negative
B	No change	Changes from positive to negative
C	Doubles	No change
D	Halves	No change

Your answer ☐

[Total 1 mark]

Topic P2 — Forces

3   A stationary red ball is hit by a blue ball with mass 4.5 × 10⁻¹ kg and velocity 3.0 m/s. The balls collide elastically then move off together at 2.5 m/s.

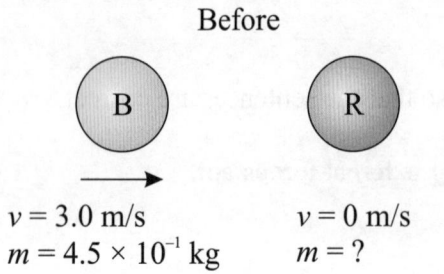

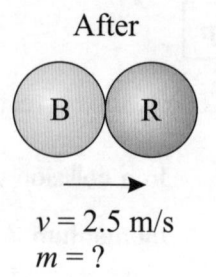

Before

B   R

$v = 3.0$ m/s $v = 0$ m/s
$m = 4.5 \times 10^{-1}$ kg $m = ?$

After

B R

$v = 2.5$ m/s
$m = ?$

a) Calculate the mass of the red ball.

Mass = ... kg
[3]

b) What is meant by an elastic collision?

....

....
[1]
[Total 4 marks]

4   Ball A has a mass of 2.0 kg. Ball B has a mass of 3.0 kg. Both are moving in the same direction. Ball A is moving faster than ball B, so the two collide. After the collision, both balls move off together in the same direction.

Just before the collision, ball A has a velocity of 1.7 m/s and ball B has a velocity of 1.2 m/s.
3.0 s after the collision, the two balls have a velocity of 0.50 m/s.
Calculate the magnitude of the frictional force acting on the two balls after the collision.
Show your working.

Force = ... N
[Total 5 marks]

Topic P2 — Forces

Mass, Weight and Gravity

Warm-Up

State whether each of the following statements are true or false.

1) The gravitational field strength on Earth is 10 N/kg. ....

2) The larger an object, the smaller its gravitational field strength. ....

3) The weight of an object is the same everywhere in the universe. ....

4) The mass of an object is the same everywhere in the universe. ....

1 Mia weighs 650 N on Earth. *Grade 4-6*

a) Define the term weight.

....
[1]

b) Calculate Mia's mass on Earth. Use: gravitational field strength (g) = 10 N/kg.

Mass = ... kg
[2]
[Total 3 marks]

2 An astronaut on the Moon drops her screwdriver. *Grade 6-7*

Use data from the table to calculate the acceleration of the screwdriver as it falls towards the Moon. Use: g = 10 N/kg. Give your answer to **2** significant figures.

	On Earth	On the Moon
Weight (N)	4.6×10^{-1}	7.5×10^{-2}

Acceleration = ... m/s²
[Total 4 marks]

Exam Practice Tip

When astronauts are in space they experience what we call weightlessness — they do still have a mass, they're just not close enough to a planet or moon to feel its gravitational effect. And remember weight is a force with unit newtons (N).

Topic P2 — Forces

Mechanical Energy Stores

1 Sarah has a mass of 65 kg and climbs up some stairs from the ground floor of a building to a height of 10 m.

Calculate the amount of energy in Sarah's gravitational potential energy store at the top of the stairs.

Energy = ... J

[Total 3 marks]

2 Cars A-D are all travelling at a constant speed.

a) The masses and speeds of the cars are shown in the table. Which car has the **most** energy in its kinetic energy store?

	Mass (kg)	Speed (m/s)
A	1500	11
B	1000	15
C	1800	10
D	2000	8

Your answer ☐

[1]

Car A is parked at the top of a hill. The driver releases the handbrake and allows the car to roll freely down the hill. When the car reaches the bottom of the hill, it is travelling at 43.2 km/hr. If you ignore friction and air resistance, the energy in the kinetic energy store of the car at the bottom of the hill equals the energy in the gravitational potential energy store of the car at the top of the hill.

b) Calculate the height of the hill. Use: gravitational field strength (g) = 10 N/kg.

Height = ... m

[4]

[Total 5 marks]

Topic P2 — Forces

Work Done and Power

1 All bulbs have a power rating. *(Grade 4-6)*

a) Which statement is **correct** for a 60 W bulb?

    A It transfers 60 J of energy every second.
    B It transfers 60 J of energy every 2 seconds.
    C It transfers 60 J of energy every hour.
    D It transfers 60 kJ of energy every second.

Your answer ☐

[1]

b) How much energy will a 40 W bulb transfer in 1 minute?

    A 40 J
    B 40 kJ
    C 2400 J
    D 2400 W

Your answer ☐

[1]
[Total 2 marks]

2 A box is pulled along a frozen pond by an electric winch with a 21.0 N force. It takes 12.5 s for the box to be dragged 35.0 m to the edge of the pond. You can assume the friction between the box and the ice is negligible. *(Grade 6-7)*

a) i) Calculate the work done on the box.

Work done = ... Unit ....
[3]

ii) Calculate the power of the winch.

Power = ... W
[2]

b) The force pulling the box is removed at the edge of the pond. The box then slides onto a paved path, where it slows down to a stop. The frictional force acting on the box from the path is 17.5 N. Calculate the distance the box travels before stopping.

Distance = ... m
[3]
[Total 8 marks]

Topic P2 — Forces

3   Siobhan needs a motor with a power of 0.6 W for her experiment. She finds four unlabelled motors in her lab. She sets up the experiment shown on the right and times how long it takes each motor to lift a 5000 g mass over the distance labelled X in the diagram.

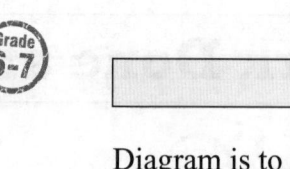

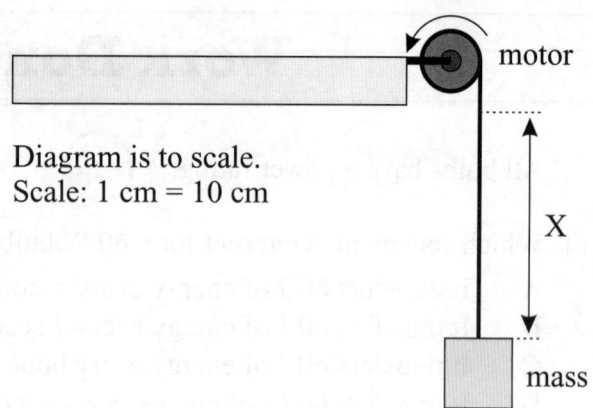

Diagram is to scale.
Scale: 1 cm = 10 cm

Her results are shown in the table below. Which motor should Siobhan use?
Use the formula: **potential energy = mass × height × gravitational field strength (10 N/kg)**

Motor	Time (s)
A	0.4
B	16
C	25
D	40

Your answer ☐

[Total 1 mark]

4   A car manufacturer is testing the brakes on a new brand of sports car. At top speed, the brakes bring the car to a stop in 365 m. The brakes work with a force of 8.1×10^3 N and the mass of the car is 1225 kg.

Calculate the top speed of the car.
Show your working.

Speed = ... m/s
[Total 4 marks]

Exam Practice Tip
When work is done on a object, energy is transferred to an energy store of the object, e.g. the kinetic energy store of an object being pushed. So you might have to use multiple equations in one question, e.g. work done and kinetic energy.

Topic P2 — Forces

Forces, Elasticity and Hooke's Law

1 Claire wants to stretch a spring of resting length 72 mm and spring constant 24 N/m.

a) What is the minimum number of forces Claire must apply to the spring in order to stretch it?

....
[1]

Claire clamps the spring at one end and pulls the other end. It stretches to 87 mm.

b) i) Calculate the force that Claire is applying to the spring.

Force = ... N
[3]

ii) Calculate the energy transferred to the spring during this stretching.
Use the formula: **energy transferred in stretching = 0.5 × spring constant × (extension)²**
Give the unit.

Energy = ... Unit ....
[2]

c) The spring displays elastic deformation. What does this mean?

....
[1]

[Total 7 marks]

2 Spring A has a smaller spring constant than spring B. They both reach their elastic limit when they have been extended by the same amount.

Which of the following correctly shows the force-extension graphs for both springs?
The elastic limits are marked with a dot.

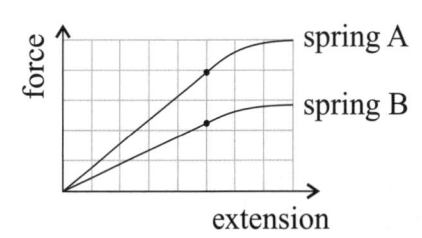

A — spring B (upper), spring A (lower)

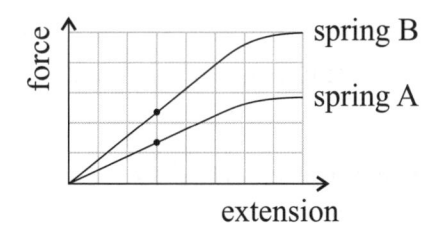

B — spring A (upper), spring B (lower)

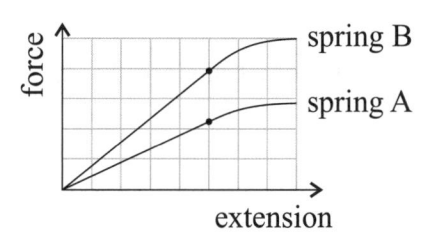

C — spring B (upper), spring A (lower)

D — spring B (upper), spring A (lower)

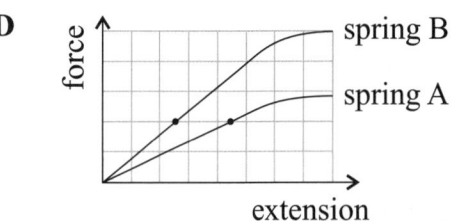

Your answer ☐

[Total 1 mark]

PRACTICAL

3 Michael is investigating the effect of force on the extension of two different springs, X and Y. For each spring, he clamps the top of the spring and hangs different numbers of 1 N weights from the bottom of the spring, then measures the extension with a ruler. A table of Michael's results and a graph of spring X is shown below.

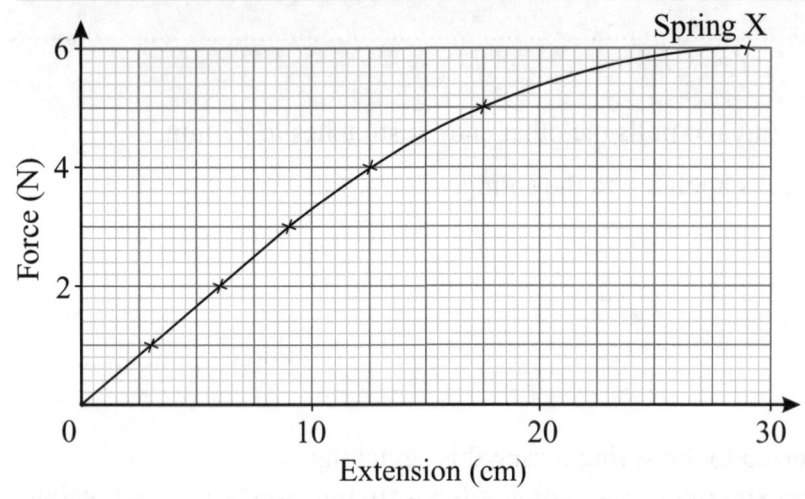

Grade 7-9

Force (N)	Extension (cm) X	Extension (cm) Y
0	0	0
1	3.0	4.0
2	6.0	8.0
3	9.0	12.0
4	12.5	16.9
5	17.5	30.0
6	29.0	—

a) i) The force-extension graph for spring X is shown above.
Draw the force-extension graph for spring Y on the same axes.
[3]

ii) Describe and explain the shape of the graph you have drawn.

....
....
....
....
....
[4]

b) Using the graph you have drawn, calculate the spring constant of **spring Y**.

Spring constant = ... N/m
[3]

c) Use the graph to find the energy transferred to **spring X** as it was extended by 12.5 cm to 17.5 cm, assuming it has not passed its elastic limit.

Energy transferred = ... J
[2]

[Total 12 marks]

Exam Practice Tip
That was a long topic, with lots of equations, some of which can be used together to answer questions. Make sure you know how the equations can be applied to different situations, so you'll be ready for anything the examiners throw at you.

Topic P2 — Forces

Topic P3 — Electricity and Magnetism

Static Electricity

1 Static electricity is the build up of charge on an object.

a) Which of the following statements is **true**?
- A   When two conductors are rubbed together, protons pass from one to the other.
- B   When two insulators are rubbed together, electrons pass from one to the other.
- C   When an object loses electrons, it becomes negatively charged.
- D   When an object gains electrons, it becomes positively charged.

Your answer ☐

[1]

b) All matter contains charge, but some matter is electrically neutral.
Explain why.

....

....

[2]

[Total 3 marks]

2 Kavita rubs a plastic acetate rod with a cloth. A positive static charge builds up on the rod.

a) Explain how a static charge has built up on the rod.

....

....

....

[2]

b) i) Kavita holds the rod close to some small scraps of paper. The scraps 'jump' towards the rod. Why does this happen?

....

....

....

....

....

[3]

ii) Kavita then tries the same experiment with a metal rod, but the paper doesn't jump. Suggest why the experiment doesn't work with a metal rod.

....

....

....

[3]

[Total 8 marks]

Current and Potential Difference

Warm-Up

Use the words below to correctly fill in the gaps in the passage.
You don't have to use every word, but each word can only be used once.

.... is the rate of flow of electric charge (electrons) around a circuit.

The driving force that pushes current around a circuit is called the ....

It is the .... transferred per unit charge. A current will flow around a circuit

if the circuit is .... and there is a source of ....

potential difference   energy   closed   current   potential difference

1 A simple circuit is shown on the right. *(Grade 4-6)*

a) How much charge passes through the light bulb in 120 seconds?

  A 420 V
  B 34 V
  C 420 C
  D 34 C

  Your answer ☐ *[1]*

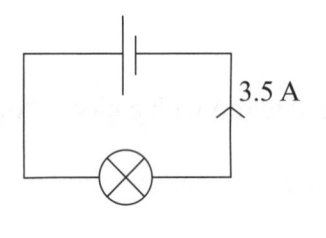

b) Calculate how long it will take for 770 C to pass through the light bulb. Show your working.

Time = ... s
[3]
[Total 4 marks]

2 It takes 2.5 mins and 276 kJ of energy for a kettle to boil water using a supply at 230 V. *(Grade 6-7)*

a) Calculate the amount of charge that passes through the kettle.
Use the formula: **energy transferred = charge × potential difference**

Charge = ... C
[3]

b) Calculate the current that is flowing through the circuit. Give the unit.

Current = ... unit ....
[3]
[Total 6 marks]

Topic P3 — Electricity and Magnetism

Circuits and Resistance

Warm-Up

Draw lines from each symbol to the name of the component that they represent.

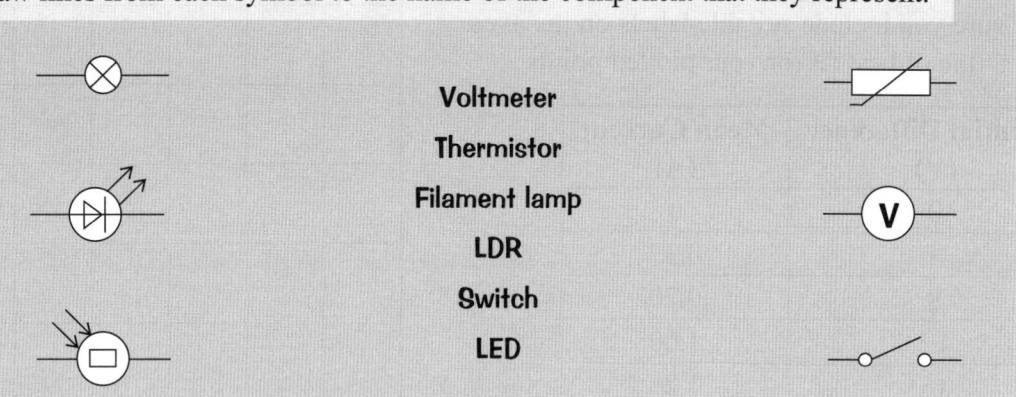

Voltmeter
Thermistor
Filament lamp
LDR
Switch
LED

1 A current of 350 mA flows through a 5 Ω resistor. Calculate the potential difference across the resistor. *(Grade 4-6)*

Potential difference = ... V
[Total 3 marks]

2 A circuit contains a cell and a variable resistor in series and an ammeter, which is used to measure the current. *(Grade 6-7)*

a) Draw a diagram to show this circuit.

[3]

b) A current of 2.4 A flows when the resistor has a resistance of 2.5 Ω.

What should the variable resistor be set to for a current of 4.0 A to flow?

A   6 Ω
B   0.7 Ω
C   24 Ω
D   1.5 Ω

Your answer ☐

[1]
[Total 4 marks]

Topic P3 — Electricity and Magnetism

PRACTICAL

3 A student uses a circuit to investigate the *I-V* characteristics of a filament lamp. Her results are given below.

a) Plot the results on the grid on the right.
Make sure you include suitable labels on the axes.
Draw a line of best fit for your plotted points.

Potential Difference (V)	Mean Current (A)
0	0
4	0.37
8	0.70
12	1.00
16	1.25
20	1.40
24	1.50

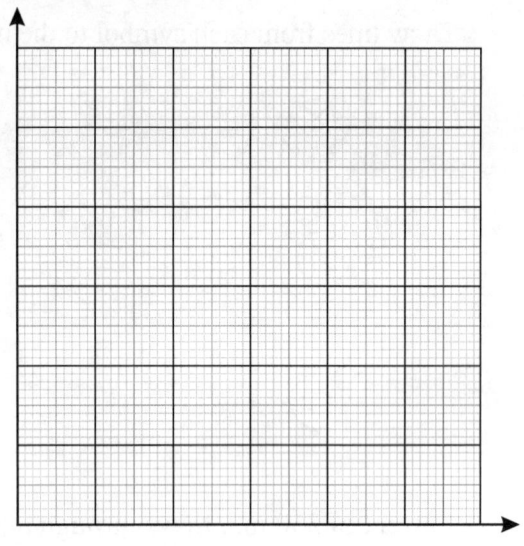

[4]

b) Explain the shape of the *I-V* graph of the filament lamp.

....

....

....

[3]

[Total 7 marks]

PRACTICAL

4* James is investigating the resistance of a diode. He sets up a circuit as shown on the right.

Describe how James could use this circuit to accurately and reliably investigate how the resistance of the diode changes with the current.

....

....

....

....

....

....

....

[Total 6 marks]

Topic P3 — Electricity and Magnetism

Circuit Devices

1 The resistance of a thermistor varies with temperature. *(Grade 4-6)*

a) Sketch a graph on the axes to show how the resistance of a thermistor changes with temperature.

[2]

b) Which is the correct *I-V* graph for a thermistor in constant conditions?

A   B   C   D

Your answer ☐

[1]

[Total 3 marks]

2 Diodes only let current flow in one direction. *(Grade 4-6)*

a) Why doesn't the current flow in both directions in a diode?

....

[1]

b) Give **one** use of a diode.

....

[1]

[Total 2 marks]

3 The circuit diagram for an automatic night-light in a garden is shown on the right. *(Grade 7-9)*

Explain what happens in this circuit as night falls.

....

....

....

....

....

[Total 4 marks]

Topic P3 — Electricity and Magnetism

Series and Parallel Circuits

Warm-Up

For the sentences below, state whether they are describing a series circuit, a parallel circuit or both.

Each component can be turned on and off separately. ....

The current through each component is always identical. ....

The potential difference across each component is the same. ....

1 A circuit diagram is shown on the right. *(Grade 4-6)*

a) Are the components in this circuit connected in series or parallel?

....
[1]

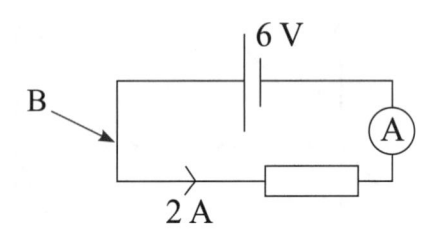

b) What is the current at the ammeter?

Current = ... A
[1]

c) A resistor is added to the circuit at the point marked B. What happens to the ammeter reading?

....
[1]

[Total 3 marks]

2 Two resistors are connected in a circuit with an ammeter, as shown in the diagram on the right. *(Grade 6-7)*

a) Calculate the current flowing through the ammeter.

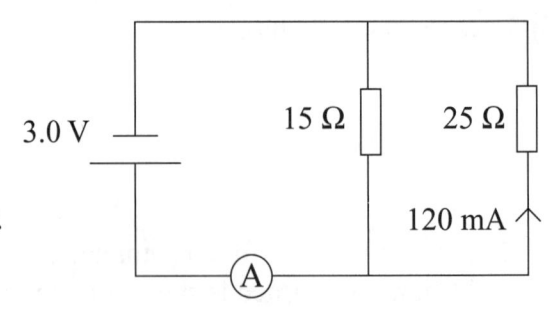

Current = ... A
[4]

b) Which of the following statements is **true** for the total resistance of this circuit?

    A   Total resistance = 35 Ω
    B   Total resistance = 15 Ω
    C   Total resistance < 15 Ω
    D   Total resistance > 25 Ω

Your answer ☐
[1]

[Total 5 marks]

Topic P3 — Electricity and Magnetism

3 Ian is investigating series and parallel circuits, using bulbs which are labelled as having the same resistance. He sets up the circuit shown in the diagram on the right.

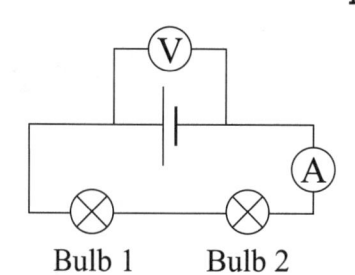

The voltmeter reads 12 V and the ammeter reads 0.5 A.
Ian uses these values to calculate the resistance of each bulb.

a) Calculate the resistance of each bulb.

Resistance = ... Ω
[2]

b) i) Ian then adds an identical third bulb in parallel, as shown in the diagram on the right.

Calculate the new current through the ammeter.

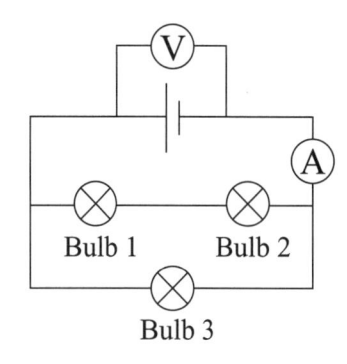

Current = ... A
[3]

ii) Ian observes that bulb 3 is brighter than bulbs 1 and 2. Explain why.

....
....
....
....
....
....
....
[5]

c) Ian now places an ammeter next to bulb 3 and a voltmeter in parallel around it, and uses the values to calculate its resistance.
Why might the resistance differ from the one he calculated earlier?

....
....
[1]

[Total 11 marks]

Exam Practice Tip
You could be asked a question about any component placed in series or parallel in a circuit. The ideas are the same though, so try not to panic. Just make sure you really understand how potential difference, current and resistance change.

Topic P3 — Electricity and Magnetism

Energy and Power in Circuits

1 A circuit component has a power of 1.5×10^{-2} kW. *(Grade 4-6)*

a) What is meant by '**power**'?

....
[1]

b) Calculate the energy transferred by the component over 24 hours.

Energy = ... kWh
[2]

[Total 3 marks]

2 Jane is shopping for a lawn mower. *(Grade 6-7)*
She finds the information in the table online.

Lawn Mower	Operating Power
Lawnmagic	920 J per s
Lawn-o-matic	3.24×10^6 J per hr
Bustagrass	1.16 kW

a) Which lawn mower is the most powerful?
Show your working.

Lawn mower = ...
[3]

Jane buys the Lawnmagic, and will run it using the mains supply (230 V).
However, the lawn mower needs a fuse fitting in the plug before use.
The fuse used should be rated just a little higher than the operating current of the appliance.

b) Which fuse should Jane fit in the lawn mower plug?

  A 2 A
  B 3 A
  C 5 A
  D 7 A

  Your answer ☐

[1]

[Total 4 marks]

Exam Practice Tip

Just make sure you know how to work with standard form on your calculator, and practise doing so. And remember, it's not scary, it's just a short-hand way of writing long numbers. For example, $1.5 \times 10^{-2} = 0.015$.

Topic P3 — Electricity and Magnetism

Magnets and Magnetic Fields

1 Field lines are used to represent the magnetic field around a magnet. *(Grade 4-6)*

a) Which statement is **correct** for magnetic field lines?
A   They always point from a south pole to a north pole.
B   They are used to show which direction a charged particle would move in the field.
C   They can only be straight lines.
D   They get closer together when the magnetic field is stronger.

Your answer ☐

[1]

b) i) Sketch on the diagram the field lines between the poles of these two bar magnets.

N   S

[2]

ii) State whether there will be attraction or repulsion between these two poles.

....

[1]
[Total 4 marks]

2 A student places two metal bars next to each other. One of the bars is a permanent magnet and the other is a magnetic material. She covers both the bars with a piece of paper and scatters iron filings over the top, to show the magnetic field lines around them. *(Grade 6-7)*

a) The diagram shows the pattern of the iron filings when they are scattered on the paper.
Add labels to show the poles on both bars and arrows to the 'field lines' to complete the diagram.

Permanent bar magnet   Magnetic material

[3]

b) The permanent magnet is removed and the filings are re-sprinkled above the magnetic material. The iron filings no longer show field lines around the magnetic material. Explain why.

....
....

[1]

c) Name **one** other piece of equipment that can be used to show field lines.

....

[1]
[Total 5 marks]

Topic P3 — Electricity and Magnetism

Electromagnetism

1 Sketch a graph on the axes below to show what happens to the magnetic field strength as you get further from a current-carrying wire.

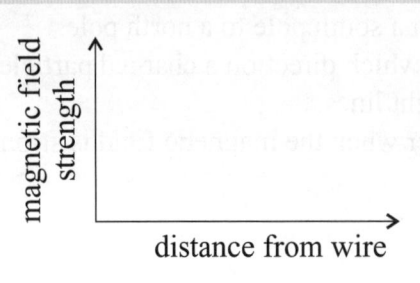

[y-axis: magnetic field strength; x-axis: distance from wire]

[Total 2 marks]

2 The diagram shows the field lines around a current-carrying wire.

The current through the wire is **decreased**. Which row correctly describes what happens to the field lines around the wire?

	Distance apart	Direction
A	Increases	Reverses
B	Decreases	Stays the same
C	Decreases	Reverses
D	Increases	Stays the same

Your answer ☐

[Total 1 mark]

3 A current-carrying solenoid has a magnetic field outside it similar to a bar magnet.

a) What happens to the magnetic effect of a solenoid if the number of turns per unit length increases?

....

[1]

b) The north pole of a magnet is brought near to the current-carrying solenoid as shown in the diagram. State whether the north pole is **attracted** or **repelled** by the solenoid. Explain why.

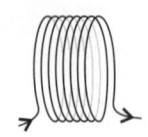

....

....

....

[3]

[Total 4 marks]

Exam Practice Tip

Use your right hand to find the magnetic field direction around a current-carrying wire. Stick your thumb in the direction of the current and curl your fingers — your fingers will be pointing in the direction of the field lines round the wire.

Topic P3 — Electricity and Magnetism

Magnetic Forces

Warm-Up

The diagram shows a left hand being used for Fleming's left hand rule.
Using **three** of the labels below, label the thumb and fingers in the diagram.

Force
Current
Voltage
Magnet
Wire
Magnetic field

1 How could the force acting on a current-carrying wire in a magnetic field be increased?

    A By decreasing the length of the wire.
    B By decreasing the current through the wire.
    C By reversing the direction of the current.
    D By increasing the strength of the magnetic field.

Your answer ☐

[Total 1 mark]

2 A 30 cm long current-carrying wire is placed between magnetic poles as shown below.

wire (current coming 'out' of the page)

S • N

a) The magnetic flux density is 2.2 T and the current through the wire is 15 A.
Calculate the force acting on the wire. Give the unit.
Use the equation: **Force on a conductor = magnetic flux density × current × length**

Force = ... unit = ...
[3]

b) Why does the wire experience a force?

....
....
....
[1]
[Total 4 marks]

Topic P3 — Electricity and Magnetism

3 The diagram shows a current-carrying wire between two magnetic poles. A current of 2.6 A is flowing through the wire, from left to right. A force of 0.0183 N is acting on the wire. Its direction is out of the paper, towards you.

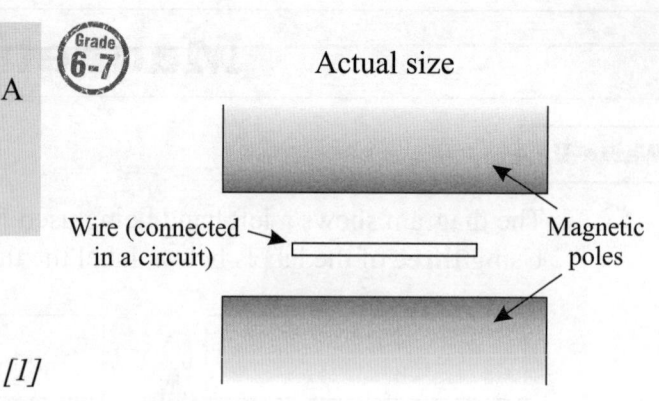

a) Label **each pole** to show if it is a north or south pole.

[1]

b) Calculate the magnetic flux density between the poles.
Give your answer to **2** significant figures.
Use the formula: **Force on a conductor = magnetic flux density × current × length**

Magnetic flux density = ... T
[4]

c) The wire is moved so that the current is now running parallel to the magnetic field.
What size force is acting on the wire now?

Force = ... N
[1]

[Total 6 marks]

4 Holly carries out an experiment using a horseshoe magnet and an iron bar connected in a circuit. Part of the set-up is shown below.

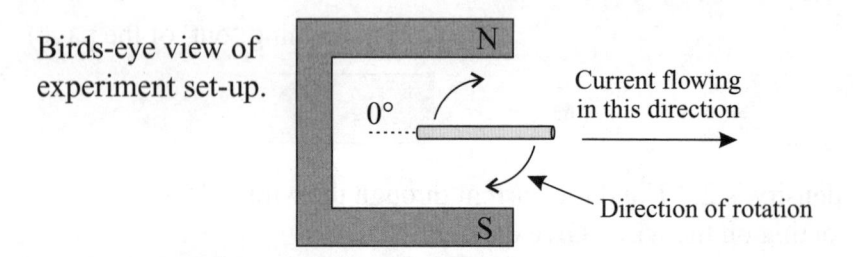

Holly rotates the iron bar 90° clockwise and measures the force acting on the bar as she does so. She then plots her results on a graph of force, F, against angle of rotation, θ.

Which of the following graphs shows a sketch of her results?

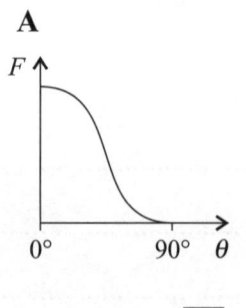

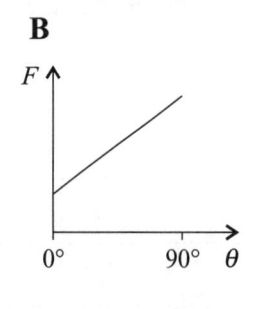

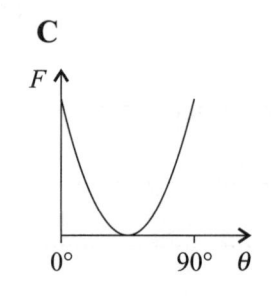

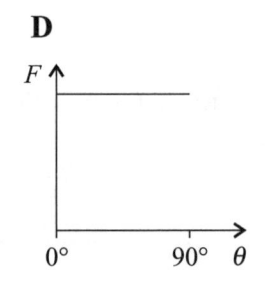

Your answer ☐

[Total 1 mark]

Topic P3 — Electricity and Magnetism

Motors

1 Eva has drawn a diagram of a simple motor. It's shown on the right.

Grade 4-6

She has made **two mistakes**.
Circle her mistakes.
Describe how to correct them.

1. ....

2. ....
[2 marks]

2 A simple d.c. motor consists of a magnetic north pole, a magnetic south pole and a rotating coil of wire connected to a circuit.

Grade 4-6

a) i) Describe how a simple motor works.

....

....

....

....
[4]

ii) Give **one** way in which the direction of the coil's rotation can be reversed.

....
[1]

b) The size of the current flowing through a motor affects the speed of rotation of the motor.
State **two** other factors which determine the speed of rotation of the motor.

1. ....

2. ....
[2]
[Total 7 marks]

3 Decreasing the current through the coil in a motor will decrease the speed of the motor (assuming all other factors stay the same).

Grade 6-7

Use the formula: **force on a conductor = magnetic flux density × current × length** to explain why.

....

....

....
[Total 2 marks]

Topic P3 — Electricity and Magnetism

Topic P4 — Waves and Radioactivity

Wave Basics

Warm-Up

Add the labels below to the diagram of the wave.

amplitude   crest
rest position
wavelength   trough

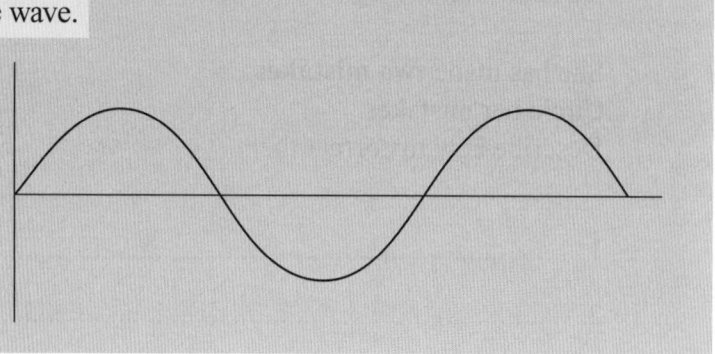

1 Which of the following is **not** a transverse wave?

    A   radio waves
    B   light waves
    C   sound
    D   ripples in water

Your answer ☐

[Total 1 mark]

2 Waves can be either transverse or longitudinal.

a) Describe the difference between longitudinal and transverse waves.

....
....
....
....
[2]

b) A transverse wave has a frequency of 1.60×10^4 Hz. Calculate the period of the wave. Give the unit.

Period = ... unit ....
[3]

[Total 5 marks]

3 Which of these is equal to the frequency of a longitudinal wave?

    A   The number of seconds taken for a complete cycle of the wave to pass a point.
    B   The number of compressions passing a point per second.
    C   The number of compressions plus the number of rarefactions passing a point per second.
    D   The number of rarefactions passing a point per minute.

Your answer ☐

[Total 1 mark]

4 A child throws a stone into a pond. The stone creates ripples when it hits the water, which spread across the pond.

a) The ripples pass a leaf floating on the pond.
Explain why the ripples do not carry the leaf to the edge of the pond.

....

....

....
[1]

b) The ripples have a wavelength of 1.5 cm. Given that their frequency is 14 Hz, calculate their speed in m/s. Show your working.

Speed = ... m/s
[3]
[Total 4 marks]

5 A vibrating violin string produces a sound wave.

A violinist is practising in a village hall. Her teacher sits at the back of the hall to listen.

a) What medium do the sound waves produced by the violin travel through to reach the teacher?

....
[1]

b) The violinist plays a note with a frequency 2.49 kHz. The sound waves have a speed of 340 m/s. Calculate the wavelength of the sound waves. Give your answer to **2** significant figures.

Wavelength = ... m
[4]

c) The violinist then plays a note with a frequency of 220 Hz.
The violinist plays this note for 5.0 seconds.
Calculate how many complete waves are produced by the vibrating string in this time.

Number of waves = ...
[2]
[Total 7 marks]

Exam Practice Tip
Don't be caught out by measurements given in different units. If a frequency is given in kHz or MHz, you'll need to convert to the correct units before using the value in an equation. You should watch out for different units of length too.

Topic P4 — Waves and Radioactivity

Wave Experiments

PRACTICAL

1 A student is investigating water waves in a ripple tank. She sets up the equipment shown below.

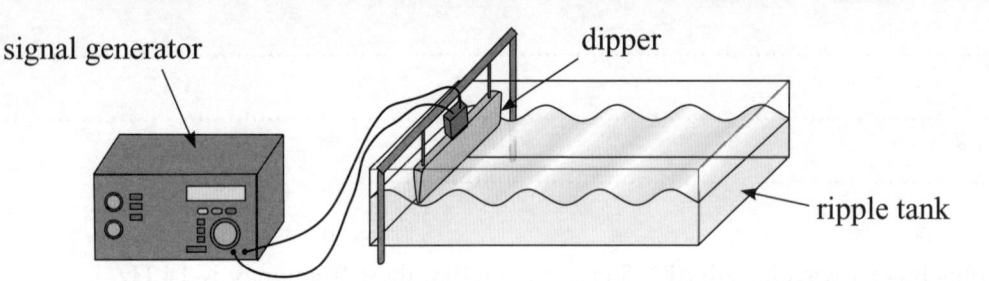

signal generator, dipper, ripple tank

a) The student wants to measure the frequency of the ripples. She floats a cork in the ripple tank and counts how many times it bobs up in 30 seconds. The student repeats her experiment five times. She does not adjust the signal generator between repeats.

State **two** other factors that should remain the same between repeats.

....

....
[2]

b) The table below shows the student's results. She recorded one of the results incorrectly.

Trial	1	2	3	4	5
Number of bobs in 30 seconds	36	33	63	33	42

Calculate the average number of times the cork bobbed up in 30 seconds, ignoring the anomalous result.

Number of bobs = ...
[2]

c) Using your answer to **part b)**, calculate the frequency of the ripples.

Frequency = ... Hz
[1]

d) A second student suggests they could also measure the speed of the ripples. Describe a method they could use.

....

....

....

....

....
[3]

[Total 8 marks]

Topic P4 — Waves and Radioactivity

Reflection and Refraction

1 A ray of light meets the boundary between two media.

What is meant by the 'normal' of a boundary?

- **A** A line at right angles to the boundary.
- **B** A line parallel to the boundary.
- **C** A line at right angles to the incident ray at the boundary.
- **D** A line that represents the boundary.

Your answer ☐

[Total 1 mark]

2 The diagram below shows light passing from air into a block of glass. The light meets the boundary at an angle of 90°.

Which of the following statements is **correct**?

- **A** Most of the light will be refracted.
- **B** Most of the light will be absorbed.
- **C** Most of the light will be transmitted.
- **D** Most of the light will be reflected.

Your answer ☐

[Total 1 mark]

3 Two rays of light hit a mirror and are reflected. The diagram on the right shows the paths of the two reflected rays.

Which diagram below correctly shows the paths of the incident rays?

A

B

C

D

Your answer ☐

[Total 1 mark]

Topic P4 — Waves and Radioactivity

4   A light ray crosses the boundary between two materials, as shown in the diagram on the right.

a) Material A is less optically dense than material B. How can you tell this from the diagram above?

....
[1]

b) Material B is a type of glass. The light ray passes out of material B into a vacuum.

i) On the diagram below, sketch the path of the ray as it leaves material B.

[2]

ii) Explain what happens to the ray's frequency, wavelength and speed as it leaves material B.

....
....
....
....
[4]
[Total 7 marks]

5   A student shines a ray of white light through a block of clear plastic. The path of the light ray is shown on the right.

The student notices that the emergent ray is not pure white. One side of the emergent ray has a red tinge, whilst the other side looks slightly purple. Explain why this may have happened.

....
....
....
....
....
....
....
[Total 4 marks]

Topic P4 — Waves and Radioactivity

More on Reflection

PRACTICAL

1 Scott is investigating the reflection of blue light by a mirror. *Grade 6-7*

He places a mirror on a sheet of paper, then draws a normal to the mirror on the sheet of paper. He then shines a ray of blue light towards the point where the normal meets the mirror.

Scott varies the angle between the ray from the light box and the normal, and traces the path of the ray on the paper. He then measures the angle of incidence and the angle of reflection for each ray.

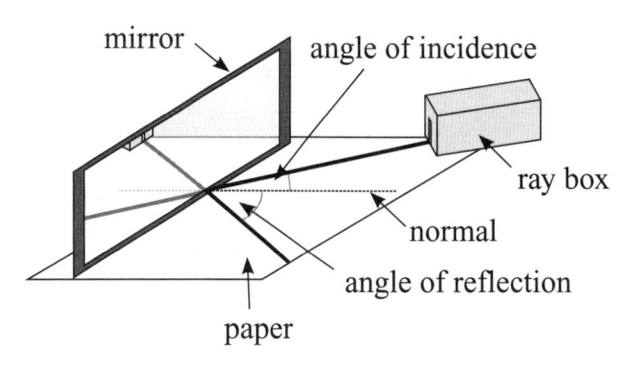

The table below shows Scott's results.

Angle of incidence / °	15	30	45	60	75
Angle of reflection / °	18	33	48	63	78

a) State what kind of error these results show, and suggest what may have caused it.

....

....
[2]

b) Two of Scott's classmates, Jiahui and Francis, do the same experiment. Their results are shown below.

Jiahui's results:

Angle of incidence / °	Angle of reflection / °		
	trial 1	trial 2	trial 3
15	15	14	13
30	31	30	31
45	43	45	44
60	60	61	60
75	74	75	77

Francis' results:

Angle of incidence / °	Angle of reflection / °		
	trial 1	trial 2	trial 3
15	18	12	14
30	33	32	36
45	45	43	49
60	57	64	62
75	70	73	76

Jiahui's results are more repeatable than Francis' results.
Suggest **one** reason for the difference in repeatability of their results.

....
[1]

c) Francis repeats the experiment using red light. Explain how this will affect his results.

....

....

....
[2]
[Total 5 marks]

Topic P4 — Waves and Radioactivity

More on Refraction

PRACTICAL

Warm-Up

Use the words below to correctly fill in the gaps in the passage.
You don't have to use every word, but each word can only be used once.

Different colours of light have .... When they cross a

material boundary, different colours refract .... If you

shine white light through a prism, you get ....

| an image | a spectrum | by different amounts | a normal |
| different speeds in air | by the same amount | a shadow | different wavelengths |

---

1 A student wants to investigate the effect of wavelength on how much a ray of light refracts when it passes through a glass block. He uses the equipment shown below.

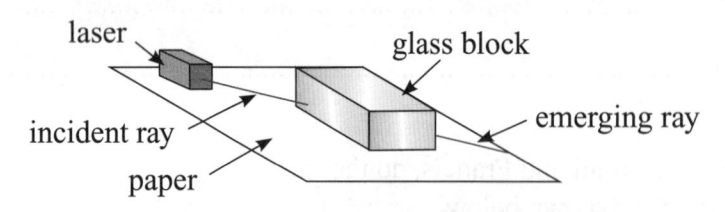

Grade 6-7

The student shines rays of light with different wavelengths through the glass block.
He traces the path of the incident and emerging rays onto the paper, then joins the two together to find the path of the refracted ray through the block.
On his diagram, he then measures the angle of incidence and the angle of refraction for each ray as it enters the block.

a) i) What is the **independent** variable in this experiment?

....
[1]

ii) What is the **dependent** variable in this experiment?

....
[1]

b) State **two** variables that the student will need to keep the same to make sure the experiment is a fair test. Give reasons for your answers.

....
....
....
....
[4]

[Total 6 marks]

Topic P4 — Waves and Radioactivity

EM Waves and Their Uses

Warm-Up

Using the words in the box, put the waves of the electromagnetic spectrum in the table below, in order of frequency.

low frequency ⟶ high frequency

....	....	....	....	....	....	....
....	....	....	....	....	....	....

microwaves   ultra-violet   visible light   gamma rays
infra-red   X-rays   radio waves

---

1 Which of the following is a type of ionising radiation? *Grade 4-6*

  A ultra-violet
  B microwaves
  C visible light
  D infra-red

  Your answer ☐

[Total 1 mark]

---

2 Which of these statements about the electromagnetic spectrum is **not** true? *Grade 4-6*

  A All electromagnetic waves travel at the same speed in a vacuum.
  B The longer the wavelength of an electromagnetic wave, the more energy it carries.
  C Our eyes can only detect a small part of the electromagnetic spectrum.
  D Electromagnetic waves transfer energy from a source to an absorber.

  Your answer ☐

[Total 1 mark]

---

3 Radio waves have the longest wavelengths in the electromagnetic spectrum. Gamma rays have the shortest. *Grade 4-6*

  a) Radio waves are used to broadcast TV and radio shows. Give **one** other use of radio waves.

  ....
  [1]

  b) Give **one** use of gamma rays.

  ....
  [1]

  [Total 2 marks]

Topic P4 — Waves and Radioactivity

4 A naturalist uses a night vision camera to capture an image of a fox, as shown below.

Explain how the night vision camera allowed this image to be taken.

....

....

....

....

[Total 2 marks]

5 X-rays are used in hospitals to diagnose broken bones.

The X-rays are generated by accelerating electrons to high speeds then firing them at a metal plate. When the electrons hit the plate, X-rays are produced.

a) Explain how these X-rays can be used to generate an image of a bone.

....

....

....

....

....

....

[3]

b) Staff who work with X-ray machines wear badges that monitor the levels of radiation they have been exposed to.

Explain why it is important to make sure hospital staff are exposed to as little X-ray radiation as possible.

....

....

....

....

[2]

[Total 5 marks]

Topic P4 — Waves and Radioactivity

6 Microwaves and visible light can both be used to transmit telephone calls. *(Grade 6-7)*

a) Explain how visible light is used to transmit phone signals.

....

....

....

....
[2]

b) Land-line calls are usually transmitted using visible light.
However, microwaves are sometimes used to transmit long-distance calls via satellites.

Suggest **one** advantage to using microwaves rather than
light waves to transmit phone signals over long distances.

....

....
[1]

c) Radio waves are also used in communications.
Which row on the table below correctly describes the conditions needed to generate radio waves?

	Changing electric field?	Changing magnetic field?
A	no	no
B	no	yes
C	yes	no
D	yes	yes

Your answer ☐

[1]

[Total 4 marks]

7 Researchers are currently investigating if it would be possibly to send humans to Mars. *(Grade 7-9)*
One of the concerns would be the increased risk of cancer.

Suggest and explain **one** possible reason for this increased risk.

....

....

....

....

....

[Total 3 marks]

Exam Practice Tip

You could be asked about any part of the EM spectrum, so make sure you know how the wavelength and frequencies change for each type of wave, plus you should know at least one example of a use for each type of wave.

Topic P4 — Waves and Radioactivity

Isotopes and Radioactive Decay

Warm-Up

The standard notation used to represent atoms is shown. Use the words below to correctly fill in the labels. You don't have to use every phrase, but each phrase can only be used once.

[ ] → A
[ ] ← $_Z^A X$
[ ] → Z

electron number
neutron number
mass number
chemical symbol
charge   atomic number

1 One isotope of sodium is $^{23}_{11}$Na. *Grade 4-6*

a) i) How many protons are in a sodium nucleus?

....
[1]

ii) Calculate the number of neutrons in the sodium nucleus.

Number of neutrons = ...
[1]

b) Describe what is meant by the term isotope.

....

....
[2]

[Total 4 marks]

2 Unstable isotopes can emit nuclear radiation, such as alpha particles. *Grade 4-6*

a) What is an alpha particle made up of?

   A Two neutrons and two protons.
   B An electron.
   C Gamma rays.
   D Four neutrons and two protons.

Your answer [ ]
[1]

b) Some isotopes will emit an electromagnetic wave as well as an alpha particle.
Name the wave. Give its charge and mass.

Name: ....

Charge: .... Mass: ....
[3]

[Total 4 marks]

Topic P4 — Waves and Radioactivity

Radiation Properties and Decay Equations

1. A polonium nucleus, $^{210}_{84}Po$, can occasionally decay to a lead nucleus (Pb) by releasing alpha and gamma radiation. Write a balanced equation to show this decay.

   ....

   [Total 3 marks]

2. Anandi carries out an experiment to investigate two different radioactive sources. A setup of her experiment is shown. She changes the material between the source and the Geiger-Muller tube and measures the count rate. A table of her results is also shown.

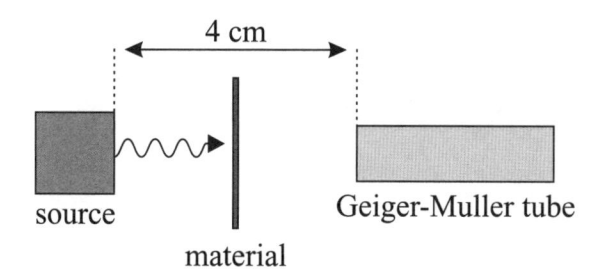

Material	Count rate (counts per minute) Source A	Count rate (counts per minute) Source B
No material	854	1203
Paper	7	1200
Aluminium	6	8
Lead	6	7

   a) What happens to the mass and charge of the nuclei of source A when they decay?

   ....
   ....
   [2]

   b) Source B is an isotope of carbon (C), which has a mass number of 14 and an atomic number of 6. The carbon nuclei decay to nitrogen (N) nuclei. Write a balanced equation to show this decay.

   ....
   [4]

   c) Anandi removes the material and moves source B from **4 cm** to **1 m** away from the detector. Explain what will happen to the count rate as she moves the source.

   ....
   ....
   ....
   [2]

   [Total 8 marks]

Exam Practice Tip
You need to know how the penetration properties of alpha, beta and gamma radiation differ — gamma radiation has the longest range in air and alpha radiation has the shortest. Beta radiation sits somewhere in-between.

Topic P4 — Waves and Radioactivity

Electron Energy Levels

Warm-Up

Use the words in the box to correctly fill in the gaps in the passage.
You don't have to use every word, but each word can only be used once.

Words: absorb, ionised, excited, release, energy, frequency

The electrons around an atom sit in different .... levels, or shells.

An electron is said to be .... when it moves up an energy level.

An electron that falls back down an energy level will .... radiation.

---

1 An alpha particle collides with a neutral atom, as shown in the diagram below. *(Grade 4-6)*

a) Complete the sentence:

The atom has now become...

A ... neutralised.
B ... ionised.
C ... contaminated.
D ... a beta particle.

Your answer ☐

[1]

b) What kind of **charge** does the atom have after the collision?

....

[1]
[Total 2 marks]

---

2 A fluorescent tube light contains mercury vapour and has a chemical coating on the inside, which contains manganese. When the light is on, electrons in the atoms of the mercury are excited, which results in them emitting UV radiation. This radiation is absorbed by the manganese atoms in the coating, causing them to emit visible light. *(Grade 7-9)*

a) Explain why the mercury atoms release radiation.

....

....

[2]

b) Why do the mercury and manganese atoms emit different forms of electromagnetic radiation?

....

....

....

[3]
[Total 5 marks]

Topic P4 — Waves and Radioactivity

209

Half-Life

1 The half-life of a radioactive source can be found from an activity-time graph like the one shown below. *(Grade 4-6)*

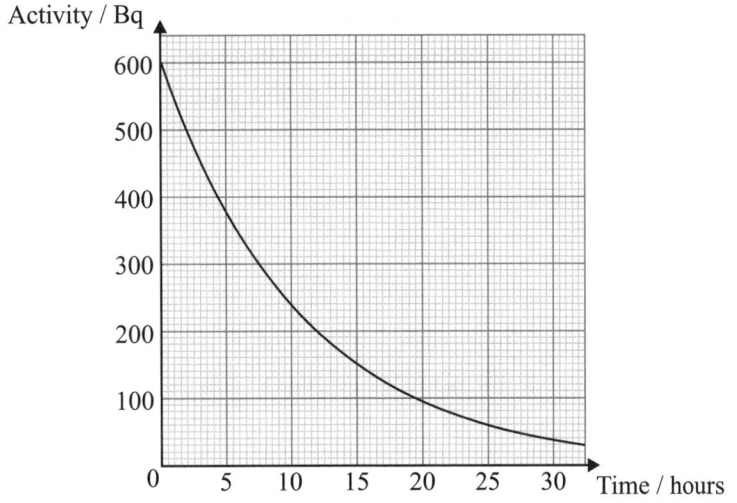

[Graph: Activity / Bq vs Time / hours, showing exponential decay from 600 Bq at t=0]

a) Define the term half-life.

....
[1]

b) Use the graph to determine the half-life of the source.

Half-life = ... hours
[1]

c) A different source with a half-life of 300 minutes has an initial activity of 400 Bq. Show how its activity will change in the first 20 hours on the graph above.
[3]

[Total 5 marks]

2 A radioactive source initially has an activity of 6000 Bq. *(Grade 6-7)*

a) After 6 years, the source has an activity of 750 Bq. What is the half-life of the source?

Half-life = ... Unit ....
[3]

b) A sample of the same source has an initial activity of 64 Bq. Calculate the net decline in activity, expressed as a ratio, during radioactive emission after 2 half-lives for this source.

Ratio = ...
[3]

[Total 6 marks]

Topic P4 — Waves and Radioactivity

Dangers of Radioactivity

1 Which of the following statements is **true**? *Grade 4-6*

    A Contamination and irradiation only last as long as the original source is present.
    B Contamination is temporary, but irradiation lasts longer.
    C Irradiation is temporary, but contamination lasts longer.
    D Contamination and irradiation last even after the original source has been removed.

Your answer ☐

[Total 1 mark]

2 Rebekah is looking at the radioactive sources they use in her lab. A table showing the properties of the sources is given. *Grade 6-7*

Source	Radiation Emitted	Form
A	Alpha	Solid
B	Alpha and gamma	Gas
C	Gamma	Gas

a) Which source poses the greatest risk to those using it? Explain your answer.

....
....
....
....

[3]

Rebekah writes out some safe handling instructions for the lab.

Safety precautions for working with radioactive sources
• Always wear gloves when working with radioactive sources.
• Keep sources as close to you as possible at all times.
• Use tongs to handle any solid radioactive material.
• Place sources in a lead lined box when not in use.

She has made **one** mistake.

b) Circle the incorrect statement. Why is this statement incorrect?

....
....
....

[3]

[Total 6 marks]

Topic P4 — Waves and Radioactivity

Topic P5 — Energy

Conservation of Energy

Warm-Up

For each example, name the energy store that energy is being transferred away from.

1) A skydiver falling from an aeroplane. ....
2) A substance undergoing a nuclear reaction. ....
3) A stretched rubber band springing back to its original shape. ....
4) A piece of burning coal. ....

1 A kettle of cold water is plugged into the mains and brought to the boil. Energy is transferred from the mains to the water.

Grade 4-6

a) Name the energy store of the water that the energy is transferred **to**.

....

[1]

b) How is energy transferred from the mains to the kettle?

A mechanically
B by heating
C by radiation
D electrically

Your answer ☐

[1]

c) i) State the law of conservation of energy.

....
....

[2]

ii) Assuming the kettle is a closed system, describe the change in total energy that takes place as the water boils.

....

[1]

[Total 5 marks]

2 Sonja is riding her bike. She takes her feet off the pedals to freewheel down a hill.

Grade 6-7

Describe the energy transfers that take place as the bike travels down the hill. Ignore friction and air resistance.

....
....
....

[Total 3 marks]

Topic P5 — Energy

Efficiency

1 Which of the following washing machines is the most efficient? *Grade 4-6*

Washing machine	Input energy (J)	Useful output energy (J)
A	4×10^4	2.52×10^4
B	4×10^4	2.80×10^4
C	4×10^4	2.95×10^4
D	4×10^4	2.98×10^4

Your answer ☐

[Total 1 mark]

2 An electric fan transfers 7250 J of energy. 2 kJ of this is wasted energy. *Grade 6-7*

a) Suggest **one** way in which energy is wasted by the fan.

....
[1]

b) Calculate the efficiency of the fan. Give your answer as a decimal to **2** significant figures.

Efficiency = ...
[4]

[Total 5 marks]

3 An electric kettle has an efficiency of 76%. 2500 J of energy is transferred from the mains to the kettle every second. When the kettle is full, it needs to transfer 418 000 J of energy to the thermal energy store of the water to boil it. *Grade 7-9*

How long does a full kettle need to be switched on for in order to boil the water?

A 2.8 minutes
B 22 seconds
C 167 seconds
D 220 seconds

Your answer ☐

[Total 1 mark]

Exam Practice Tip
No device is 100% efficient as some energy will always be wasted. For example, energy is carried away by sound waves — you can probably hear an electrical appliance in your home if it's turned on, even if it's just a quiet hum.

Topic P5 — Energy

Energy Transfer by Heating

1 Water in a bucket heats up by conduction and convection when a lump of hot coal is put in it. *(Grade 4-6)*

a) Explain how energy is transferred through the water by conduction, causing its temperature to rise.

....

....

....

....

....
[4]

b) Another lump of hot coal is buried under some sand. Why doesn't the sand heat up by convection?

....
[1]
[Total 5 marks]

2 A matt black pan full of hot water is left to cool in a room. The initial temperature of the water is 85°C and after 30 minutes it has cooled down to 43°C. The water loses 441 000 J of energy in this time. The specific heat capacity of water is 4200 J/kg °C. *(Grade 6-7)*

a) Calculate the mass of water in the pan. Show your working. Use the formula:
change in thermal energy = mass × specific heat capacity × change in temperature

Mass = ... kg
[3]

b) i) Energy is transferred away from the surface of the **pan** in **three** ways. Name them.

1. ....

2. ....

3. ....
[3]

ii) Explain why the **pan** would cool down at a slower rate if it was shiny and silver in colour.

....

....

....
[2]
[Total 8 marks]

Topic P5 — Energy

Reducing Unwanted Energy Transfers

1 Randeesh is cycling in a race. Before the race, he puts oil on the bike chain. *Grade 4-6*

Explain, using ideas about energy, how adding oil will affect the efficiency of Randeesh's cycling.

....

....

....

....

[Total 4 marks]

2 Camilla is building an energy-efficient house. *Grade 6-7*

She has four brick brands to choose from for the walls.

Brand	Thermal conductivity (m²/s)	Brick thickness (cm)
A	5.2×10^{-7}	10
B	5.2×10^{-7}	15
C	2.7×10^{-7}	10
D	2.7×10^{-7}	15

a) Based on the information in the table above, explain which brick brand she should use.

....

....

....

....

[4]

b)* Describe **other ways** that Camilla could make her house energy-efficient.
   Include how each of your suggestions reduce energy losses.

....

....

....

....

....

....

....

[6]

[Total 10 marks]

Topic P5 — Energy

Mechanical and Electrical Energy Transfers

Warm-Up

Use the words below to correctly fill in the gaps in the passage.
You don't have to use every word, and words can be used more than once.

As a rubber ball falls, it experiences .... due to gravity. .... is done on the ball and energy is transferred from the ball's .... energy store to its .... energy store. The ball compresses when it hits the ground. Energy is transferred from the ball's .... energy store to its .... energy store.

| a force | work | chemical potential | kinetic |
| elastic potential | radiation | gravitational potential | friction |

1 An electric heater with a power rating of 3 kW is connected to the mains. *Grade 4-6*

a) Which statement correctly describes the energy transfer occurring when the heater is switched on?
- **A** Energy is transferred electrically to the kinetic energy store of the heater.
- **B** Energy is transferred by heating to the kinetic energy store of the heater.
- **C** Energy is transferred electrically to the thermal energy store of the heater.
- **D** Energy is transferred by heating to the thermal energy store of the heater.

Your answer ☐

[1]

b) What is meant by the power rating of an appliance?

....
[1]

c) The heater is on for 5 hours. How much work is done by the mains in that time?
Use the formula: **energy transferred = power × time**. Give the unit.

Work done = ... unit = ...
[2]

[Total 4 marks]

2 A 0.1 kg toy contains a compressed spring. When the spring is released, the toy flies 0.5 m upwards from ground level. *Grade 4-6*

Calculate the energy stored in the toy's gravitational potential energy store at its highest point.

Energy = ... J
[Total 3 marks]

Topic P5 — Energy

3 Dylan is investigating the speed at which a light foam ball (9×10^{-3} kg), dropped from up to 2 m, hits the floor. He plans to use a 30 cm ruler to record the initial height of the ball and a light gate connected to a computer to find the final velocity.

His teacher tells him that the ruler is inappropriate for this experiment.

a) Give **one** reason why. Suggest equipment he could use instead of the ruler.

....

....
[2]

Dylan's results are shown in the table.

Height (m)	Attempt 1 (m/s)	Attempt 2 (m/s)	Attempt 3 (m/s)	Mean Speed (m/s)
0.5	3.06	3.08	3.10	3.08
1.0	4.27	4.36	4.31	4.31
1.5	5.10	5.12	5.08	5.10
2.0	5.96	5.98	6.01	

b) i) Complete the table by calculating the missing value.
[1]

ii) Explain the trend shown by the data in terms of the transfer of energy between different stores.

....

....

....

....

....
[3]

c) i) Using the idea of energy transfers, calculate the speed at which the ball should hit the floor from a height of **5 m**. Use: gravitational field strength (g) = 10 N/kg.

Speed = ... m/s
[4]

ii) Dylan measures the speed of the ball dropped from 5 m and finds it to be **lower** than that calculated in **c) i)**. Suggest why.

....

....

....
[2]

[Total 12 marks]

Topic P5 — Energy

4 An empty lift has a mass of 1150 kg. The lift always moves at the same steady speed between each floor, and the distance between each floor is 4.00 m.

a) How much energy is transferred to the lift's gravitational potential energy store when it moves from the second floor to the sixth floor? Use: $g = 10$ N/kg.

    A 1.84×10^5 J
    B   18.4 kJ
    C   46 000 kJ
    D 4.6×10^3 J

Your answer ☐

[1]

b) A motor is used to move the lift. The lift takes 10.0 s to move up four floors. Calculate the power of the motor if it has an efficiency of 0.80.

Power = ... W
[3]
[Total 4 marks]

5 Amy and Ben fire identical 10.0 g ball bearings from different catapults. The rubber band of each catapult is elastically extended by 0.100 m and then released to fire the ball bearings.

a) The rubber band in Ben's catapult has a spring constant of **1.44 N/cm**. How much energy is transferred to the kinetic energy store of Ben's ball bearing? Use the formula: **energy transferred in stretching = 0.5 × spring constant × (extension)²**

    A   0.0072 J
    B   0.072 J
    C   0.72 J
    D   7.2 J

Your answer ☐

[1]

b) The initial speed of Amy's ball bearing is twice as fast as Ben's ball bearing. Calculate the spring constant of Amy's rubber band. Show your working.

Spring constant = ... N/m
[5]
[Total 6 marks]

Exam Practice Tip

A tricky few pages here, but it's not really as bad as it seems. Just make sure you learn the equations for power and for calculating kinetic, gravitational potential and elastic potential energy store values. Then it's just a matter of working out how the energy is being transferred between the different stores and whether there's any energy being wasted or not.

Topic P5 — Energy

Topic P6 — Global Challenges

Everyday Speeds and Accelerations

Warm-Up

Circle the correct typical speed for each scenario below.

A pedestrian walking down a quiet street — 1.4 m/s   OR   14 m/s   OR   140 m/s

A car on a motorway — 13 m/s   OR   31 m/s   OR   3100 m/s

Speed of sound in air — 34 m/s   OR   340 m/s   OR   3400 m/s

A person running in a race — 0.3 m/s   OR   3 m/s   OR   30 m/s

---

1 A train is travelling at 95 mph. *(Grade 6-7)*

What is the speed of the train in m/s?

A   15 m/s
B   210 m/s
C   42 m/s
D   26 m/s

Your answer ☐

[Total 1 mark]

---

2 A cyclist is travelling along a main road. *(Grade 6-7)*

a) The cyclist is wearing a helmet which contains a layer of foam covered in plastic.
Explain how the foam in the helmet would help to protect the cyclist in the event of a crash.

....
....
....
....
....

[3]

b) The cyclist stops at a red light. When the light changes to green, the cyclist rides away, accelerating up to a speed of 21 km/hr.

Estimate the cyclist's acceleration. Give your answer in **m/s²**.

Acceleration = ... m/s²

[4]

[Total 7 marks]

Stopping Distances and Reaction Times

1 A student is measuring their reaction time using a computer program. *(Grade 4-6)*

a) What is a typical value for a person's reaction time?

    A 500 milliseconds
    B 50 seconds
    C 50 milliseconds
    D 5 seconds

Your answer ☐
[1]

b) The student presses the enter key on the computer keyboard to start the program. After a random time interval, the computer sounds a buzzer. The student presses the enter key again as soon as they hear the buzzer. The computer then calculates their reaction time.

Describe how the computer might calculate the student's reaction time.

....

....
[1]

c) The student repeats the experiment three times and calculates an average reaction time. Explain why this is done.

....

....
[1]
[Total 3 marks]

2 A car manufacturer tests the brakes of a new model of car. *(Grade 7-9)*

The car is driven at a steady speed of 15 m/s in dry conditions.
The driver applies the brakes when told to. The velocity-time graph of the test is shown below.

On the same axes, sketch the graph you would expect if the test was repeated at the same speed, with the same driver, but in **wet** conditions.
Assume the driver is told to stop at the same time in both tests.

[Total 2 marks]

Exam Practice Tip
You need to be neat, even if you're just sketching a graph — the examiner needs to see what you're trying to show. Remember to use a pencil, so you can correct any mistakes, and if you're drawing a straight line use a ruler.

Topic P6 — Global Challenges

Energy Sources

1 Which row **only** lists non-renewable energy resources?

	Energy Sources
A	uranium, bio-fuels, coal
B	uranium, gas, hydro-electricity
C	wind, hydro-electricity, oil
D	oil, uranium, coal

Your answer ☐

[Total 1 mark]

2 The amount of electricity generated by wind turbines is increasing in the UK.

a) How do wind turbines generate electricity?

....

....

[2]

b) Why might people want to increase the amount of electricity generated by wind turbines?

....

....

[2]

[Total 4 marks]

3* Compare how a coal power station and a nuclear power station work, including a description of the energy transfers that take place.

....

....

....

....

....

....

....

....

....

[Total 6 marks]

Topic P6 — Global Challenges

4 Electricity can be generated by burning bio-fuels, such as animal waste collected from farms or specially grown crops like sugar cane. *Grade 6-7*

a) Are bio-fuels a renewable or non-renewable energy source? Explain your answer.

....

....
[2]

b) Suggest **one advantage** and **one disadvantage** of growing crops for use as bio-fuel compared to burning waste.

Advantage: ....

....

....

Disadvantage: ....

....
[2]
[Total 4 marks]

5 A sunny coastal country is debating replacing a coal-fired power station with a different form of electricity generation. *Grade 6-7*

a) Give **three** reasons why the country might want to stop using coal as a source of energy.

....

....

....

....
[3]

b) Suggest **two** sensible replacement energy sources for this country. Compare their use to coal.

....

....

....

....

....

....
[5]
[Total 8 marks]

Topic P6 — Global Challenges

6 The bar chart below shows the electricity generated from renewable and non-renewable energy sources in a small country over 20 years.

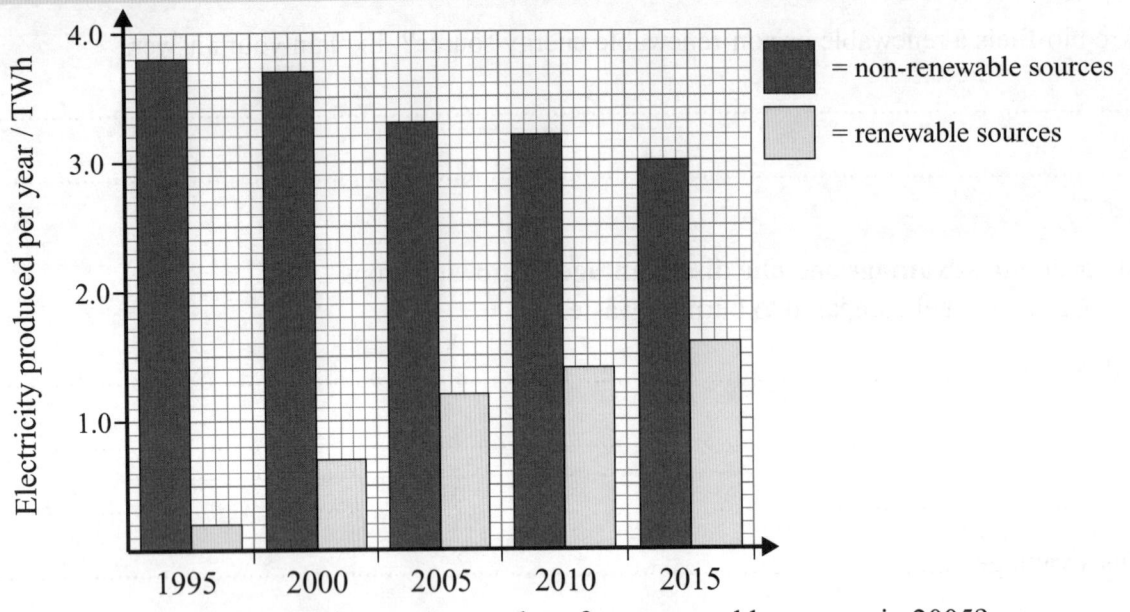

Grade 6-7

a) How much electricity did the country produce from renewable sources in 2005?

.... TWh
[1]

b) i) How much **more** electricity did the country produce per year in 2015 than in 1995?

.... TWh
[2]

ii) Suggest **one** reason why the country needed to produce more electricity.

....
[1]

c) Describe the trends in use of energy sources shown by the graph.
Suggest reasons for these trends. Use data from the graph in your answer.

....
....
....
....
....
....
....
[4]

[Total 8 marks]

Exam Practice Tip
If you're asked a compare or discuss question in the exam, like compare the advantages and disadvantages of different types of energy source, make sure your answer is clear, doesn't contain any waffle and uses physics terminology correctly.

Topic P6 — Global Challenges

Electricity and the National Grid

1 Electricity is supplied to homes in the UK through the national grid. *(Grade 4-6)*

a) The electricity supply of the UK has an alternating voltage. What does this mean?

....

....
[1]

b) State the potential difference and frequency of the UK mains electricity.

....
[1]

[Total 2 marks]

2 Electricity is transmitted across the national grid at 400 000 V. *(Grade 6-7)*

a) Explain why electricity is transmitted across the national grid at a high potential difference.

....

....

....

....

....
[3]

b) The diagram on the right shows a transformer at a sub-station. It changes the potential difference generated by a wind farm from 12 000 V to 400 000 V.

primary coil: 12 000 V, 300 A

secondary coil: 400 000 V, ? A

i) Calculate the current in the secondary coil of the transformer. Use the formula:

$$\text{potential difference across primary coil} \times \text{current in primary coil} = \text{potential difference across secondary coil} \times \text{current in secondary coil}$$

Current = ... A
[2]

ii) Explain whether this is a step-up or step-down transformer.

....

....
[1]

[Total 6 marks]

Wiring in the Home

Warm-Up

Draw lines to match the type of wire to its colour in a typical plug.

| LIVE WIRE | EARTH WIRE | NEUTRAL WIRE |

blue   brown   green and yellow

1 Explain why touching the live wire in a socket is dangerous. *(Grade 4-6)*

....

....

....

[Total 2 marks]

2 A student is examining two kettles. One of the kettles has a plastic casing. The other has a metal casing. The student notices that the earth pins on the plugs of the kettles are made from different materials, as shown below. *(Grade 7-9)*

Metal Kettle: — Metal Earth Pin

Plastic Kettle: — Plastic Earth Pin

a) An earth pin connects to the earth wire. Explain why the plastic kettle doesn't need a metal pin.

....

....

....

[3]

b) The metal kettle develops a fault and the live wire inside the kettle is touching the metal casing. Explain how the earth wire and the fuse act to keep the kettle safe when it is switched on.

....

....

....

[3]

[Total 6 marks]

Exam Practice Tip

Don't forget — its not just the colour of the wires in the plug that you need to remember, you need to understand the different functions of the wires and the potential differences between them too. It could come up in the exam.

Topic P6 — Global Challenges

Biology Mixed Questions

1   Alcohol is metabolised in the liver using alcohol dehydrogenase enzymes.

   a) One of the functions of the liver is to break down excess amino acids.

      i) Which of the following molecules is made up of amino acids?

         A   a carbohydrate
         B   a protein
         C   a lipid
         D   glycerol

         Your answer ☐

         [1]

      ii) What word is used to describe a molecule that is made up of smaller repeating units, such as amino acids?

         ....
         [1]

   b) Which of the following sentences about enzymes is **true**?

      A   Enzymes speed up chemical reactions in living organisms.
      B   Enzymes are used up in chemical reactions.
      C   Enzymes are products of digestion.
      D   Enzymes are the building blocks of all living organisms.

      Your answer ☐

      [1]

   c) A scientist was investigating the effect of pH on the rate of activity of alcohol dehydrogenase. The graph below shows his results.

      i) What is the optimum pH for the enzyme?

         ....
         [1]

      ii) Suggest and explain the effect an acid with a pH of 1 would have on the enzyme.

         ....
         ....
         ....
         [3]

d) Which of the following statements about alcohol is **false**?

A High alcohol consumption can cause liver disease.
B High alcohol consumption is a risk factor for cancer.
C High alcohol consumption decreases blood pressure.
D High alcohol consumption can lead to heart disease.

Your answer ☐

[1]

[Total 8 marks]

2 The diagram below shows a plant cell with one of its sub-cellular structures magnified. The overall movement of four molecules into and out of the sub-cellular structure are also shown.

Grade 4-6

IN — carbon dioxide + water
OUT — glucose + oxygen
45 mm

a) i) Look at the movements of carbon dioxide, water, glucose and oxygen in the diagram. What reaction do these movements suggest is taking place in the magnified sub-cellular structure?

....

[1]

ii) What is the name of the magnified sub-cellular structure in the diagram above?

....

[1]

b) The width of the sub-cellular structure when viewed using a microscope is 45 mm. What is the width of the magnified image in μm?

A 4.5 μm
B 0.045 μm
C 45 000 μm
D 4500 μm

Your answer ☐

[1]

c) The cell in the diagram is from a leaf.

i) Describe how carbon dioxide enters a leaf.

....
....

[2]

ii) What is the name of the process which transports water up a plant and into the leaves?

....
[1]

d) After glucose has been produced by a plant cell, some of it leaves the cell to be transported around the plant. What is the name of the transportation process?

....
[1]

[Total 7 marks]

3 Aerobic respiration transfers energy from glucose. *Grade 6-7*

a) i) Name the sub-cellular structures where aerobic respiration takes place.

....
[1]

ii) What would you expect to happen to the carbon dioxide concentration in a person's blood if their rate of respiration increased? Explain your answer.

....

....

....
[2]

b) Glucose is obtained through the diet in animals.

i) Once it has passed through the digestive system, glucose is transported around the body in the blood. Name the liquid component of blood.

....
[1]

ii) Some of the excess glucose from the diet is converted into glycogen and stored in the liver. Explain what happens to this glycogen if the blood glucose concentration falls below normal.

....

....
[2]

c) Cells respire anaerobically when they cannot get enough oxygen. During anaerobic respiration, glucose is only partially broken down.

i) Name the substance that is produced during anaerobic respiration in animals.

....
[1]

ii) Give an example of a situation in which a plant's cells may respire anaerobically.

....
[1]

[Total 8 marks]

4 Crops can be genetically modified so that they produce substances that they wouldn't normally. An example of this is Golden Rice™. Read the information about Golden Rice™ below.

> Golden Rice™ is a variety of rice that has been genetically modified to produce beta-carotene. Beta-carotene is used in the body to produce vitamin A.
>
> Vitamin A deficiency is a major health problem in some developing countries because many people struggle to get enough beta-carotene and vitamin A in their diet. Golden Rice™ could be used in these countries to help tackle vitamin A deficiency.
>
> Golden Rice™ was genetically engineered using a rice plant, a gene from a maize plant and a gene from a soil bacterium.

a) Explain whether vitamin A deficiency is a communicable or non-communicable disease.

....

....
[1]

b) Explain why the genome of Golden Rice™ will be different to the genome of normal rice.

....

....
[1]

c) Describe the process that may have been used to produce Golden Rice™.

....

....

....

....

....

....

....

....
[4]

d) Crops can also be genetically modified to produce higher food yields. Suggest **one** way in which plants can be genetically engineered to produce an increased yield.

....

....
[1]

[Total 7 marks]

Mixed Questions

5 In pea plants, seed shape is controlled by a single gene.

The allele for round seed shape is R and the allele for wrinkled seed shape is r.
R is a dominant allele and r is recessive.

a) i) What is the genotype of a pea plant that is homozygous dominant for seed shape?

....
[1]

ii) What is the phenotype of a pea plant that is heterozygous for seed shape?

....
[1]

b) Two pea plants were crossed. All of the offspring produced had the genotype **Rr**.
Construct a genetic diagram to find the genotypes of the parent plants.

Genotypes: .... and ....
[3]
[Total 5 marks]

6 The endocrine system uses hormones to produce effects within the body.
Hormones only affect particular cells, called target cells, in particular places.

a) Briefly explain why target cells only respond to certain hormones.

....
....
[2]

b) State how the speed and effects of a hormone are different to that of a nervous impulse.

....
....
[2]

c) Insulin is a hormone. A person has a mutation in their DNA which causes the structure of insulin to change. The mutation means that insulin is unable to carry out its normal function.

i) What does insulin control?

....
[1]

ii) Suggest the disease that this person will have as a result of having non-functional insulin.

....
[1]

d) The menstrual cycle is controlled by hormones.

The diagram below shows the change in the levels of these hormones during one menstrual cycle. It also shows the change in the lining of the uterus.

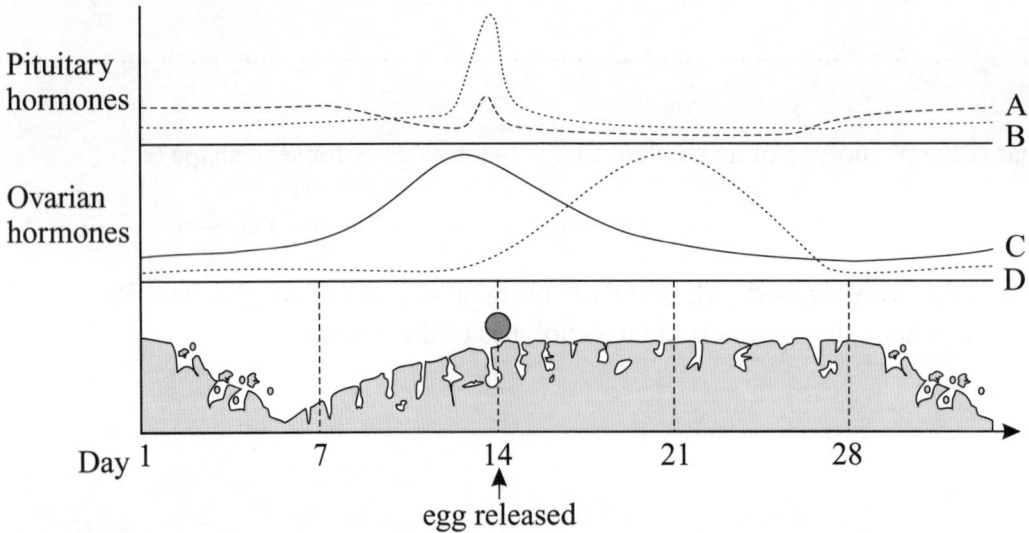

i) Which of the following hormones does line **B** represent in the diagram above.

A   LH
B   FSH
C   Oestrogen
D   Progesterone

Your answer ☐

[1]

ii) Which of the following hormones does line **C** represent in the diagram above.

A   LH
B   FSH
C   Oestrogen
D   Progesterone

Your answer ☐

[1]

iii) Where in the body is progesterone produced?

....

[1]

iv) Describe how a high progesterone level affects the secretion of hormones from the pituitary gland.

....

....

[2]

[Total 11 marks]

Mixed Questions

7 A student was investigating the effect of limiting factors on the rate of photosynthesis by green algae.

The student set up two boiling tubes as shown in the diagram on the right. She also set up a third tube that did not contain any algae. The colour of the indicator solution changes as follows:

- At atmospheric CO_2 concentration, the indicator is red.
- At low CO_2 concentrations, the indicator is purple.
- At high CO_2 concentrations, the indicator is yellow.

The student covered one of the boiling tubes containing algae with foil. All three tubes were left for several hours at room temperature with a constant light source. The colour of the indicator solution was then recorded. The results are shown in the table.

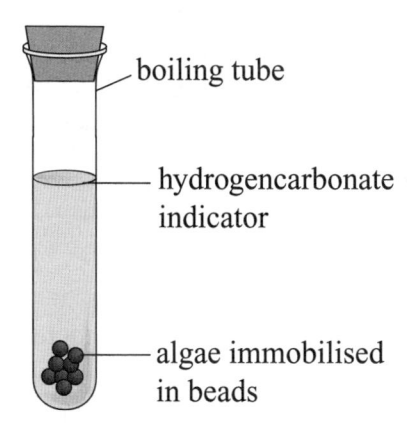

	Algae?	Foil?	Indicator colour at start	Indicator colour at end
Tube 1	yes	yes	red	yellow
Tube 2	yes	no	red	purple
Tube 3	no	no	red	red

a) At the end of the experiment, which tube has the highest carbon dioxide concentration?

Tube ....
[1]

b) Explain the results seen in Tube **1** and Tube **2**.

[4]

c) State the limiting factor of photosynthesis that is being investigated in this experiment.

[1]

d) Give **two** variables that needed to be controlled in this experiment.

[2]

Mixed Questions

A scientist investigating the effect of limiting factors on photosynthesis sketched this graph.

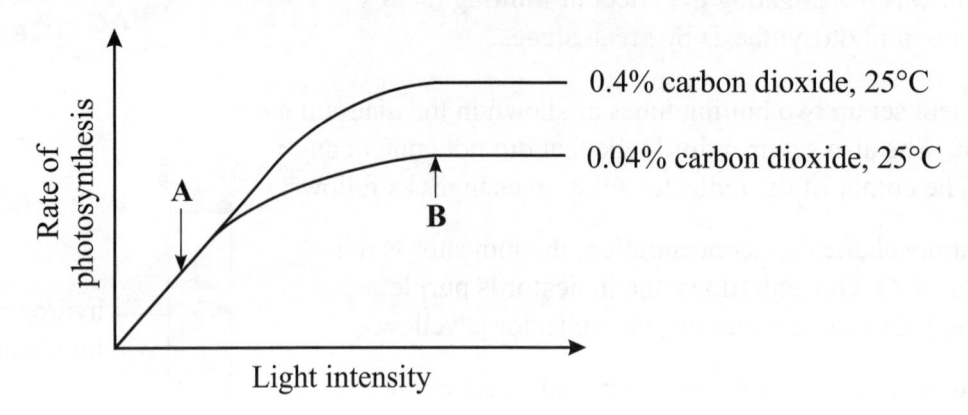

e) What is the limiting factor at point **A**? Explain your answer.

....

....
[2]

f) Name the limiting factor at point **B**.

....
[1]

[Total 11 marks]

8 Sickle cell anaemia is a genetic disorder caused by homozygous recessive alleles. The disorder affects the shape and structure of red blood cells, so they lose their flexibility and become sickle-shaped. This can cause the red blood cells to become stuck in the capillaries.

a) David does not suffer from sickle cell anaemia.
Which of the following genotypes does David **not** have?

 A   SS
 B   Ss
 C   sS
 D   ss

Your answer ☐
[1]

b) What aspect of the capillaries' structure makes sickle-shaped red blood cells more likely to become stuck in them rather than in arteries and veins?

....
[1]

c) Sickle cell anaemia can sometimes be treated with a bone marrow transplant.
Bone marrow contains adult stem cells. Explain how a bone marrow transplant could help to treat sickle cell anaemia.

....

....

....
[2]

[Total 4 marks]

Mixed Questions

Chemistry Mixed Questions

1 Fractional distillation separates crude oil into fractions.
Which of the following fractions is extracted **above** petrol in the fractionating column?

    A   Kerosene
    B   LPG
    C   Diesel
    D   Naphtha

Your answer ☐

[Total 1 mark]

2 When calcium metal is added to a solution of copper(II) nitrate, $Cu(NO_3)_2$, a displacement reaction takes place.

  a) Write a balanced symbol equation for this reaction.

    ....
    [2]

  b) This reaction is a redox reaction.
    Identify the oxidising agent and the reducing agent in this reaction.

    Oxidising agent: ....

    Reducing agent: ....
    [1]

[Total 3 marks]

3 Rubidium is an element from Group 1 of the periodic table.
Fluorine is an element from Group 7.
Rubidium metal, Rb, and fluorine gas, F_2, react violently to produce a single product.

  a) Write a balanced symbol equation for the reaction of rubidium metal and fluorine gas.

    ....
    [2]

  b) What type of bonding exists in the product of this reaction?

    ....
    [1]

  c) Would you expect the product of this reaction to have a high or low melting point?
    Explain your answer in terms of the forces within the compound.

    ....

    ....

    ....

    ....
    [2]

[Total 5 marks]

4 A solution of a metal salt is electrolysed.
During the electrolysis, a gas is produced at each electrode.

a) The gases produced at the electrodes are collected and tested.

i) The gas produced at the anode is found to relight a glowing splint.
What is the gas produced at the **anode**?

....
[1]

ii) The gas produced at the cathode is found to burn with a squeaky pop.
What is the gas produced at the **cathode**?

....
[1]

b) The salt in the solution is composed of a metal ion and a non-metal ion.

i) What do the identities of the gases produced during the electrolysis
tell you about the reactivity of the **metal** that forms the ions in the salt?

....

....
[1]

ii) What do the identities of the gases produced during the electrolysis
tell you about the identity of the **non-metal ion** in the salt?

....

....
[1]

[Total 4 marks]

5 A scientist wants to produce a batch of aluminium sulfate for an experiment.
She plans to do this by reacting aluminium with an excess of sulfuric acid.
A chemical supplier offers three options to provide the quantity of aluminium she needs.

Which of these options will allow the scientist to complete her reaction in the **shortest** time?

A 1 aluminium cube with side length 8 cm.
B 8 aluminium cubes, each with side length 4 cm.
C 64 aluminium cubes, each with side length 2 cm.
D They will all take the same length of time.

Your answer ☐

[Total 1 mark]

6 The atomic number of every atom of a certain element, X, is the same. The value of the atomic number is equal to the relative atomic mass of X. Which of the following statements must be **true** for element X?

- **A** Atoms of element X contain no neutrons.
- **B** Element X only has one isotope.
- **C** Atoms of element X have a full outer electron shell.
- **D** Atoms of element X have an equal number of protons and neutrons.

Your answer ☐

[Total 1 mark]

7 Aluminium can be obtained by electrolysis of the ore bauxite, Al_2O_3.

The overall equation for this reaction is:

$$2Al_2O_{3\,(l)} \rightarrow 4Al_{(l)} + 3O_{2\,(g)}$$

a) Explain why this reaction is an example of a redox reaction.

....

....
[1]

b) Before the electrolysis of aluminium ore can be carried out, the bauxite needs to be molten. Explain why this is necessary.

....

....

....
[2]

c) Iron can be extracted from its ores by heating with carbon. Explain why this method is **not** suitable for the extraction of aluminium from its ore.

....

....

....

....
[2]

d) Give **two** advantages of recycling aluminium.

1. ....

....

2. ....

....
[2]
[Total 7 marks]

Mixed Questions

8 Some elements have several different isotopes. Look at the bar chart.
It shows the percentage of the atoms of some elements that exist as each of their isotopes.

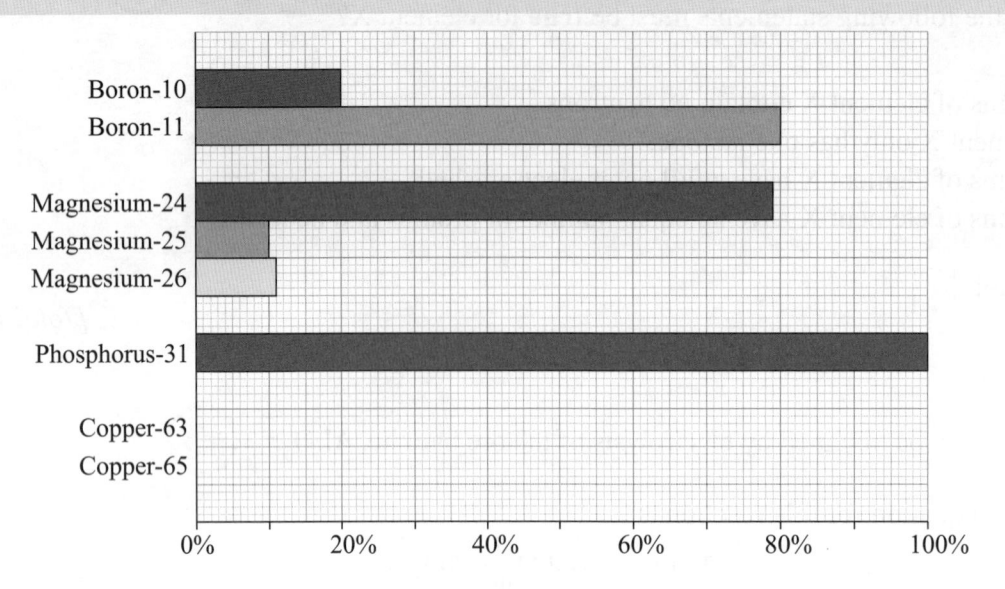

a) 69% of copper atoms are copper-63 and the rest are copper-65.
Complete the bar chart by adding bars for the two isotopes of copper.

[2]

b) Explain why the relative atomic mass of phosphorus is a whole number, while the relative atomic masses of boron, magnesium and copper are not.

....

....

....

....

....

....

[3]

c) One mole of boron atoms contains 6.022×10^{23} atoms.
How many boron-10 atoms would you expect to find in one mole of boron atoms?
Give your answer to **three** significant figures.

.... atoms

[2]

d) The atomic number of magnesium is 12. Magnesium forms ions with a 2+ charge.
How many electrons are there in one Mg^{2+} ion? Explain your answer.

....

....

....

[2]

[Total 9 marks]

Mixed Questions

9 Chlorine water reacts with potassium iodide solution according to the following reaction. *(Grade 6-7)*

$$Cl_{2\,(aq)} + 2KI_{(aq)} \rightarrow 2KCl_{(aq)} + I_{2\,(aq)}$$

a) Describe what you would observe if you added chlorine water to potassium iodide solution.

....
[1]

b) Explain why this reaction takes place.
Give your answer in terms of the reactivity of the elements involved.

....

....
[2]

c) Write a balanced ionic equation for the reaction between chlorine and potassium iodide.

....
[2]

d) Write balanced half equations to show what happens to chlorine and potassium during this reaction. Use e⁻ to represent an electron.

Chlorine: ....

Potassium: ....
[2]
[Total 7 marks]

10 A scientist carries out an experiment to investigate the rate of reaction between zinc and hydrochloric acid. He prepares three different blocks of zinc metal. The table below shows some information about the three blocks of zinc. *(Grade 7-9)*

	length (cm)	width (cm)	height (cm)	surface area (cm²)	volume (cm³)
Block X	60	1	1	242	60
Block Y	15	2	2	128	60
Block Z	5	3	4	94	60

Which block of zinc would you expect to react **more quickly**?
Explain your answer.

....

....

....

....

....
[Total 2 marks]

Mixed Questions

11 Boron nitride, BN, is a compound which can form giant covalent structures. Two forms of boron nitride are shown below.

● = boron atom
○ = nitrogen atom
— = covalent bond
---- = intermolecular force

hexagonal boron nitride

cubic boron nitride

a) One of the two forms of boron nitride shown above is used to make drill bits. The other can be used as a lubricant. Using your knowledge of similar giant covalent structures to suggest which is which, complete the following sentences using either 'cubic' or 'hexagonal'.

i) .... boron nitride is used to make cutting tools.

ii) .... boron nitride is used as a lubricant.

[1]

b) Explain why the structure of boron nitride you have suggested in part a) i) would make it suitable to use to make drill bits.

....
....
....
....

[2]

c) Explain why the structure of boron nitride you have suggested in part a) ii) makes it suitable to use as a lubricant.

....
....
....
....

[2]

d) The main difference between the properties of hexagonal boron nitride and the closest equivalent carbon structure is that hexagonal boron nitride cannot conduct electricity, but its carbon equivalent can. What does this difference suggest about the structure of hexagonal boron nitride?

....
....

[1]

[Total 6 marks]

Mixed Questions

Physics Mixed Questions

PRACTICAL

1 A scientist is carrying out an experiment to find the specific heat capacity of water. A sketch of her experiment and her results are given below. *(Grade 4-6)*

She heats 0.64 kg of water in a large grey sealed box using a 336.0 W electric heater. The heater is on for 120.0 s and she records the temperature of the water before and after this time.

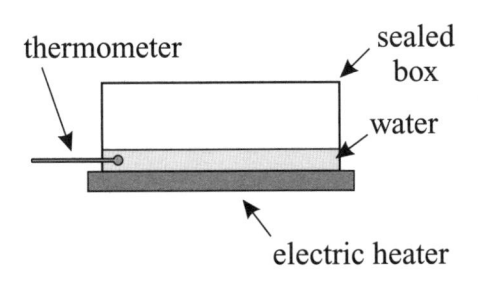

Attempt	Temperature before (°C)	Temperature after (°C)	Change in temperature (°C)
1	19.0	33.6	14.6
2	22.2	37.8	
3	25.7	40.5	14.8
		Mean change in temperature	

a) Fill in the **two** missing values in the table.

[2]

b) Assuming there are no energy losses, calculate the energy transferred to the water by the heater.

Energy transferred = ... J

[2]

c) Find the specific heat capacity of the water and give the unit. Use the formula:
change in thermal energy = mass × specific heat capacity × change in temperature

Specific heat capacity = ... Unit ....

[3]

d) The specific heat capacity of water is actually lower than the value calculated by the student. What colour container should the student have used to make her results more accurate?

A silver
B maroon
C black
D brown

Your answer ☐

[1]

e) The student now heats the water to 100 °C, causing all the water to boil and become water vapour. Explain what will happen to the pressure inside the box as the temperature rises above 100 °C.

....

....

....

[3]

[Total 11 marks]

240

2 X-rays and gamma rays are types of electromagnetic waves. *(Grade 4-6)*

a) What is the frequency of an X-ray travelling at 3×10^8 m/s with a wavelength of 4.8×10^{-9} m?

    A 1.60×10^{16} Hz
    B 1.25×10^{16} Hz
    C 6.25×10^{16} Hz
    D 1.44×10^{16} Hz

Your answer ☐

[1]

b) State **one** use of each of the following electromagnetic waves.

X-ray: ....

Gamma ray: ....

[2]

c) The equation shows a nucleus emitting a gamma ray. State what values A and B should be.

$$^{202}_{81}\text{Tl} \rightarrow\ ^{A}_{81}\text{Tl} + ^{B}_{0}\gamma$$

A = ...   B = ...

[2]

[Total 5 marks]

3 The diagram shows a solenoid with a current flowing through it. Five points mark where a compass has been placed. *(Grade 4-6)*

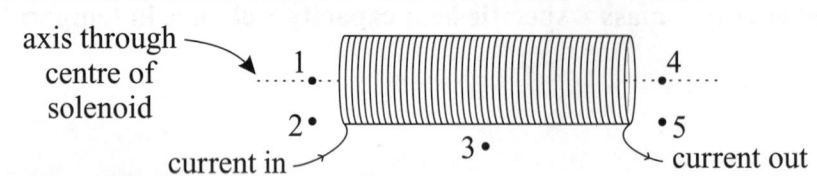

a) Which two points will have the compass needle pointing in the same direction?

    A   1 and 2
    B   1 and 4
    C   2 and 5
    D   3 and 5

Your answer ☐

[1]

b) The solenoid is connected in series with a 12.0 V power supply. A current of 3.20 A flows through the solenoid. Calculate the resistance of the wire of the solenoid.

Resistance = ... Ω

[3]

[Total 4 marks]

Mixed Questions

4 An electric hob has four separate rings. One ring is used to heat a pan of water. (Grade 6-7)

a) The ring has an input voltage of 230 V and a current of 6.0 A through it.
What is its power?

A 1.38 kW
B 13.8 kW
C 38.3 kW
D 2.76 kW

Your answer ☐

[1]

b) i) For every 2200 J of energy transferred to the hob, 1496 J of energy is transferred to the thermal energy store of the water. Calculate the efficiency of the hob.
(You can assume the pan conducts energy perfectly and is 100% efficient.)

Efficiency = ...
[2]

ii) Suggest how energy is **lost** from the system.

....
....
[1]

c) The water in the pan requires 24 288 J of energy to increase its temperature from 18 °C to 22 °C.
Calculate how long the ring needs to be on for to increase the temperature by this much.
Give your answer to **2** significant figures.

Time = ... s
[4]

d) i) The four rings of the hob are all connected in parallel to the mains supply.
Describe **two** advantages of connecting the rings in parallel.

....
....
[2]

ii) One of the rings has a **lower** resistance than the other three. How will the amount of current flowing through it differ to the current flowing through the other rings?

....
[1]

[Total 11 marks]

Mixed Questions

5   Oona is investigating how the compression of a spring affects the velocity of a trolley. She sets up her experiment as shown below. She pushes the trolley to compress the spring. Then she releases the trolley and measures its velocity as it passes through the light gate. She repeats the experiment, altering the amount of compression each time.

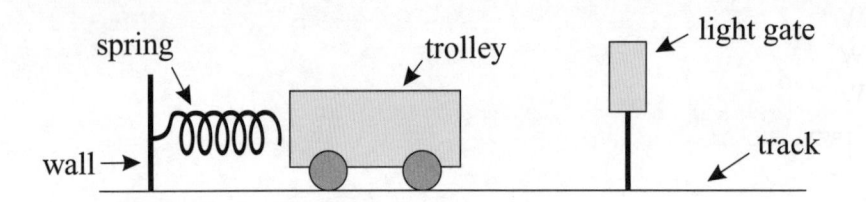

Grade 6-7

a) i) State the **independent** and **dependent** variables in this experiment.

Independent variable: ....

Dependent variable: ....
[2]

ii) Suggest **two** things Oona should do to make this a fair test.

....

....
[2]

b) The trolley has a weight of 8.80 N. What is its mass? Use: $g = 10$ N/kg.

A 8.8×10^1 kg
B 8.8×10^{-1} kg
C 8.8×10^{-2} g
D   0.0088 kg

Your answer □
[1]

When the spring was compressed by 0.0400 m, the trolley's velocity was 0.600 m/s at the light gate.

c) i) Ignoring friction and air resistance, calculate the spring constant of the spring. Use the formula: **energy transferred in stretching = 0.5 × spring constant × (extension)^2**

Spring constant = ... N/kg
[4]

ii) The spring constant of the spring is actually higher than the value calculated in **c) i)**. Explain why.

....

....

....
[2]
[Total 11 marks]

Mixed Questions

6 The diagram shows a Van de Graaff generator which is used to generate a positive charge on a metal dome.

The Van de Graaff generator consists of a metal dome and a belt made of insulating material wrapped round two wheels. The wheels turn in order to turn the belt.

The bottom of the belt continuously brushes past metal comb A, which is positively charged. The top of the belt continuously brushes past metal comb B, which is attached to the metal dome.

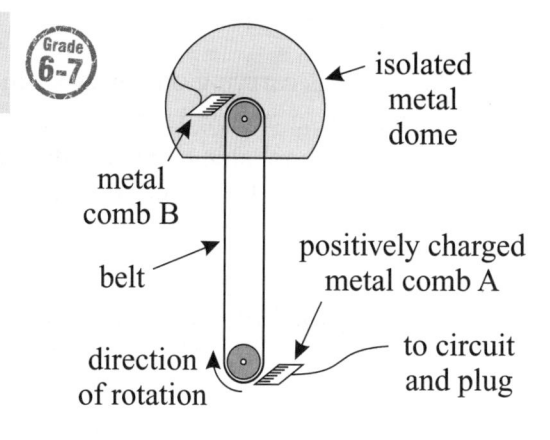

a) Explain how a charge builds up on the dome.

....
....
....
....
....
....
[5]

b) Explain why the metal dome of a Van de Graaff generator is not connected to an earth wire.

....
....
[2]

An earthed piece of metal is brought near to the charged dome.

c) i) Explain what you'd expect to happen now.

....
....
[2]

ii) Just before the metal was brought close, a charge of 15 μC had built up on the dome and the potential difference between the dome and the earthed piece of metal was 320 kV. Calculate the energy transferred away from the dome during the event described in c) i). Show your working.

Energy = ... J
[4]
[Total 13 marks]

Mixed Questions

7 A student is carrying out an experiment to find the frictional force acting on a trolley. He releases a trolley from a marked position at the top of a ramp. The trolley rolls down the ramp, along a horizontal track and then up a second ramp at the other side. The diagram below shows the experimental setup.

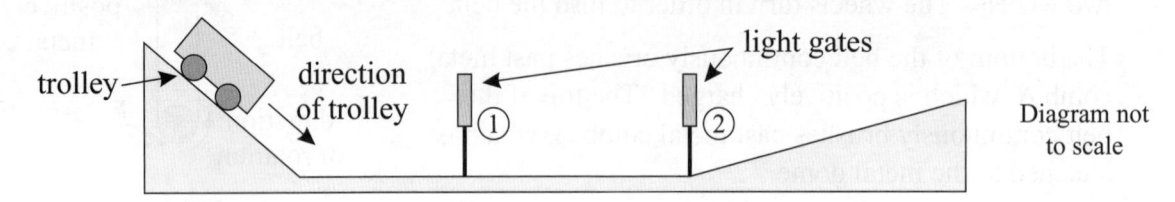

a) i) The table shows his results. Fill in the final column in the table.

Repeat	Speed at light gate 1 (m/s)	Speed at light gate 2 (m/s)	Time taken to travel between light gates 1 and 2 (s)	Acceleration (m/s^2)
1	1.22	0.76	2.00	
2	1.16	0.62	2.25	
3	1.19	0.75	2.00	

[3]

ii) The mass of the trolley is 300 g. Use information in the table to calculate the **magnitude** of the frictional force acting on the trolley.

Force = ... N
[4]

b) Complete the free body force diagram to show the forces acting on the trolley when it's moving along the horizontal part of the track.

[3]

The student sticks sandpaper onto the horizontal part of the track and repeats the experiment.

c) What effect will the sandpaper have on the height reached by the trolley on the second ramp? Explain your answer.

....
....
....
....
....
[5]
[Total 15 marks]